REAL LIFE,

Real Choices

A Young Adult Life Reference Book

REAL LIFE,

Real Choices

A Young Adult Life Reference Book

Kijana Martin

COPIOUS PUBLISHING

Irving, Texas

Cover and interior design by Kijana Martin
Cover Graphics by Logan Fisher

Notice: This book is designed to provide information and be used a life reference tool. It is sold with the understanding that the publisher and author are not engaged in rendering legal, psychological, medicinal, financial or other professional services. Such topic discussed herein is for illustrative purposes only. If you need legal, financial, medicinal or other professional assistance, you should use the services of an appropriately qualified professional.

Every attempt has been made to make this book at complete and accurate as possible. There may be errors both typographical and in content. This book should be used as a general reference book.

The purpose of this book is to educate and entertain. The author and Copious Publishing shall have neither liability nor responsibility to any person or entity with respect to any loss or damage caused, or alleged to have been caused, directly or indirectly, by the information contained in this book.

If you do not wish to be bound by the above, you may return this book to the place where you purchased or to the publisher for a full refund.

ISBN: 978-0-9843210-0-1

10 9 8 7 6 5 4 3 2 1

Published by Copious Publishing
Irving, TX

Acknowledgments

I thank my Creator for my strength, endurance, persistence, and love. I am grateful that I don't give up.

To my boys, Nikko, Khabir, and Jelani: thank you for patience, understanding, and unconditional love.

There are several people who have impacted my life in ways that I can never forget, mostly by their continuous love, belief in me, and true friendship.

Thank you Deborah Martin (Ganny) for giving me life and setting the example of a strong woman. Thank you Alisa Martin, Reginald Martin, Ejeama Martin, Dr. Marietta Greer-Thompson, Michelle Sims, Larry Tankson, Heru Uaxsaktun El, Rob Davis, Terrence Holmes, Mary Dobbins (from Greensboro, NC), Tony Smith, Roderick Norman, Cynthia De La Pena, Randy McKinley, and Ade Adekoye for believing in me.

I'd like to extend a special thank you to Principal Terry, Mr. Hunt of the English Literature Department, and students of Oak Cliff High School Classes of 2001 and 2002 for their kindness during a difficult time.

JaMarris and TeVorris Carter; I will always love you dearly.

To Oprah Winfrey and Montel Williams I extend a special acknowledgment for being extraordinary people. Thank you for being beacons of inspiration. Life is much more interesting with you two in it.

Thank you to everyone who has crossed my path, touched my soul, and played their part in this great play of "Kijana's Life." Most of all, I thank God for Divine Order.

*This book is dedicated to my three loving sons, Nikko, Khabir, and Jelani. Remember to always be yourself and that you always have a choice in any situation that can **immediately** change your life.*

Contents

REAL LIFE,

Real Choices

A Young Adult Life Reference Book

This preface purposely addresses parents and young adults in different sections.

Parents

Parents, how different would you be if your parents had educated you about life, supplying the most important information that would have helped you survive emotionally, physically, mentally, financially and spiritually? When wisdom and knowledge gained by living and learning is passed down to the next generation, they are allowed to make educated choices, waste less time, and prosper. Unfortunately, this has not been the case in many families and is being perpetuated today.

Today, communication between parent and child is better than previous generations, but is still a work in progress. Parents are in a constant battle with negative influences of peers, music, television, and society.

Children are not being taught the most important resources for adulthood due to their parents:

- Repeating their parent's actions

- Not being knowledgeable about various topics
- Inability to verbally express
- Being a product of a particular environment
- Being a child raising a child
- Not being active in their children's lives
- Not having enough time
- Many parents are caught up in the rat race trying to manage their time between work, family, life goals, and personal relationships. Important thoughts or lessons parents desire to communicate to their children are often forgotten.

In an attempt to fill the gap, explain sensitive subjects with real life experience, or to be accessible when a parent or guardian isn't, I've shared my life in a down to earth fashion to be referenced for a lifetime.

My goal is to show young adults that they are not the first person to experience a situation; and though it may seem difficult to overcome, they will. No matter what, they can keep their heads held high and proceed through life knowing that with each challenge they are learning themselves and becoming seasoned with wisdom.

Young Adults

Freedom is what you anticipate as a young adult. We all grow up awaiting and counting down the years to freedom, 18 years old by society's standards. At 18, you're free to apply for credit, rent an apartment, sign contracts, and create bills. However, how many of you have been taught to manage your financial affairs?

You are now free to date, befriend, or establish a relationship with whomever you desire. How many of you are educated on the importance of loving self, responsibility, sex, birth control, relationships, and respect?

You are now able to decide if you will continue your education, get a job, or start a business. Again, how many of you are prepared to make these decisions?

Much of the afore mentioned information goes undisclosed by

parents for many different reasons. Parents are not to be blamed. They are products of their environment. They are the parents they needed to be to you. Every experience you've had thus far has set up the life lessons you must overcome as an adult.

In an attempt to help you find your way, I am sharing what I have learned and some of what I am still digesting in hopes that some of your unanswered questions will be answered.

This book contains information on self-development, mental development, care of the physical body, sexuality, relationships, career, education, and finances. As you read, absorb the information and choose what feels right to you. You will discover your own truth as you progress through life. Do not disregard truth because it's not what you want to hear at the time.

Life is like a box of chocolates. The first time you open the box, choose and bite a candy, you don't know what you're going to get. However, if you remember how it looks, tastes, and how it made you feel, you'll know whether you want to experience it again. That's experience and knowledge gained. Using the power of choice, you can either choose another experience or have that nasty taste in your mouth again.

Regardless of your circumstances or background, you can obtain anything you desire. Whichever route you take, you're always going to wind up where you're supposed to be. Life has a way of working itself out. As long as you desire and strive for the best, you will achieve greatness. You fail when you don't believe in yourself. Never forget the power of choice and free will. This is your life, live it, choose your experiences, make educated decisions, and ride it 'til the wheels fall off!

REAL LIFE,
Real Choices
A Young Adult Life Reference Book

As a young adult, in my mid-twenties, I'd often question why I had been through so much in my life at such a young age. This puzzled me. I'd look back and review how different my life was than I had envisioned it would be; my being an artist and business owner. My life was different for a reason and with as much heartache as I'd experienced, mainly due to lack of communication, I wanted to make sure I touched and helped as many people as possible through communication.

My life hasn't been all bad and I have enjoyed significant portions of it. To help you understand why I am passionate about helping young adults I will give you a brief history of the experiences that had a negative impact on my life because these are the situations people usually carry and reflect on for years.

My mother is a great woman and my father was a loving man. They were young when they started their family and did only what they knew to do. Their inexperience as adults and parents definitely impacted my life and my siblings' lives.

My father graduated high school but impregnated my mother soon after. My mother dropped out of her senior year of high school due to her pregnancy and my parents were married.

My father was big on education, very playful and interacted with the children more than my mother.

We moved around often due my father's inconsistent employment. My parents stayed married for about ten years or so and eventually divorced due to my father's infidelity. After they divorced, my siblings and I missed the interaction with our father.

My mother proved to be the breadwinner of the family and stabilized our family after divorcing my father. My mother's day consisted of her going to work, sometimes cooking dinner and spending the majority of her time in her bedroom.

We were not an extremely poor family but it was definitely a challenge for my mother to raise four children with minimal support from my father. I will never forget lying in bed with my mother as we counted pennies to be able to buy food until her next payday.

As a child, I witnessed many things that a child should not have to see or experience. Those experiences affected me, my perception of what love is, judgment, how I should relate to men, how I should behave as a young lady/woman, and my general perception of life.

To help you understand more quickly, I am going to bullet point portions of which I feel would have been quite different had I had a communicative family.

1. My mother loved to a fault.
2. My father was an adulterer and abusive.
3. My father had children out of wedlock.
4. I excelled in school not only because I loved school but also because it was a way for me to get attention from my father.
5. My father died when I was fifteen.
6. I lost my virginity, became pregnant and aborted a child at age fifteen.
7. I was an A-B student who eventually brought home straight F's.

8. I unknowingly suffered from depression.

9. I didn't go to college due to my parent not understanding financial aid and my not realizing I could have applied for college on my own.

10. I allowed people to negatively influence me.

11. I had difficulty saying "no" because I didn't want to hurt people's feelings.

12. I was expected to do great things with my life and a lot of people were disappointed.

13. I graduated high school from summer school because although I had completed my final paper in one class I didn't hand it in and I failed another class.

14. I had my first child at age twenty.

15. I suffered financially because I had a boyfriend whom I didn't know was on drugs.

16. I always saw the good in people instead of being realistic about the whole personality of the person.

17. If I had given in to all the peer pressure I would have been an extreme product of the ghetto.

The above points affected my life. How? You will learn that as you read various chapters in this book. I am sharing my life because I want you to understand that you are not alone or the only person to have had or are having a particular experience. The above list of experiences set me up for growth and development. I am sharing my experiences with hope that what I share will be what you need when you need it. This book is not a novel but a reference book in which you can turn to a particular topic for advice. The stories in this book are experiences that can assist you from your teenage years well into adulthood. I hope that you will use this book and cherish it as you age and pass it down when you're able. Thank you for this opportunity to share. Enjoy.

Self

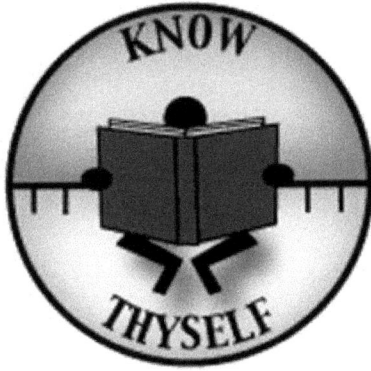

REAL LIFE, REAL CHOICES: A YOUNG ADULT LIFE REFERENCE BOOK

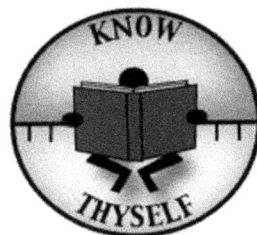

SELF INTRODUCTION

Self- the distinct characteristic, individuality, or identity of any person or thing -Webster's Illustrated Contemporary Dictionary

You are unique. There is no one truly identical to you. You may ask, "What about identical twins?" Even they are not truly identical. They may look the same but their personalities are quite different. The innermost person, that if you closed your eyes and could not see the person's form; their spirit, is *self*, and is identical to no one.

Your most valuable asset in this lifetime is your self. You are rare in its rarest form. When you have nothing else in this world, you still have self. When you're all alone, you have self to remember, laugh, smile, and reflect.

If you lose everything, you still have self and the knowledge that is contained within you to rebuild and become greater than you were before.

Becoming the greatest you can become begins with self-love. If you don't love and take care of you, you can't fully love anyone else.

Taking care of self involves making choices and considering the effect they can have on you and others. Make the choice for the higher good. Never sacrifice by putting yourself in a "bad" position or one that's not beneficial to you in one way or another; mentally, spiritually, emotionally, or physically. Continue to develop your self by analysis, reading, relating, listening and by staying in touch with your Creator. Eliminate as much baggage as possible.

Never forget that you have self and when no one else believes in you or is available to cheer you up, you still have self-motivation. Live your dreams and create your own expectations of self. **Always protect yourself; you are your most valuable asset.**

SELF-LOVE

*Self is the essence of **you**.*

Take a good look at yourself in the mirror. Yes, I'm talking to you. Look at your face, hands... your whole body. Notice your hair, your smile, your teeth and eyes, everything that identifies you as being you and then come back and finish reading.

Now, what if I took away all of the features that you identify with as being you – your self – would you still be you? What is self? Think about it for a minute. While you're thinking, continue reading and I'll tell you a couple of stories.

There once was a fetus living inside his mother. His mother's body nourished and protected him, as he was unable to survive without her. Though everyone knew he existed, his features and personality could not identify him. But his mother knew him. She knew that he liked to kick a lot at night; that when she ate, he'd calm down. She knew he'd relax when she played music. She knew all these things about her son, yet he had not yet been born.

Nine months later, his mother gave birth and this baby was now able to breathe on his own. Everyone could then see him. They knew his physical features and would soon know his personality. He was given a name, Aaron.

Aaron became a person, an individual who could be identified by his characteristics and physical appearance. Before he was an individual, his mother identified him by his personal energy. She knew the essence of him: his spirit, which is the most important aspect of defining *self*.

Self is the essence of you, your spirit, which makes up who you are regardless of what vessel of identity you are in. Your body is the way in which others are able to easily identify you. It is the house for your spirit. Your mind, with your spirit controls the mechanisms of your body.

Okay, I may be getting a little too deep. What I really want you to understand is that no matter what your physical appearance, you still know you, your *self*. To really simplify it, if I were to peel the skin off an apple and paste it on an orange, would it be an apple or an orange? The core or essence of it would be an orange, which happens to have a new appearance because some goofball pasted apple skin to it. The core of you is self; your spirit.

Love

If you try to define love, you may think of words such as passion, devotion, and affection. These words are descriptive of the emotions or feelings that come along with love, but they don't truly define love.

> **Self-love starts with self acceptance.**

Love is complex but when you feel it, you know that there is just about nothing that you wouldn't do for someone that you love. Love can be overwhelming. Some want to love so badly that they do that which is unloving; giving so much in the name of love that they forget to love themselves.

This chapter is first on purpose. If you can grasp self-love, you can save yourself a lot of pain and lessons about taking care of you.

As a teenager, my family was by no means wealthy or even middle class. Though we carried ourselves well, financially we were just getting by.

I had a boyfriend whose family was less fortunate than mine. Between the tender ages of 16 and 19, he and I were in a relationship in which I did many things in the name of love. I allowed him to use my car that he crashed. I gave him an ATM card, which he abused and I had to pay back the money that he overdrafted. Eventually, he stole several hundreds of dollars, my jewelry and other valuables. But it took years to learn that I did not love my *self*. I allowed him to trample over my feelings, my accomplishments, and me. Though I went out of my way to help him in his life and express my love, he didn't have the same respect, care, or concern for me. I subjected myself to pain, heartache, and serious financial repercussions.

You set the tone for how people will treat you.

I gave to and took care of not only him, but many others except the person that mattered most, me.

Self-love is one of the most difficult things to do consistently because you must remain aware of all your relationships, your one-on-one conversations with self, and how you allow others to treat you.

How we perceive an experience can create negative relationships, thoughts we have of ourselves, and situations. Our self-esteem is affected, as well as the perception others may have of us. When we allow others (by having them in our lives) or we negatively affect our esteem, the likelihood that we allow unhealthy influences into our lives, is heightened, and increased insecurities and doubts within ourselves are also heightened. But if we love ourselves, this possibility is decreased.

Self-love starts with self-acceptance. We are our best and worst critics. We talk about ourselves to ourselves. If only I looked that way. If only I were as smart as so-and-so. If only I could lose x number of pounds. If only I had this or that.

GOD DOESN'T MAKE MISTAKES! You are who you are and you look the way you look for a reason. The package that makes up you was designed to complete a specific goal and you had to have the proper tools to do it. The benefit of being a co-creator in your life is that you are able to change or improve upon any aspect of you that makes you unhappy.

Begin to love you

Self-love entails more than physical care. You must nurture your emotions, spirit, body, and mind. This may include:

- *Healthy relationships*

Choose positive relationships. In some of your relationships, you will experience conflict, which is often a learning process. But if you are continually unhappy, angry, or depressed when relating to a person, you need to choose again.

- *Spiritual foundation*

A spiritual foundation is your relationship with your Creator/ God; with whomever you identify for higher knowledge. The spiritual foundation is extremely important because it helps you identify with your *self*, existence, and the meaning of your life.

Spirituality helps you discover your reason/purpose of being and to ascend to a higher level of consciousness or awareness. Spiritual development can include reviewing your life experiences, the positive or negative impacts, making corrections, or not repeating the same. By doing this, your life and experiences change.

- *Exercise and proper nutrition*

What you don't use you lose. This saying is quite true concerning the human body. As we age, we either stay active or become less active. Less activity can equal less flexibility, a slower metabolism, weight gain, and health issues. Exercise keeps the body strong, flexible, and healthier. It helps to decrease aches and pains and disease.

Proper nutrition is important to nourish your body. With proper nutrition you can extend your life, increase good health and overall wellness.

- *Continuous learning - feed the mind*

Feeding the mind keeps it active. Instead of decreasing your memory and mental abilities, keep your mind young by reading, hobbies, and personal development activities. Don't limit your knowledge and ability to continually discover the newness of this wonderful world.

Teach others how to treat you by first loving and respecting yourself.

AFFIRMATION
Begin to love yourself by saying to yourself, "I love you. You are the perfect you and I accept and love you for you."

ACTION
• Work daily on the things that you can change about yourself. Make a list and make sure you do something for yourself daily.
• Commit to loving yourself by taking time for you.
• Guard your mouth and your thoughts. Replace every negative thought immediately with a positive one.
• Be mindful of your relationships. The next time you're placed in a compromising position that will not have a positive effect on your life, do what's best for you.

CHOICE

Use the power of choice by choosing what is right for you.

As a child, one of my favorite days was the day I had enough money to go to the candy store. The candy store was actually called the "Corner Store" because it was located on the corner, on the first floor of an old brownstone building.

This store was unique within itself because after you passed the two heavy entrance doors, you stepped into a small standing area of about six by four feet and were surrounded by gates. The gates were there to eliminate stealing, I guess. So you'd place your order and someone would get your chips, candy, or other requests.

One thing I knew for sure was that when I was there, I had all sorts of candy to choose from; from tootsie rolls to wine candy (jolly ranchers), and bubble gum.

My friends and I would each leave the store with a fat brown bag of candy full of our selections that we carefully held to avoid a tear.

Every now and then we'd choose a new candy and if we liked it, it became part of our normal selection.

If we didn't like it, we'd never buy it again. We'd utilize the power of choice by choosing what we liked.

Life is somewhat like a visit to the candy store. We choose our experiences and, if we learn our lessons, we never choose the bad ones again. We hold on to the good choices and they become part of our happy memories but all our experiences become wisdom.

Responsible choices come with thinking harder about situations that can negatively impact your life, body, or well-being.

> **Listen carefully to people. Pay attention to their actions and the situations that you find yourself in.**

Whenever you begin a statement with, "I'd be happier if", "If only I could", "I'd rather be", "This doesn't feel right", you may need to make a choice. **Make a choice if:**

- Something doesn't "fit" you or if you have outgrown it
- You are not happy or growing from an experience or feel stagnated
- You're in a situation only because you don't want to hurt someone's feelings
- You're spinning your wheels and going nowhere
- You're in an abusive situation or sense danger
- You have a dream that's yearning for expression and you haven't expressed it due to fear.

Responsibility

A word that is synonymous with adulthood is responsibility. In every aspect of an adult life, responsibility rings loud and clear. As an adult you are responsible for your possessions, family, and relationships.

Responsibility in making choices is no different. For example, if you allow someone to yell at you and you don't immediately set him or her straight, from that point forward, they think it's okay. So when they yell at you in front of others and embarrass you, you must take responsibility for your choice of allowing them to disrespect you.

Another example: if you know that your bill is due on the 15th of the month and you wait until the 25th to pay it and incur a twenty-five dollar late fee, you made the choice – take responsibility for incurring unnecessary debt and wasting money that could have paid another bill.

A final example: if you choose to sleep with someone unprotected and contract an STD, you can't put the whole blame on that person because you chose to not protect yourself.

If you find yourself in a difficult situation, ask yourself, "How did I get here?" Trace the choices you made. This will help you understand what you need to do differently.

Choosing Again

We all make choices that we later think about and ask ourselves, "What was I thinking?" The choices that we make will impact our lives until we are ready to forgive and leave the past in the past. Sometimes we are presented with a similar situation (a re-do), which affords us the opportunity to apply the knowledge gained from a previous choice.

This is your opportunity to use the power of choice appropriately and responsibly. Don't wait until you're crying, broke, unhappy, or worse. Immediately do what you know you should do. **Take responsibility for you, love you, and choose wisely.**

AFFIRMATION
Everyday I am making choices that positively impact my life.

ACTION
When presented with situations/experiences, before rushing into them, pay attention to how your body feels. If you feel any uneasiness or have thoughts that it isn't right for you, take heed. Don't allow peer pressure or the fear of disappointing someone make you do something you know isn't good for you.
Ask yourself why you are doing it. If you can't find a positive answer or one that will benefit you, choose again!

SELF-SACRIFICE

> *Create a balance through self-love, self-respect, and educated choices.*

There are three types of people: those who direct their focus outwardly, those who focus inwardly, and those who know how to balance.

Those who focus outwardly tend to do for others instead of first doing for themselves. They will often find themselves consumed with the daily tasks of helping others, which becomes their lives. Often you will hear them complain, "I never have time for myself." That's because they have fallen into the habit of sacrificing self. Although this may be due to many different reasons, the primary reason is that it's easier to deal with others than to understand, develop, and love yourself.

Little girls are groomed to take care of others. Young ladies, did you play mostly with a doll as a child? You were probably taught to care for your doll by feeding and clothing it as if it were real. How many of you were actually taught to take care of yourself and ensure your happiness first? Many women fall prey to catering to everyone in their lives, putting their dreams on hold. In their later years, they eventually learn to take time for themselves and pursue what makes them happy.

Those who are often called selfish are those who focus inwardly.

31

There is nothing wrong with being selfish, depending on the degree of selfishness or how you define it. If you are selfish in the sense that you are into yourself, your happiness, and what is best for you in life...wonderful. If you are selfish in the sense of being greedy, mean, and unable to help others, that's not good. If you are unable to give, how do you expect to receive? To be able to admit to the latter takes a lot. If you're able to do so, you're well on your way to creating a balanced you.

We are rewarded for our good deeds in life.

I mentioned helping others because we are not here to be alone. We are here to relate by developing relationships. Each relationship you have is a give-and-take situation. Each person is there for the mutual exchange. If you are selfish and think only about self in the negative sense, you are greatly limiting your capabilities and potential for satisfaction. We are often rewarded throughout life for our good deeds by receiving good fortune mentally, physically, spiritually, emotionally, and financially.

Create balance by learning your limits, setting boundaries, and not overextending yourself. Those who have been given the direction of self-preservation are blessed with a head start. With balance, you are less likely to be torn between what you desire to do for yourself and pleasing others. You do what you desire most in life without allowing someone to dictate your life to you. If someone truly loves you and has your best interest at heart, he or she won't try to hinder you from advancing. People have a right to express opinions, but you must choose what is best for you in all areas of your life.

Sacrificing and helping others is a part of life but never sacrifice yourself to your detriment. Create a balance through self-love, self-respect, and educated choices.

AFFIRMATION
I am actively balancing my time, efforts and attention while giving myself the love, attention and peace of mind I need.

ACTION

If you are in the habit of doing for others all the time, set aside some "me time." Take time for yourself each day. Use this time to learn yourself by being still, exploring, or trying something you've always wanted to do.

Sometime people who focus outwardly don't want to have time for self because they don't want to deal with their personal issues such as getting better grades or working on their health. They always have what they're doing for others as an excuse for not having time for themselves. It takes courage and self-love to stop this.

Do not sacrifice yourself to the point that you lose you, fail to complete your goals, damage your health, and make yourself unhappy. Create balance by learning and actually saying, "No." Learn it now and you'll be less likely to forget about taking time for you.

SELF-DEVELOPMENT

Repetition creates habit, thus creating change.

I've been outspoken since I was a child. Without considering others' feelings, I stated how I felt about whatever the issue. At my eighth birthday party, my best friend gave me a necklace. I didn't know to consider her feelings before stating how I felt. "This is ugly!" I blurted, hurting her feelings, damaging our friendship, and getting myself into trouble. My mother reprimanded me and made me apologize. I felt bad and the lesson stayed with me to this day.

The affect it had on me caused me to not say things that I thought would be hurtful to others. Sometimes I held everything in, even at times when I should have spoken to protect or defend myself. At other times, I would become angry and everything that I'd been holding in would explode. I verbally thrashed the person to whom it was directed.

As an adult, I've sought balance. I have learned to tailor my conversation to the person with whom I am speaking. My balance is to say what I feel at the appropriate time and sometimes preface it with a disclaimer. I have practiced self-development, which has helped me.

Self-development is a continuous process. I'd be surprised if you one day wake up and feel like you can't improve yourself and the decision isn't based on your giving up. If you do, please email me. I'd love to see you; the perfect human specimen.

Self-development is working on self to increase your capabilities and maturity to become a better you. This happens by acknowledging who you are right now, recognizing that no one is perfect and taking action to improve upon your character and personality.

Self-development can be as simple as being on time, eliminating procrastination, or answering the telephone politely when the norm for you is the opposite.

How do you know what you need to develop? It's simple. Identify a trait or comment that more than one person has made about you that is not positive. Choose a "flaw" you've identified in yourself. Think of what you can do to enhance your life. You'll have identified three things you can work on.

When you identify the traits or flaws you wish to change about yourself, you may find that this is something you've been aware of for quite some time. If so, there may be a reason that you have obstructed change.

A friend of mine had a problem with communicating. Though she was aware of it, she didn't know how or where to begin proper communication. She first had to find the root of the problem, which actually stemmed from a childhood trauma. Once she acknowledged where the problem originated, she was then on a path to healing and change.

Self-development often requires you to take long hard looks at yourself and your life. You will find the beautiful and the ugly. The ugly makes it difficult, but it also poses a challenge and opportunity for growth. When you tackle the "uglies", you become stronger, more mature, respectable, and admirable among other things.

If your change is a matter of consistently doing something, consider committing to twenty-one days of repetition. Repetition creates habit, thus creating change. After twenty-one days, it should be easy to continue what you've made habit. Reward yourself and acknowledge your progress. Look in the mirror and say to yourself "(insert your name) I am proud of you."**Apply development in every aspect of your life.** This is a lifelong work. You will have a more fulfilling life and be an inspiration to others with your ability to share your lessons or as they silently watch you grow.

AFFIRMATION

I freely acknowledge the aspects of myself that I can improve upon. Daily I am changing and molding myself to be the best I can be.

ACTION

1.   Make a list of changes you like to make. Make a list of what you'd like to learn. Set goals by setting a date by which you wish to have accomplished these things.

2.   Each day review your list and do one something. You will gradually see a change in you.

THOUGHTS ARE THINGS

You give power to that on which you focus.

Thousands of thoughts will pass through your mind everyday. Thoughts affect your feelings, health, energy and happiness. Thoughts are powerful.

Take a moment to be still and pay attention to your mind. Pay attention to your thoughts and how they quickly move from one thing to the next. Pay attention to how your emotions change as the thoughts change.

Each day, your body feels every emotion that you experience and therefore affects the functions of your body. If you stress, your body is stressed. Stress causes hormonal imbalances, can create fat, and throw off the body processes. People under stress may rapidly gain or lose weight, have insomnia, constipation or diarrhea, or other dysfunctions.

It is a known fact that when you are happy, your body will produce endorphins, which is a group of hormones that affect pain and emotion. These are good hormones that make you feel good.

Be mindful of your thoughts for a day. Realize your thought process; the conversations you have with yourself about yourself and others. How many of your thoughts are negative? How many of your thoughts, if said out loud would hurt others or yourself even? How many of your thoughts are you dwelling on past events? Are these happy times or sad times? How do they make you feel? Pay attention to your emotional and bodily reactions while you're thinking.

Now do this exercise. Take a moment and take in your surroundings: the scents, sounds, lighting, and activity. Pay attention to your mind and your thoughts. What you're involved in at this very moment is "now." When you focus on "now", you are not engrossed in your past or worried about your future. You are dealing with what is present at this time. This way you eliminate rehashing your past hurts by leaving them in the past. You eliminate the worry of tomorrow by focusing on your gift, which is the present.

> Practice countering your thoughts all day every day.

Can you actually change your thoughts? Yes you can. There is an aspect of us that attempts to keep us focused on the drama in our lives. You can learn to control this. Pay attention to your thoughts. If you are thinking negatively, counter it with something positive. If you find yourself lost in the past, change your focus to the present.

For example, if you find yourself degrading yourself or others, counter this action by finding something positive or kind to say. If you really want to get to the bottom of this thought process, you have to go within and figure out why you think such things. Why are you insecure? Why do you feel you have to speak badly about yourself or someone else? Does it gratify you, if so, why? Don't you think it would create better energy in your body if you say kind things and have kind thoughts? **Master your thoughts and you can master your mind.**

AFFIRMATION

I am focused on the now, the present and all that is good. I know by doing this I am becoming a Master of my mind.

ACTION

Every thought you have affects your life, your experiences and health. Focus on good/positive for yourself and others. See yourself happy and doing positive things. You give power to that on which you focus.

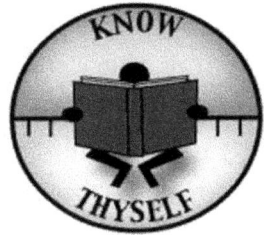

SELF-MOTIVATION

{ *You set the finish line.* }

A friend of mine told me a story of how he grew up as a young boy without the expectation of his family being there for him.

As a young boy, Ray grew up in one of the, if not the poorest towns in the U.S. Ray loved sports. Though it was a challenge to get to practice, his team didn't have a nice field or turf to play on, and his parents never drove him, Ray always made it to practice because he was passionate about playing ball.

I asked Ray, "Did your parents attend your games?" He replied, "No." I then asked, "How did you feel about that?" He said, "It didn't faze me. I was okay with it."

I told Ray that his response is what I'd expect many "manly men" to say. What child wouldn't want their parents cheering them on? It took Ray a while to comment as he digested what I said. He concluded that he grew up pushing himself to become a better person because that's what he desired.

He went on to tell me a story about how he and a friend dreamed of becoming successful, mirroring themselves to soap opera businessmen.

One thing they realized was that many people in their town didn't enunciate and some even used words in the wrong context. They even made up words because they couldn't pronounce words correctly. Ray and his friend made it a point to practice enunciating words daily in an effort to better themselves. They were self-motivated.

If you had no friends or family for support but you had many dreams and goals, how would you accomplish your dreams? If you had no one to motivate you, to tell you to keep going, would you give up?

The only person you need is with you at all times. You have self, and within self, you have all that you need through inner strength and divination.

You can't depend on others to get you through life or help you reach your goals. You have to want badly to succeed. You have to tell yourself to get up when the sun hasn't risen. You have to tell yourself to stay awake and complete the task when the sun is rising and you haven't had any sleep. You have to pat yourself on the back, jump up and down and cheer for yourself when you make a baby step. You must be your everything to get you through. You have to be that little voice that won't go away and keeps affirming, "Don't give up. I have faith in you. You can make it. You have something to share with the world. If you don't do it, who will? If you don't make a name for yourself, how will anyone ever know that you existed?"

When you feel you can't go on, do something that you know will give you that extra boost. Put on your favorite song. Dance. Pray. Sing. Do whatever you feel is necessary to put you in the mood for success.

Be passionate about you. Be passionate about achieving. Chase your dreams, your desires, and goals. You set the finish line. Don't look to your left or right and expect anyone to be there supporting you. Look in the mirror and remember you have all the necessary tools for success.

Who wouldn't want someone in their life supporting them? If you have a supportive person, acknowledge but do not depend on them to motivate you. Definitely appreciate their presence; they are a bonus.

Most importantly, you have all you need within. Now succeed!

AFFIRMATION

Success flows through me. I was born to succeed. I am already successful. I am focused. I use my inner wisdom. I attract others that are excited and can help me to easily attain my goals.

ACTION

Envision yourself having already completed your goal or tasks. Feel it. Live in the moment daily. Be thankful, say thank you, and ask your higher power to bless you with more.

BAGGAGE

{ *Choose your destiny.* }

I am the middle child in my family. If you know anyone who is a middle child, I'm sure they'll have some stories to share.

In my opinion, I grew up seeking attention, so I excelled in school or did extra things to get attention. I felt like I was the last person to get clothes so I eventually got a job or earned extra money to buy my own. One year, I think I was about nine years old, it was the dead of winter in Chicago, there was ice on the streets and my shoes were worn out. Actually they were talking, meaning the sole separated from the upper portion of the shoe, so I wore my mother's bowling shoes to school, slipping and sliding all the way to the bus stop, down the school halls and back home.

The baggage I incurred was:

- Desiring love

- Desiring attention

- Self-sacrifice instead of self-preservation for the sake of love and attention

Each of the experiences I've had, and you've had, are a part of us. These experiences create challenges, pain, strength and a variety of other emotions. As we get older, the experiences change, leaving us with new lessons to learn. When the experience is one that you don't agree with, may have hurt you, or you keep repeating, you reflect on that experience when confronted with one that's similar and/or build up fear and walls to protect yourself. Though your reactions/actions may not be appropriate for the current situation, it is what it is – fear.

Baggage is fear and emotions that you are holding onto. We hold them because we have not healed. If not released, fear will repetitively attract the same thing/experience causing you to feel the same emotions.

Use the feeling, fear, to understand what you desire in life. Dissect what is bothering you and more than likely, your desire will be the opposite of what you fear. Release fear by confronting the issue. Allow the experience to guide you to make sure you don't have the same experience again.

Heavy duty bags or cheap bags?

Have you ever heard the song "Bag Lady" by Erykah Badu? This song discusses how people carry baggage from relationship to relationship and miss opportunities, because we've crowded our space with hurt from the past, blocking fresh starts.

By never confronting the issues that have caused us pain, we store loads of hurt feelings, denial, anger, as well as so many other emotions that we could fill bags with it – hence baggage.

Bags are used to store and transport items from one destination to another. Eventually the items that are placed in the bag are taken out and the bag is discarded.

Too many people have invested in heavy-duty emotional bags, the most durable they could find so they can continue to transport their baggage from place to place for the rest of their lives. This is one time that you want a cheap bag so that when you get a hole in it, all the baggage will have leaked out by the time you have reached your next destination.

43

> ## Release fear by confronting the issue.

At some point in your lifetime, you must experience pain in order to know joy. Pain is such an intense feeling that we carry the experience that has caused it until we can understand and discard it or it's replaced by a temporary distraction. The distraction takes your mind away until another experience triggers the old emotions, creating a floodgate.

No matter at what point you are impacted, it is your responsibility to empty your bags to create a void to be filled with a new experience. This may be a different approach to what you have considered baggage to be. We don't usually focus on the growth; we focus on the pain or what we feel we've lacked. By looking at it as a challenge or opportunity to make you a better person, you take the stronger view and become the captain of the ship. From that moment on, you choose your destiny.

Every circumstance, be it positive or negative, has made you who you are today. Each childhood experience establishes the questions you want answered as an adult. Each inadequacy or sufficiency you feel is an accumulation of experiences you will decipher and change, or use as you develop. As an adult, you must take control and heal yourself through healthy expression without causing harm to others.

How do you heal?

To help you grow and understand why you went through these changes of life, I suggest keeping a journal. Writing is therapeutic and one of the most powerful healing tools available. Within you are all the answers. By writing and keeping a journal, you learn about yourself and your patterns. You get to see your growth as a person. You always have a sounding board: your pen and paper. You never have to curb what you want to say. You can express yourself without holding back.

- *Start a journal*

You can buy an ordinary notebook or purchase an actual journal and just start writing. Write about whatever you feel; what hurts you, has made you happy, or anything you have not resolved. Write about it until you feel better. The more you write, the more you converse with self. The majority of the time you will receive your answers to all the "whys" from within. With writing comes understanding. It may take some time for closure. Nevertheless, one day it will come.

Start to write about that childhood baggage that is still affecting you today. Write about the kids who harassed you, the time you wanted to go out with your friends and you couldn't, that mean teacher, or the abuse you experienced. Write everything you ever wanted to say to the people who hurt you, release the pain and you'll release yourself from the prison you've been in.

> **The answers are within.**

You are not responsible for actions forced upon you as a child. You did not control the situations you were in. As an adult, you can now take control and heal yourself.

- *Talk it out*

Express to a friend or loved one how you feel and how the particular experiences have affected your life. If necessary, seek the help of a professional therapist. The more you talk, the less you will hurt. You will release the pain through expression.

- *Confront the issue*

Speak to the other party to the experience. Don't just point fingers; take responsibility for your actions. As you express, use the words "I feel" or "I was hurt by" to release. Do not expect the person to apologize. Just use this time to release.

- *Cry*

We have tears for a reason. At the time of the event, tears may not have been appropriate or for whatever reason they did not come out. In privacy, you can let go. Release the pain from the depths of your soul. Free yourself.

- *Artistic Expression*

If you feel that pain makes you feel aggressive, go to a gym, punch a punching bag, play a musical instrument, write a song, draw, or run.

Never harm another because of the pain you feel.

To alleviate baggage, stay conscious of your emotions. Recognize signs that you may be adding to your bag.

- Did you express yourself concerning the situation?
- Are you feeling any pain or tension?
- Are you angry after the fact?
- Do you have tears waiting to come out?
- Are you holding in emotions?

If you recognize any of these signs, don't wait days or months to start healing yourself. Realize why you are in pain. Accept your feelings; validate them. It's okay to hurt. If you're journaling, write the reasons why you hurt. Ask yourself how you contributed to the situation. Take responsibility for your actions. Release every thought and emotion you have in a way that helps you but doesn't cause harm to others. If need be, repeat the steps you take for healing until the pain subsides. If necessary, incorporate a variety of methods such as talking to a confidant as well as journaling. If you continue to do this throughout life, you can experience each experience for what it's worth and appreciate it. You will understand the exchange you share in each experience, why you experienced it and have the ability to move on without filling your bag and carrying it to another relationship.

We experience some things in order to be a voice, inspiration, or support to others. You can definitely turn lemons into lemonade. **Don't miss out on what life has to offer. See the forest and the trees.**

AFFIRMATION
I release and let go of the past, pain and all things that are not good for my mind, body, and spirit. I know that by focusing on the now, I relieve myself of past worries, pain, and concerns. I know life had greater and more beautiful experiences in store for me and I openly accept them now.

ACTION
Heal in a positive way by not harming yourself or others. You may have experienced some things that were terrible or pain that is unimaginable. How can you use that same experience to help someone else?

MEASURING UP

> *Yours are the only standards you have to measure up to.*

Whoo hoo! The end of a marking period and grade time was always exciting in the Martin household. At least it was for me. I was always excited to get my grades, but even more excited because the child with the best grades would get a monetary award. Thanks to my dad, the tradition continued until he passed away. My siblings and I would rush home to compare our grades to see who would win the money. Lucky me; I won just about every time. My motivation wasn't the money. I was trying to please my father. I wanted his approval.

As children, we are conditioned to do positive things to benefit from the result be it a kind word, praise, or a reward. We're craving the feelings derived from praise and ultimately love that comes with approval.

As a young adult, you will be challenged to do what will make you happy instead of compromising to gain someone's approval. You'll have to decide whom you love most, yourself or another person. Are you doing what you do for praise and love from someone or because you simply desire to?

To gain love we sometimes do what will please someone else because we think it will make him or her love us more, but do you love yourself?

We go through life trying to make people we love proud of us. Parents have a tendency to push their own desires and dreams on their children because they did not do what they yearned to do, possibly because their parents did the same to them. This causes lost time and delay of accomplishments. When you finally realize that what you're doing is not what you desire and that you're trying to measure up to someone else's expectations, half of your life has passed you by. You then have to redefine self and identify what you really want to do and create your own path instead of following the one that others predestined for you.

You have to choose and recognize that the only person's standards you have to measure up to are your own. You are responsible for your happiness and accomplishments. When you're an elderly person, you are the one who must look back on your life and say to yourself, "If only I had..."

Avoid this by experiencing what interests you. Explore life and all that it has to offer. Set no limits on yourself. Be the best you that you can be. That starts with loving self first and making yourself happy before anyone else. Time is precious. Do not waste it pursuing dreams that are not your own. **Dare yourself to be you!**

AFFIRMATION
I love myself. In my life I am pursuing that which will make me happy. I attract positive healthy experiences that will allow me to become the best I can be. I am attracting only that which complements my desires, my highest high in this lifetime. I release all judgments and guilt that I may have for not following someone else's desires and replace them with peace and happiness. I have created a void that I now fill with my own desires.

ACTION
Make a list of your true goals. Make an action plan – a list of smaller tasks that will help you reach your goal. Act on it. Be accepting of yourself. You may question what you are doing because of fear or wanting approval from others. Ask yourself are you happy when you're completing your goals? Allow that answer to direct you.

SELF DEFENSE

{ *Be aware and stay safe!* }

This information is not intended to be used as a sole resource for self-defense. It is merely supplied to provide tips for protection. You are urged to seek the advice of a professional to learn techniques as well as other protective measures. **Use at your own discretion.**

1. Always be aware of your surroundings. Criminals are more likely to attack people who are not attentive.

2. If you must go out late at night, take someone with you.

3. If you notice someone near or under your car, do not proceed to your car; go in a different direction, get an escort, return to the place you were leaving.

4. Carry your keys in your hand to be used as a weapon.

5. If you feel someone is following or approaching you, act as if you are crazy. Talk loud, be abrasive, and flail your arms; do whatever you need to do to attract attention to yourself. Call out for help.

6. If the person is near you, turn to them with a mean expression on your face, and scream in your crazy voice, "What do you want

from me? I am not in the mood! Get away before I hurt you!"

7. Women, place your purse strap over your head and under your arm for added security.

8. Women with ponytails and long hair are targets. Your hair can be used against you. Always be aware of your surroundings.

9. Always look around you as you walk.

10. Look inside your car before entering and lock your doors as soon as you get in your car.

11. If the door of your home is open (not as you left it), do not enter. Go to a neighbor's home and call the police.

12. If a suspicious person is lurking outside your home or knocks on your door, speak loudly as if someone is in the house with you. Never appear to be alone. Never open your door to strangers. Never invite them in for any reason.

If you are attacked:

13. Run away.

14. Scream! Call attention to yourself.

15. Gouge their eyes or scratch them.

16. Use the heel of your shoe as a weapon. Raise your knee as high as possible and slam your heel down with all your strength on their toes.

17. If your attacker is male, grab his private parts and squeeze until he faints. If your attacker is female, grab her breast and don't let go.

18. Grab the pit of your attacker's underarm and squeeze. It's an extremely sensitive area.

19. Knee your attacker in the genitals.

20. Bite hard enough to rip off whatever body part you can sink your teeth into.

21. If attacked from behind, do the same heel technique described in #4 and send a swift jab to your attacker's ribs with your elbow.

22. If you're on the ground, kick, kick, kick.

It's a Girl Thing!

GIRL THING INTRODUCTION

> ## *Allow the world to complement you by first complementing yourself!*

This is the girl section – intended for girls! Okay. For guys who are brave enough to delve into the pages and learn about women, you can read it too.

Woooo Hoo! Girl Power!

It is a wonderful time to be alive and have so many strong intelligent role models.

Take a moment and think about women such as, Mae Jamison, Oprah Winfrey, Sandra Day O'Connor, and Hillary Clinton. With such incredible role models, you should never doubt your capabilities.

Each of these women has achieved success in one or several aspects of their lives. They are respected because of their accomplishments and their image. They are respected because they first respect themselves. You must have self-respect to gain the respect of others. The way you are treated is decided by how you allow others to treat you.

Independence is often coupled with self-respect. Being an independent woman means you can take care of yourself and anything anyone does for you or gives you is a bonus. Remain an individual. Allow men to be men.

Allow him to complement your efforts and help you when he can.

Take your time in life. Court and choose "the best male bird". Allow a man to come to you. Don't give away the kitchen sink before he buys the house. Learn men. Respect men that deserve respect. Remember that tears don't detract from manhood.

When you're ready to marry, be the best wife you can be. Don't forget what you did to deserve that man. Do the same to keep him.

Learn your body. Respect your body. Take care of your body. Learn your spirit. Respect your spirit. Take care of your spirit!

Love you always!

THE IMPORTANCE OF SELF-RESPECT FOR WOMEN

You set the example of what your expectations of others are concerning your treatment.

I remember being in the midst of several young ladies freely calling one another "bitch." I also remember one day listening to adult females refer to themselves as "bitch."

I've been to clubs and watched young ladies being sexually harassed and assaulted, only for them to giggle about it. I've also watched as they danced and flashed everyone with their butts and breasts and either allowed men to touch them or got upset when someone did.

What I don't understand, how could these women/young ladies ever expect respect when they don't respect themselves?

Women are under attack by the disrespect displayed on television and in today's music. Women are not seen for their uniqueness, appreciated for their love, honored nor respected as the glue that keeps families together. Women are defamed daily and viewed as sex objects who are not seen or acknowledged for their continuing struggle to maintain an increasing number of fatherless households. Women are nothing but "the one" for the night, discarded for the next.

What happened to the respect that we had for our mothers? What happened to the fathers who demanded respect for women? Where are the fathers who once trained men to be men? Ladies, they are close to extinction. It is your responsibility to claim your respect. It is your responsibility to demand it.

- ***Put your clothes back on.***

Remove the profane language and the careless disrespect of your counterparts. Take back what is rightfully yours – your self-respect. If you don't do it, you condone it. You accept that it's okay each time a man calls you other than your name, treats you as a piece of meat, or touches you without permission.

- ***Your body is your property.***

You are the caretaker of you. You are setting an example of your expectations of others concerning your treatment. If you allow someone to call you a profane name and you laugh it off, or you permit a man to use your body as a garbage dump at his whim, how could you ever expect anything different?

- ***You are to dictate your treatment; what you will and will not accept in your life.***

Respect yourself by treating yourself in the highest regard possible. Act like a lady and don't give anyone an opportunity to challenge your morals or dignity.

- ***You attract what you put out.***

If you desire fillet mignon and you're acting like a fast food queen, get ready for a dollar menu meal. If you freely call yourself a female dog, the next person will feel it is okay to call you one as well. Do you really consider yourself to be a genital-licking, scrap-eating dog? Check yourself.

- ***Self-respect will carry you through life.***

It will allow you to enter various arenas and decrease, if not eliminate, disrespectful situations. **Allow the world to complement you by first complementing yourself.**

AFFIRMATION

I realize that I am a beautiful creation of my Creator. I know that as I respect myself I command respect from others. I walk with honor, represent love, and exude the beauty of all this is.

ACTION

- Buy clothes your size and dress less provocatively.
- Stop referring to yourself as a bitch. Don't call your friends bitches, hoes, or any other profane name.
- If necessary, find yourself a new group of friends that respect themselves.
- Don't use your body to get attention. If someone really likes you they will be interested in what you have to say, spending time with you, etc.
- Wait to have sex with someone. Sex doesn't equal love.
- Devote time to discovering yourself. Just because you grew up in a sexual environment doesn't mean you have to be that way. You attract what you put out.

INDEPENDENT WOMEN

> *As an independent woman, your success is not dependent upon whether or not someone can foot the bill.*

The song "Independent Women" by Destiny's Child is one of my theme songs and some of you may want to make it yours, too. This song is about a woman and her ability to clothes, treat, and take care of herself. You should depend on you and only you, and not any other individual. Anything extra is a bonus.

Independence increases self-esteem, self worth, self-love, and respect. The respect comes not only from you but your peers and family as well. However, what you think of yourself is what matters most.

There is nothing like the feeling of knowing you can take care of yourself and you are in full control of your being. It not only relieves you of stress, but it also relieves the people who are in your comfort zone (the people the matter to you and you to them) because they don't have to worry about your needs and wants.

Your attitude toward life is different as an independent woman. You are self-assured because you are in control of what, when, why, and how you do what you do. Your accomplishments are not based on whether someone can afford to foot the bill. You don't have to depend on someone else supporting you.

> **Never give up your power.
> Never give up your will.**

Being independent frees you. You don't have to compromise yourself, your standards or beliefs, or deny your self-expression. You don't have to do something other than what your heart desires because of fear that your support will be cut off.

Everything beyond what you do or are capable of doing for yourself is a bonus. The money or efforts of others is a complement to your actions, an enhancement to your success. Others' efforts do not dictate your success or failure.

In marriages or other relationships, the ability to depend on someone and them not disrespect or mistreat you does exist. These types of relationships are wonderful.

However, there are some men who need women to validate them or make them feel manly by having women depend on them. These men usually have low self-esteem and need to be able to control something in their lives, so they give you everything they can possibly give. They create a dependency on your part (make you feel like you need him in your life because he supports you). He develops control, controlling and overriding your will (what you desire), because he now has one up on you. You now expect a standard of living that you can't afford yourself. This is when you start to compromise yourself, bite your tongue, or do undesirable things for fear of losing these materialistic items.

> **Never stay in a situation that makes you fearful.**

If you notice this occurring in your life and you have the courage, this is where you might start to become that independent woman, so you can "throw your hands up at me!"

Money is being manufactured all the time. I don't think they'll be running out of it anytime soon. The same money your supporter is making and spending on you; you can make and spend too.

I hope that you are reading this information before you've become dependent on someone. This way you know what not to do.

If you're already in a dependent position, I recommend change. You don't have to leave or eliminate this person from your life. You do, however, need to gain power and control of your life. You can reclaim your power by eliminating your dependence on this person.

You need a source of income. Look at your standard of living and learn how much money it takes to maintain it. What is your education level? At this point in your life, how much money are you capable of making? Is your standard of living much higher than your potential income could maintain? If so, it's time to do a few things.

Find out how much this person that you're dependent on really loves and cares about you by requesting they pay for your education. This may not happen because they may think you're trying to become independent and they'll lose you.

If your supporter won't support you, go back to school on your own steam. Get financial aid, grants or whatever is necessary and get it done!

Think about what has always interested you and pursue a career that will utilize the talents you already have.

Get a part time job while you're in school. No matter what your pay is, you'll feel good receiving a check with your name on it and knowing that you've earned your own money.

If you're already educated, then get busy girl! What have you been waiting on? Let everything your supporter provides become a bonus rather than a necessity in your life. It's time for you to save, invest, and set yourself up for the rest of your life.

Being an independent woman will help you in more ways than you'll ever know. Have you ever seen the commercial on television where the husband dies with no life insurance or savings, and the wife is left alone with a family to take care of? She has no money. She either has an education and hasn't worked in a quadrillion years or has no education because her goal was to be a mother forever. All she'd done for the last few decades was stay at home being a mother and wife. The husband took care of everything. She didn't even know how to use a checkbook. All this because she gave up her will, never explored herself and her capabilities, and created a dependency on her husband. In the meantime, she lost her identity and didn't develop beyond being a mother. She didn't develop skills that would allow her to support her family.

It is wonderful to have a relationship where you divide the responsibilities of taking care of the family. But, you should still learn all aspects of maintaining the household. No one is promised tomorrow. Your life can change in the blink of an eye. So why are you depending on what can change in a heartbeat?

Never become that lost woman. If you allow yourself to be sheltered, you will miss out on much of life. You should be able to ask yourself, "What did I accomplish for myself this year?" Be able to give an answer.

Please never stop developing yourself. Never stop learning. Never stop pursuing your goals and dreams. Never give up self for anyone! **You can share you, but never forget your number one priority… YOU!**

AFFIRMATION

I am an independent woman. All that I need, I have within me. I know that my creator has more in store for me. I openly accept the goodness of the divine. Thank you Creator and give me more.

ACTION

- Develop an action plan by listing your desires.
- Follow your plan. If you encounter difficulty, don't give up. You have to experience the "bad" before you experience the "good". Things often get stressful right before the break through.
- If necessary seek help or advice.

THE BEST MALE BIRD

Value yourself and allow a man to earn your love.

NOW, THROW YOUR HANDS UP AT ME!

I watched a PBS television documentary on evolution and survival. It showed how several bird species went through their mating process. What ruled supreme was the female being the chooser. She dictated with whom and when she would mate.

What really struck me as interesting is how the female birds knew this and used it to their advantage. By being particular in their choice of mate, they dictated and controlled the survival of their species by choosing the best male bird.

The male birds danced, sang, and even showed off their feathers to get the female's attention. They set out to impress a female bird to have the honor of mating with her. Many males approached the ladybird and she just sat and watched until finally the best male bird came along. He was the bird that exerted the most masculinity, strength, and survival instincts. He had traits that assured her that her offspring would survive and carry on as a strong generation.

This documentary went on to explore other bird species as well, and the female birds remained very selective in choosing their mates. They would even fight off males that weren't right for them.

As I watched the program, I actually became upset with myself. I am the mother of three sons whose fathers don't participate in their lives. I've raised my boys by myself and I realized that I didn't pick the best male bird. I didn't take the time to get to know myself to decipher my definite desires nor did I get to know the fathers of my sons well enough to determine whether they were quality men who would be there. I didn't pay attention to their personality flaws because I was too busy trying to focus on their positive qualities. I didn't acknowledge their family history or their survival instincts in relation to how their DNA could affect my children. I was looking for the good and trying to get them to realize their self-worth. I should have kept my legs closed, learned them, and continued looking for the best male bird.

As I reflect, I realize I am a product of my environment. I was never taught about being a lady, how to deal with men, or anything about choosing the best. My father died just when I needed him the most. I knew not what to look for. My life has been a continuous lesson of learning about putting myself first, holding myself in high regard and learning to show my "being" only to the best male bird.

In this society, some parents teach their daughters to choose the best male bird. Can you guess whom? They would be the "upper class" – those who consider it terrible to date someone without a name. Why are they like this? Think for a moment. If I were in that class, the best male bird would be someone from a wealthy family, a good family history, who takes his earnings and invests them properly, strong in character, and knows how to treat a woman of my caliber. This way, we'd pass down wealth to our children, a good family history, survival instincts, and good character – the same thing the birds do.

We all fit into a certain group or class of people. As we get older, we may change our class through our successes or failures in our lifetime. Through it all, you learn who the best male bird would be for you. You know within your heart what caliber of woman you are and what caliber of man you deserve.

If no one took the time to teach you about being choosy, putting yourself first, and only allowing the best into your life, then it's time to teach yourself. This does not mean that you have to be a snob or act stuck up. It simply means do not compromise your desires due to what may seem to be a good thing. Let that man dance, sing, and show off his feathers to gain your attention. Allow him to prove to you that he is the best male bird.

Keep your legs closed so that you don't wind up with any permanent attachments to your suitor. A man who thinks you're worth the time will put forth effort and patience. Men like a challenge anyway.

Along the way, we have gotten away from being courted. Women are now giving away everything before they get married or even get an engagement ring.

It has now become the norm to have sex and live with someone before you get married. Women are not being taught the power of being a woman and the fact that a man gladly takes on a challenge that he feels is worthwhile. Ladies slow down. If he is interested, he will take his time.

When you live with a man you regard as your boyfriend, you are giving him every comfort of a marriage without the commitment. Men are taking advantage of women everyday who don't know any better. Value yourself and allow a man to earn your love. Let him earn your cooking, cleaning, running his baths, and taking care of him. If you give away the milk, why should he buy the cow? When you give him everything of yourself without a commitment, what does he have to look forward to in marriage?

During his process of courting you, make sure he's sincere in his actions by spending quality time, learning one another, experiencing both your likes and dislikes, hobbies, talents, meeting the family, etc.

Establish a good line of communication that is filled with honesty and truth. Make sure he makes his deposits in the love bank before you allow him to make a withdrawal. **Let him show you that he is the best male bird and you show him that you've been the best ladybird all the time!**

AFFIRMATION

I am a divine being, deserving the best life has to offer. I have a mate that is my complement. We love, respect, and honor one another. I know my mate will arrive in divine time.

ACTION

Define the type of mate and relationship you desire to have. Be careful in your description. The universe will give you exactly what you ask for. Spend each day focusing on how your relationship will be as if it already is.

SOME THINGS YOU SHOULD KNOW ABOUT MEN

The goal is finding someone willing to work on themselves as you do the same.

A man's attitude towards life and women is greatly influenced by his relationship with his mother and his mother's relationships. These examples will dictate or influence how he treats you, his opinion of women, and the value he places on them.

Many young men and women are being raised in a single parent household headed by a woman. Therefore, many of our men are struggling with understanding manhood and may have very different perceptions of what a woman's responsibilities are.

There are young men who:

- Think it's the woman's responsibility to take care of him or that he has to battle the women for control of the household to the extreme of setting the house at unease.

- Don't have the natural protective instinct as some men. There are those that do.

- Have watched their mothers in abusive relationships and either vow to never hit a woman because they know it's wrong or will hit woman because they think it shows love or they don't know how

66

to handle anger.

- Will associate their manhood with their ability to take care of you or the family and if you are self-sufficient they'll feel inadequate.
- Will feel confused about their role in the family because they didn't have a male example.

Seemingly, very few young men grow up in two parent households and see loving relationships and active fathers. At this rate, it's going to take a lot of patience for you to have a successful relationship. You will be dealing with your dysfunctions and his. Young ladies struggle with their roles and identities as well. The goal is finding someone willing to work on themselves as you do the same.

An example of a good relationship will be the ones where the roles and identities are eliminated and you find out how you and your mate complement one another. What is he good at? What are you good at? Allow him to do what he's good at and vice versa.

- ***Find out about his childhood, how he grew up, what he didn't like and what he loved, what his dreams and desires were/are.***

What was his household and neighborhood environment like? What did he wish he had and desire to do or become?

- ***Learn about his relationship with his father.***

Was his father in the household? Who taught him about manhood? This way you can learn what kind of man he desires to be or fears becoming. It will also let you know the type of parent he could potentially be and who his role model(s) were.

- ***Ask him about his faults.***

What does he know that he needs to correct about himself? What is he ashamed of? In the beginning, people always show you their best side. As the relationship progresses, the "real" person creeps out. The faster you get to know the "real" them, the quicker you'll know if this person is right for you.

- ***Allow him to be a man.***

Complement him instead of overriding him. Give him a chance to be himself. However, don't sacrifice yourself or your happiness to teach a man to be a man.

Points to remember:

1. You are an individual first. Always do what's best for you!

2. Ask them more questions than they ask you in the beginning. Many guys will allow you to talk so they can learn what they need to say to you to win you over. Not that it's the truth but it's what you want to hear.

3. Don't allow anyone to approach you with a conversation about sex. If you fall for it, they may peg you as somewhat "easy". Sex should not be a conversation until well in the future of your relationship. Do not discuss sex when you are initially courting.

4. Give them space and keep yours.

5. Allow them to pursue you.

6. Don't give too many chances. Stand your ground.

7. Never allow them to disrespect you verbally, emotionally, or physically.

8. Do not allow them to hit you – ever! If it happens, get out of the relationship.

9. Never give up your free will. Continue to make decisions for you that relate to your happiness.

10. Do not allow a man to dictate to you – what you can wear, where you can go or what you can do.

11. Remain independent. Anything he does for you should be a bonus.

12. If you're considering a long-term relationship with him, pay attention to his management of time, money, etc.

13. Let him earn your trust. Unfortunately, many men lie. If it sounds like a lie or feels like a lie, it's probably a lie.

14. Some men, young and old, are on a conquest to conquer as many women possible. Be aware and sure that you are getting what

you want from the relationship while he's getting what he wants. Make sure it benefits you.

15. Many young men live in the moment for as long as possible. Without some type of serious responsibility, they take their time maturing.

16. You don't have to be strong and do everything yourself. Allow him to assist you.

17. A man that appreciates you for who you are will never degrade your strength or demand you change to appear weak in order to decrease his inadequate feelings.

18. Men are visual beings. They love women to look pretty. It keeps them attracted.

19. Guard your heart and protect your body.

AFFIRMATION

I am aware and in tune with my consciousness. I listen to my body and my spirit to make decisions that are good for me. I attract positive, loving, kind, respectful men into my life.

ACTION

Stay aware of your relationships. Listen to people. If you pay attention, they will tell you everything you need to know.

BABIES FOR THE WRONG REASONS

Never have a child because you feel lonely, desire love, or are trying to keep a significant other in your life.

During one of the attempts with my son's father to work things out, we had unprotected sex. I trusted him to use the withdrawal method but he had a plan I wasn't aware of. He had the sick notion that if he impregnated me again, we would stay together and things would work out. Uh, no. That wasn't going to happen.

Usually it's the woman trying to keep the man. He flipped the script. Regardless of the situation, a child should not be a pawn in an effort to fortify a relationship.

Never have a child to get or to keep a man. It doesn't increase his love for you nor his desire to be with you. If a man is with you because you're having his child, his dedication and loyalty is to the child. It doesn't mean that he will stay with you.

Do not put yourself through the unnecessary stress, pressure, or drama that comes with this situation. If you decide to have a child and you're not in a marriage or steadfast relationship, you should take a serious look at your life.

When making the decision, weigh your options. Don't depend on child support or the child's father being in your life. You have to look at what you're capable of providing, your finances, support network, and time.

In addition, what if the child's father decides that he doesn't want to be involved in the child's life? Think about the imbalance for which you will be trying to compensate for the rest of your life. Think about your life, how you were raised, what you're able to give, and what you really want for you and your child.

> **Have a child when you are ready and willing to make the sacrifices associated with parenthood.**

Things you should know about being a single parent

- Time for yourself...what's that? When you are a custodial parent, your child will dominate your time.

- You will have to be creative and always on your toes when trying to balance the absence of the other parent.

- You are everything to your child: doctor, nurse, teacher, friend, playmate, mother, and father.

- Your dreams and goals may take a little longer to accomplish.

- You will have to rearrange your life.

- Every event of your life will have to be planned around your child.

- Before you make a major decision, you have to consider how it will affect your child's life. You no longer have the carefree option of doing things on a whim.

- Children are expensive. They are constantly growing and changing and you must have the money to keep up with their changing needs.

- You have to keep food in the house and the electricity and gas working.

- You must remain ever conscious of the people you bring around your child. You have to protect them from abuse, bad examples, and violence.

Are you ready to give up your freedom? Are you ready to do it all alone?

If you know any single parents, talk to them. Spend some time with them to digest what being a single parent really requires. It's not the easiest road in life and you have to be very special to be willing to make a sacrifice of this kind. **Be sure that you're sure!**

THE FEMALE BODY

Take care of your body and it will take care of you.

Discovering womanhood on your own is more of an everyday occurrence than not. One day you notice your breasts changing, and then your vagina and then you start menstruating.

It amazes me when I converse with adult women who don't know about their bodies, but when I think about it, I can relate. The way I learned about my body was by reading books.

If you are unknowledgeable about your body or ashamed of it, set aside all of the stories, misconceptions and shame and read on. I'll share with you what I would have told my daughter had I had one.

Never be ashamed of your body. It is a beautiful and dynamic creation. Your body was made especially for you, for your spirit to live in. Your body has an intelligence of its own, containing billions of living cells that communicate with one another to keep your body functioning.

The body is beautiful but being female is even greater. You are immensely special. You can create, carry, and nourish a life. The beginnings of these abilities start with puberty. Yes, I know you'll feel/felt a little uncomfortable because your body is/was changing, but welcome it. You are becoming a woman.

Your breasts are developing because they are mammary glands. One day you may decide to have children, so they are preparing to be able to deliver sustenance to your baby.

Your female organs are developing for the processes that will enable you to carry and birth a child. Let me explain.

Your body ovulates, which is producing and releasing an egg to be fertilized. During this time, the body is storing nutrients (contained in blood) in the lining of the uterus. The uterus is where a baby will live until it is born.

A few days before menstruation, an egg leaves one of your ovaries and travels through a fallopian tube to the uterus and floats around waiting to be fertilized by sperm. When the egg is not fertilized, it travels out of the body along with the shed lining of the uterus, through the cervix and the vaginal canal. This is menstruation; the flow of blood from your vagina which occurs on a monthly basis.

If the egg is fertilized, it will attach itself or burrow into the lining of the uterus where the embryo (baby) will develop for the next 38-40 weeks.

Menstruation is one of the biggest physical changes you will experience as a young lady.

Female body care tips

- *Apply cocoa butter, lotion or olive oil to your whole body.*

This will keep your skin supple. Massage your body to help blood circulate and remove waste.

- *Try to eat less sugar around the time of your menstrual cycle, and make sure your bowels are moving properly.*

If necessary, take a laxative. This will help to reduce or eliminate cramps.

- *Cleanse your body – every nook and cranny.*

It's not natural for you to smell bad. Bathe daily. If you notice a discharge or a foul scent that won't go away, see a gynecologist.

- ***Don't mistreat your body with drugs, alcohol, or smoking.***

It ages you and speeds up death. You make it hard for your body to heal itself.

- ***Don't give/share your body with just anyone.***

You don't owe anyone your body because they took you out to dinner or a movie. Respect yourself.

- ***Select clean partners.***

Bacteria will travel and cause infections. Women's bodies are very sensitive. Think about it: you are allowing someone inside your body.

- ***Always protect yourself.***

Never depend on your partner. You carry the ultimate responsibility and decision-making power concerning life.

- ***Love yourself first.***

If you do this, you'll be all right. You will get sidetracked sometimes. Get back on track by doing what's best for you.

For more information on the female reproductive organs, see the section entitled "Health."

CALCULATING YOUR MENSTRUAL CYCLE

Menstruation: part of the cycle of life.

Menstruation involves your body releasing an egg and the food it stored to feed the potential life that could have developed. Each month your body goes through a cycle of preparation for another life to enter the world, and when it doesn't, it removes what is then unnecessary.

Menstruation can feel like the plague when it catches you off guard. However, there is a way to anticipate when to expect your period. Each woman's cycle occurs within 28 days. To calculate your average time span between periods, circle the first date of your period on your calendar. You can anticipate your period between 20 and 28 days. The next time your period comes, circle that date. Now count from the first date to the second date and you will know how many days you have between each period.

If you want to plan a trip, a wedding, or any other event, you can calculate your next period and plan around it.

Pay attention to your body. If you notice you're having mood swings, headaches, or any other sign of PMS (pre-menstrual syndrome), check your calendar to see how many days remain until your next menstruation.

Vaginal Exam/Pap Test

> *Take care of your pocket book. You harness the most valuable aspect of being a woman...the ability to give life.*

Having your first vaginal examination is truly an experience. You have to allow someone to see what your parents have told you never to show anyone. Even worse, they're going to touch it. This is something that you have to get over quickly. (You can add this to the list of things you go through as a woman).

A vaginal exam is necessary to check the health of your vagina and other reproductive organs.

When you visit the doctor's office, you will change into a gown and be covered with a sheet. You will then be asked to either allow the bottom of your feet to touch and let your knees fall to the sides or prop your feet in stirrups. The doctor will them examine your vagina externally. Next, a lubricated speculum is inserted within your vagina to allow the doctor to examine the inside of the vagina. Sometimes the speculum will pinch you. If you feel any pain, let the doctor know so he or she can adjust it.

To conduct the Pap test, the doctor will use a small brush to remove some cells from your cervix, which will be sent to a lab to check for any abnormalities.

The doctor will them place two fingers in your vagina and press on your abdominal area to check your ovaries, fallopian tubes, and uterus. You will be asked if you feel any tenderness or pain as they check for abnormalities.

Be sure to tell the doctor about any changes you've noticed. Be honest with the doctor so they're able to diagnosis you properly. The vaginal exam is a way for the doctor to "catch" illnesses such as a STD, vaginal cancer, or other issues that can develop into more serious illness if let undetected. After the exam, the specimen is sent to a lab and the doctor's office will contact you with the results. If the doctor requests a return call or for you to return to the office, do not hesitate to return. **Always accept opportunities to heal.**

COSMETIC TIPS

Complement your inner beauty.

Who taught you how to apply makeup? Was it your friend, older sister, your mother, or did you learn to do it by yourself? Makeup today is much different from the makeup used by earlier generations. The variety available today shows that manufacturers are acknowledging every skin color and type.

Less is more. Wear makeup to complement your natural beauty. Don't look like Me Me on "The Drew Carey Show". She's a classic example of someone who applies too much makeup, uses blending and colors poorly, and really has no clue about application.

If using makeup is new to you, invest in a session with a makeup artist. They will be able to help you to choose the right foundation, liners, eye shadow, etc. You can even visit the department store counters and sales representatives will be more than happy to help you.

Wear appropriate makeup for each occasion. Save the glitter and heavier makeup for parties or after-five events. Use softer makeup for work or the daytime and get your eyebrows professionally arched. It truly makes a difference.

You don't want to be noticed for your flaws. Don't use excessive makeup to draw attention to them. Excessive makeup is associated with women who are loose or *easy to bed*. Makeup cannot hide pain or anything you dislike about yourself. They will always show through.

Less is more.

Try manufacturer Web sites for tips and tricks on makeup application. Www.youtube.com has many videos about makeup application. I like the videos shown on this site because they actually demonstrate how the products are used. You can learn how to work the brushes, sponges and other tools.

Remember, appearance does matter and will affect others' perception of you.

"MEN DON'T CRY"

If tears provide relief and help to heal, then why not cry?

Do you remember a boy from your childhood who would always get in trouble for crying? Everyone teased him and his father probably gave him something to remember for each tear that fell from his eyes.

Men are plagued with keeping up with the stereotypical tough "men don't cry" image. From childhood to adulthood they were trained to not cry and suppress their pain. The phrase "men don't cry" is damaging our men.

Think about the last time you cried hard. You cried until you couldn't cry anymore. Now think about how you would feel if you had to hold in all that emotion on a daily basis all because someone told you women don't cry?

Before you put a man down, call him a wimp or whatever creative identity you come up with for him because he sheds tears, think about what you just read.

Why did the Creator give women this mode of expression if we're not to use it? Men are equipped with eyes, tears, and a voice to release in the same manner.

The belief that "men don't cry" is damaging men because each emotion felt carries an energy or vibration. The emotion causes each person to feel a certain way. To understand this, think about something that makes you happy. Notice how you feel; the smile on your face and how your body reacts. Now think of something that angers you and notice the same.

Energy travels. When it is not allowed to travel, it stagnates. When it stagnates, whatever "vibration" it's carrying will begin to affect wherever it has taken up residence.

In this case, the residence is the human body. Reflect again on the time you cried hard. Think about what made you cry that hard, what emotion(s) you felt; how these emotions influenced you (your attitude and actions) and for how many days. Think about how it must feel to carry it around with you for a lifetime. Where does that feeling go? If it wasn't released, then the body will still carry it until it is no longer at ease; it is at dis-ease which can lead to disease.

Unhappiness and stress trigger us to do things to try to deal with the disorder we feel, such as overeating, expressing anger, mistreating others or ourselves. These things, in turn, affect the body and make it unhealthy. You're not giving the body good energy because of the unhappiness you feel. You have billions of living cells in your body that share your unhappy energy. Your cells will be trying to do their job, but production is down because they are unhappy. This is the same way production can decrease in a factory when the workers are unhappy.

If tears provide relief and help us to heal, then why not cry? Never condemn a man for crying or expressing emotion. The few tears that fall may very well extend his life.

AFFIRMATION

I accept and realize that my creator has created each of us with the necessary tools for expression. I acknowledge that all humans have feelings and tears are a mode of expression that heal. I appreciate the beauty in each of my Creator's creations.

> **ACTION**
> - Don't criticize men for crying.
> - Encourage release.
> - Allow him space and time.

Notes

Life

LIFE INTRODUCTION

Life: the period of animates existence from birth until death, or a part or specific aspect of it.

My personal belief is that a part of our lives is planned, which is whatever we are to accomplish or learn in this lifetime or fate, and there is a part that isn't. The part that isn't is how and whether or not we reach that destination. This is where the power of choice comes in.

Life presents us with situations or circumstances and it's up to us to make a choice, the highest and greatest choice we can make for everyone involved. The problem is that as children or young adults, we either don't know this, don't always think about it, and definitely don't always do it, which results in the problems we have, negativity we feel, and drama we experience.

Each time you are presented with a situation, you are empowered to do what's best for you and all involved. Take your time before you choose. Weigh your options for the greater good.

You attract to you people and lessons. If you don't like the experience, choose again. If the same type person or lesson appears again, obviously you didn't get the lesson and need to do something different this time.

A lot of times, people say they want to change their lives to be different and they're sick and tired of this or that. But what are they doing differently? The definition of insanity is doing the same thing over and over again and expecting a different result. Okay so you say, I did change but the old stuff still came my way. Why? What did you actually change? Did you remove yourself from the environment? Did you change your thought process? Did your forgive yourself or other's involved? What did you do different?

In order to change:

1. Eliminate your presence in the environment.

2. Visualize your life or the situation exactly the way you desire it to be and accept it as being reality today.

3. Counter any negative thoughts with positive thoughts.

4. Keep yourself in the "now". That means stay focused on what is presently occurring in your life at this moment. The past is occurring as each second ends.

5. If you are hurting, review the occurrence. Digest what you could have done differently and forgive yourself and others if necessary.

This is life; various lessons are presented for you to learn from and it is up to you to make sound choices, choosing the best for all involved.

COMMUNICATION

> **Communication saves lives!**

My father returned to our home after learning he had a terminal illness. He and my mother had been divorced for quite some time, but when people are at their lowest, they tend to return to the ones who love them.

My father suffered with cancer for nine long months. On a beautiful spring day, my mother arrived home and when she stepped in the house, her face said it all. I don't think she ever uttered the words that my father had died. I watched as my siblings ran in various directions seeking one another for solace. They experienced denial because they kept their distance from my father as I watched him deteriorate during his illness. I watched him go downhill daily as I cared for him in my mother or grandmother's absence. His imminent death was real to me. I expected it.

On the day of the funeral as my mother sat combing my sister's hair, she said, "If you all are going to cry, do it now because if you cry at the funeral, I'll cry." We did not cry. We were children. We knew nothing about making ourselves cry and releasing on command. We went to the funeral, told jokes, and laughed at people, I guess to keep our minds off what was really going on.

From that day on, I don't remember speaking with my mother about my feelings over my father's death. During that time, I needed to talk, vent, and understand. I was fifteen years old. My life had changed. I was changing. I was grieving and I did not have an outlet.

Our house seemed to have a dark cloud over it. Everyone went in opposite directions in search of a source of comfort or peace. I don't remember my mother asking how we felt or trying to help us through this time. I guess it was because she had lost her first love and she was raising her children alone.

I eventually found someone to talk to. He even gave me comfort. I was the perfect person for him to manipulate. He realized it and took advantage of my state of mind. My mother could see he wasn't good for me. Instead of talking to me about him, sex, pregnancy, and relationships, she told me with a stern voice, "You better not come home pregnant." That was the extent of my lesson on the birds and the bees and the most "motherly advice" I'd received from my mother in seven months. One day I came home pregnant.

The inability to communicate with my mother caused me to grieve for several years. I went from being an A or A&B student to straight F's. I was in a downward spiral, eventually wanting to commit suicide and just be done with it all. Just in time, I found a support base of family and friends that I could talk to. Communication saved me.

Non-communication is a safe haven for danger, abuse, neglect, and suffering. Each time we don't communicate, we are possibly causing harm to others or ourselves.

Contributing factors to non-communication at home

- Parents repeating the way they were raised and not changing what negatively influenced them. Therefore, many situations exist where children are not being taught about emotions, life issues, finances, sex, care of the body, etc.

- Parents who work long hours or have demanding careers have a limited amount of time with their children. Limited time equals limited communication. Quality time is what counts.

- Some parents avoid discussing subject matter they're either uncomfortable with or not knowledgeable about. On the other hand, they may have learned as a child that it was not to be discussed.

- Abusive relationships can also contribute to non-communication through fear of expression.

Effects of non-communication

Non-communication contributes to:

- Low self-esteem

- Under achievement

- Lack of self-respect

- Unhappiness in school, work, family, and other relationships

- Stress

- Mental and physical problems

- Abuse and tolerance of abuse

- Weight loss and weight gain

Understanding expression and energy

Each emotion, word, and feeling carries energy meant to be expressed. We can touch, hear, speak, or create to communicate. We have tears, laughter, and other emotions for expression. Our use of these abilities differentiates us from other living species.

To understand expressive energy, do the following exercise. While being attentive to your body's response, think about someone you love. Next, think about someone you dislike. How did your body respond? Think about the times when you held in your thoughts or feelings. Did your body hurt? Did you have an upset stomach or headache? Did you overeat?

Unexpressed emotions or non-communication is stored in the body and causes dis-ease. The body is not comfortable. In order to avoid storing harmful feelings and repressed emotions, we must communicate.

How to communicate

- *Speak.*

Open you mouth and express how you feel! For some, conversation can be difficult. If you find it hard gathering your thoughts, write a list of what you want to address. Ask the other person to allow you to complete your statements before they speak. Take a deep breath and understand that with practice you will become a great communicator. Know that it's okay to speak up and express happiness and unhappiness. Maintain a peaceful conversation instead of being accusatory and saying "You did" use the words "I feel." Try to eliminate the word "you" from the conversation.

- *Be a willing listener.*

Practice listening by waiting three seconds after a person completes their sentence. This way you can be sure they're finished, avoid interruption and show respect.

- *Be patient and don't try to hurry a person along in their story.*

What they are saying may be necessary for you to understand their point.

- *Take responsibility for your actions and avoid shifting blame.*

One of the best things you can do in life is to own up to your crap. If you know someone has made a valid point, digest it and don't respond with, "Well, you did xyz." Don't be evasive and try to turn the conversation or make a point about the other person without addressing what is currently being discussed – YOU or your actions! If you owe an explanation or apology, give it.

- *Never make fun of what a person is saying to you.*

What you may think is stupid or unnecessary may be important or serious to them.

- *Consider others' perspectives.*

Don't be one-sided. Put yourself in the other person's shoes. Doing this helps you to grow as a person. You will become more in tune with how you affect others' lives.

It takes time to develop good communication. If you take the time, you can learn about others, share an experience, keep a person from danger, save a life, or steer someone in a better direction.

Parents and future parents, talk to your children. Break the barriers. Educate your offspring about life. Save them from repeating your mistakes or lessons that would not have happened had someone communicated with you.

Young adults make an effort and practice great communication daily. I know for some it may be difficult to make that first step, especially if you've grown up in a non-communicative household; but when you do, the next step will be easier.

With communication you get answers, truth and sometimes lies but you will have an opportunity to learn, gain relief, get an understanding of who or what you're dealing with, and release.

Communication saves precious time. There is no need for suffering. **Open your mouth, write a letter, save a life; communicate.**

AFFIRMATION

I am using what my creator has given me. I am expressing. I am healing through expression. I communicate well and command respect while communicating. I am a great speaker. I am a great listener. I appreciate every opportunity I have to gain a clear understanding. Every day I am becoming the best communicator that I can be.

ACTION
- Be a great listener by focusing on the person speaking and pay attention to what they're saying.
- Wait three seconds before you respond, making sure they've completed their thought.
- Say what you feel and think in a respectful manner.

EXPECTATIONS

Expectation: The act of looking forward to as fact or truth

While researching this book, I spoke with several young adults (high school students) to gain insight into what they knew about life. One of the most interesting stories came from a young man. He told me that when he graduated, he was moving to California and his father would buy him a condo and support him for the duration of his life. I asked him, "What will you do if your father dies and doesn't leave you any money? How will you survive?" He couldn't fathom my questions. Getting a job was the furthest thing from his mind. All he relied on was his expectations.

If your parents suddenly tell you to pay your own car note because you need to be more responsible, you may be disappointed because it wasn't expected.

If you walk into your house and flick the light switch but the lights don't come on, you might become angry because you expected light until you realized you didn't pay the bill.

If your mate says, "I don't want to continue this relationship," you may be hurt because that's not what you expected. You expected your relationship to proceed as normal.

The scenarios can go on and on. On a daily basis, we build our lives around expectations; things we look subconsciously forward to as being true. We expect our parents to take care of us. We expect our partners to love us. Expectations come naturally. They evolve through relating, establishing relationships, and following patterns.

People are continually evolving every second of the day, including you. The person you are today will be slightly different tomorrow because of what you have experienced today.

While getting to know a person, you learn their habits, their likes and dislikes, their propensity to do this or that. Through repetitive actions you learn them and what to realistically expect; you create expectations. These expectations are somewhat safe. Be sensible about what you expect by acknowledging what you already know. What you know is everything they've shown you; the good, the bad, and the ugly. Do not make the mistake of focusing only on the good. This is where you'll get hurt. Recognize the whole person.

Identify the expectation and you'll discover the source of your pain.

Expectations can act as a gauge to help you determine what is right for you. If an expectation is "broken", there is a reason in every scenario. Love doesn't hurt; the hurt stems from the expectation you had of the situation.

Stay consciously aware of the people you deal with from day to day. It is not by mistake that you get to see how a person acts in different settings. This will help you to fully know the person. Pay attention to the uglies – which can be hard because the good is so much happier. But if you know a person to be a certain way, accept it. **The safest expectation is CHANGE.**

AFFIRMATION
I am aware. I acknowledge the truth in each situation. I make choices that will increase the peace and happiness in my life.

ACTION
Be truthful with yourself by recognizing and accepting what is real and make changes in your life accordingly.

CHANGE—THE ONE CONSTANT

The ability to change gives you control of your environment and experiences.

It was around 9pm on a hot summer night in Chicago. As my family was settling down for the evening, several of the locals were just beginning their day. My apartment vibrated as cars drove by with piercing bass. We heard loud talking and crack addicts pushing shopping carts down the asphalt streets. Insomnia was my new friend as I was unable to sleep.

This was now the norm for this neighborhood, which was a far cry from the reasons I originally moved into the area. The original attraction to this vicinity was the beautiful brown stone building, controlled rent, inactivity (an important consideration since I had two young boys), and peace and quiet, which no longer existed. It was nothing to now see a drug deal, gang banging, prostitutes, winos, and addicts toting their goods.

The events of this particular night were life changing. Around the corner and divided by the alley in back of my apartment building was a set of row houses from which came gun shots, screaming and screeching tires. This wasn't the first time we'd heard gun shots, but it was the last. We soon heard fire trucks and police cars. I went outside to find that an off duty security guard's home was being fired upon. As she returned fire, she mistakenly shot and killed her sister.

This was not the place to raise my boys! It was time for change.

The ability to change gives you control of your environment and experiences. If a situation isn't conducive, productive, nor influencing you in a positive way, consider your right to change. Change gives you the option to create a better reality for yourself.

Familiarity is the culprit of fear of change. Being open to newness can be a challenge for some. I've known people who have lived their lives, waking up, bathing, eating breakfast, going to work, going home, having dinner, watching television, going to bed, and repeating this pattern everyday. This mundane existence is what their lives will be until they die due to fearing the unknown (change) and lacking faith to achieve what they dream. Some never venture out of the neighborhoods or other comfort zones because they don't know what to expect. Instead of fearing the unknown, embrace it as an adventure, a chance to experience or learn something new and different. You are your ultimate decision-maker. You can become whomever and whatever you desire to be.

Control your experiences... control your destiny.

Welcome change. Control your experiences, control your destiny. Never allow anyone to shatter your dreams, your goals, or your idea of who you should be. Use change to make your life what you desire. If you don't you'll never know what could have been. You'll become one of the mundane television-watching couch potatoes wondering "If I could have, would have, where might I have been today?"

Knowing when it's time to change

How do you know when it's time to change? Ask yourself these simple questions:

1. Is this situation benefiting me?

2. Is it adding to or taking away from my happiness?

3. Am I accomplishing any goals?

4.   What will I lose by letting this situation go?

If the bad outweighs the good, then it's time to move on. Always do what is going to increase happiness and peace in your life. Make choices that will help you prosper mentally, spiritually, and emotionally for the long-term. **If you're in a "bad situation" you always have the option to change.**

AFFIRMATION

I am a co-creator working hand and hand with my creator. I know that I have the power to change my life. I accept change and am open to the wonderful possibilities of life. I know that although I can't see the unknown, I have faith in the guidance of the divine. I understand there is a blessing in every situation. I welcome change. I welcome peace, happiness, and the excitement of life.

ACTION

Choose a place you'd like to visit. It can be a museum, restaurant, school, city, or whatever will make you happy. Go there and take in the whole experience; sights, sounds, scents, and movement.

Choose something else you like to do. Go downtown. Ride the train. Just do it. Take baby steps. Open your mind, your life to something greater that the four walls of your home, four corners of your block, or the boundaries of your neighborhood. Remember to be safe in all that you do.

EXCUSES

Develop your integrity by first being honest with self.

Have you ever tried to confront someone about their actions and they had a reason for everything?

"Why were you late?" "I couldn't find my keys." The truth is they waited until the last minute to get ready.

"Why didn't you clean up?" "I forgot." Actually they just didn't want to.

No matter what you say, it's always something other than the real reason. As a friend of mine once told me, "Excuses are like butt holes. Everyone has one."

I remember as a teen ditching school and coming home late from time to time. On the way home, I would try to think of an excuse to use as my explanation which would actually equal to a lie. I would come up with all sorts of reasons and try to pick the best one. I was never a good liar so whatever lie I chose never worked.

I had this bad habit for a while which was uncharacteristic of me. In my relationships, I would try to explain why I behaved a certain way, refusing to take responsibility. As a working teen I would make up excuses to take a day off. I remember once calling in sick and then the next day I became horribly sick but had to work anyway.

Finally, I got tired of trying to avoid the truth. As situations arose, I'd do a quick self-analysis by being truthful with self, acknowledge my responsibility in the situation, and take the necessary steps for correction. This process simplified my life. I became a woman of my word, learned to apologize when necessary, and was more responsible.

Excuses usually rear their heads when you are being questioned; you know you fell short of your commitment and don't want to acknowledge what appears to be negative. Before speaking, take a moment to digest the situation. Build integrity by first being honest with yourself so you can be honest with others. You can grow by also opening yourself to accept constructive criticism; feedback that is given to help you improve – allows growth.

Decrease the possibility of making excuses for your actions, by honoring your commitments. Don't make promises you can't keep. If you can't do something, say it. Treat people the way you want to be treated.

Challenge yourself by looking yourself directly in the eyes and take responsibility for who you are. Change what you can change. **Continually better yourself until your good gets better and your better gets best!**

AFFIRMATION

Each day I am committed to being honest with myself and others. I know that by being honest with myself I am honest with others. I keep my word. I am trustworthy. I am honest. I am free.

ACTION

The next time you are being questioned, before you respond, take a deep breath. Next take a moment to be truthful with self then voice the truth appropriately. If what you have to say is something that may be hurtful to another, tell them that it may be painful.

Also, if you are in an abusive situation, use your best judgment. You don't want to cause yourself additional harm. You also need to make the necessary steps to get out of that situation.

DON'T SETTLE

You can write your own ticket in life.

Growing up, I enjoyed watching the neighborhood guys play basketball and football. Their moves were intriguing. They had a serious love for their respective sports. There were two guys in particular that caught my eyes; one loved basketball, the other loved football. The basketball player had an awesome three point shot and free throws were always a cinch. He had the slam dunk and tongue thing down before it became the Michael Jordan trademark. He never left the hood even though he had the potential to be one of the greats. The football player was arrogant with his ability and skills. He was well-known and scouted. He went to college on a scholarship, didn't stay, and to my understanding today still hangs out on the corner he hung out on as a teenager.

We all know at least one person in our lives that should have been one of the greatest in whichever path they chose. Unfortunately, that person didn't believe it. People settle on a daily basis by not pursuing happiness or what they feel will help them become a better person. They settle by accepting what they or others think of them. They settle by not chasing their dreams, striving to reach their goals, leaving bad relationships, not pursuing their educations, or not going after a better job.

Because of where or how we live, we sometimes think, "I can't have that," "That's too good for me," "I'll never be able to afford that" or "I dream too big." You are supposed to dream big and believe in yourself and your ability to have anything you are willing to work to obtain. Claim your future.

You are not in the world to be a have-not. Depending upon the environment in which you were raised, you may have to learn to think outside the box. You have to realize that the world and your opportunities are much greater than the four walls of your house, the corners of your block, or the city or state you live in.

How to think outside the box

One young lady knew she couldn't afford to eat a full course meal at Spago's in Beverly Hills but it didn't stop her from going. She'd put on her best clothes and dine with the crowd she wanted to be a part of. She'd enjoy a lunch of salad and a glass of tea in elegant surroundings, and then return to a downtrodden neighborhood, but no one knew. Eventually she could afford Spaggo's and it was part of her reality.

Take a good look at everything in your environment, your daily routine, what you do, how you do it and when. This is your box. Keeping this information in mind, venture out of your environment. Leave your neighborhood and go somewhere you'd like to be. Go somewhere you thought you wouldn't fit in but you'd like to.

Pay attention to your feeling while you're in the new environment. Take a moment and utilize all of your senses: smell, see, touch, hear, and taste. Live in the moment.

Compare your new surroundings to your environment. Note the differences. Realize that you are able to experience this as often as you'd like. You deserve to enjoy yourself and have the best.

Venturing out of the box creates new experiences. When you have one good experience, you wish to have another and another. One day you will understand that you can have anything you want. All you have to do is apply yourself. You can write your own ticket in life.

Reaching your goals by thinking outside the box

Have you ever daydreamed about something you wished you could have, be or do, and then your box slammed you back to the ground? This time, I want you to daydream and write what you desire at the top of a blank sheet of paper. Next, write down every positive point of your goal.

For example:

GRADUATING FROM HIGH SCHOOL

1. Obtaining a high school diploma
2. Option to go to college
3. Great for my resume
4. I can get a better-paying job
5. I will be proud of myself
6. I will have completed a goal

Now write down the reasons you feel you _can't_ reach your goal.

1. Not enough credits
2. Missed too much school
3. No time to party
4. I have a baby
5. My parents didn't graduate

Read each reason and reflect. For every reason why you **_can't_**, write a reason why you **_can_** next to it. Identify a way you can eliminate that negative. For every action, there is an equal and opposite reaction. Example: I tie my shoe. The opposite is I untie my shoe.

Using the list above I will write the "I cans."

- Not enough credits – I can find out how many credits I need and how long it will take to earn and receive them.

- Missed too much school – I can make sure I attend the classes I missed and complete the necessary makeup work.

- No time to party – I can wait until the weekend.

- I have a baby – I can find a sitter or a school that offers daycare. I can check into resources that will assist me with childcare.

- My parents didn't graduate – I can realize that I don't have to be like my parents and I can be the first in my family to graduate.

Read your last list. Your list of "I cans" is your action plan. Use it to complete your goals.

Never settle for less than what you consider the best for you in your life. Settling is accepting less than you deserve. You deserve the best! This means mentally, physically, spiritually, financially, and materially.

Never Settle!

Strive for great things in life. Be honest in your dealings. What you put out comes back to you. If you do positive things, positive things will come your way.

Read! Non-fiction books will expose you to the wonders of the world. The places that you read about in travel magazines or see in pictures or on television, you can actually experience close up and personal. You can have the wealth that you see, including the beautiful homes, cars, and vacations.

Many millionaires do not have college degrees. Those who weren't born wealthy did not settle. They did not let go of their dreams. Continue your education for the rest of your life. You don't have to be in a classroom to continue learning. Always aim high. **You are entitled to the riches of this world. Now get them!**

AFFIRMATION

I am a co-creator of my reality. My world expands beyond the four corners of any room, block, or city. I am receptive to divinity. I know the world is my oyster and my cup overflows with prosperity, love and happiness. My dreams are at my fingertips. I believe in myself, my abilities, and the divine. I welcome and accept all the riches of the heavenly.

ACTION

Make your lists of goals and plan the necessary steps. Act on your desires. If you get discouraged, know that you have to experience the "bad" before you experience the "good". Nature has to create a void, an empty space to fill it with the positive.

The "bad" is the void (not having). The "good" is what you've desired actually come true.

RESPONSIBILITY

{ *Plan to be responsible.* }

As I grew up, I assumed responsibilities in the form of chores in my family's home, as did my siblings. My mother was good at delegating to get a job done. Each day when she returned home she expected to find a sparkling clean home. Of course, that didn't always happen. We were so busy doing what we wanted to do that we often procrastinated until ten minutes before we expected her to walk through the door. If she could have been a fly on the wall, she would have seen us running through the house in a race against the clock surface cleaning or doing whatever we thought would pass her inspection.

Many children or teenagers want responsibilities until they get them. Life is so much easier when all you have to do is schoolwork, call your friends, listen to music, watch television, and hang out. The reality is that you have been given responsibilities such as picking up your toys, making your bed, brushing your teeth, taking a bath, doing homework, and attending class which prepares you for adulthood. You have been responsible and your responsibilities expand as you develop other relationships.

Responsibilities are known as the "have tos" of life. Adults have to take care of themselves, their homes, their offspring and mates, their businesses or work, and material items. Simply put, the way to be responsible is to not procrastinate concerning the "have tos" of life.

Planning complements responsibility.

As you develop as a teen and young adult, your responsibilities will increase. Now you may participate in extracurricular activities at school which is actually preparing you to maintain and prioritize your schedule. An important point to remember is that you are your primary responsibility. As you participate in activities, begin working or even volunteering, remember to take care of you including eating right, resting, and monitoring your stress level. Try to designate time for being alone and doing whatever makes you happy. Don't be afraid of being alone; it's good for the soul.

There are several other areas of responsibility that will be prevalent in your life, such as family, career and possessions. As an adult, if you decide to have a family, they will be the bulk of your responsibility and your motivation to provide for them. Don't forget to spend time with your loved ones. It is important to laugh, learn, and grow together. Spending quality time nourishes your relations.

As an employee, your job is a responsibility. You have made a commitment to the employer to do the necessary tasks of your particular job. You are working to assist the company making money. Putting in hours at work allows you to maintain your lifestyle and/or that of your family.

The possessions you acquire are responsibilities, such as a home, car or any other item that requires you to preserve its value for as long as possible. These are your assets. Take care of them.

Planning complements responsibility. As you gain responsibilities, especially when caring for other humans, your time shrivels away. A planner, or PDA, may be helpful for managing your schedule and reminding you of the "have tos." A Franklin Covey planner will help you balance your work, family, and personal goals to keep your life productive.

Get in the habit of writing a "to do" list of all the tasks you "have to" do for the day, week, month, or year. This list can help keep you on track so that you don't miss your appointments, a school play, getting a tune-up on your car, or a hot date.

As an adult, accept responsibility. If you don't plan your life and set goals, you are not being responsible to yourself. Take life head-on. Plan, achieve, and challenge yourself to make the most of every day of your life. Don't be the old person asking, "What did I do with my life?" **You want to be able to look around and see your successes because you were responsible.**

AFFIRMATION

I am proactive. I know what it takes to get the job done and I do it. I save myself time. I eliminate stress. I complete my goals.

ACTION

Keep a running to-do list to keep track of action items. Check off the tasks you complete and add tasks you need to complete. Continually do this and you will see your life change before your eyes. You will see progress.

LEARNING FROM EXPERIENCE

Find a balance between your mind and spirit.

My head was hardening and I became adamant about doing what I desired around fifteen or sixteen years of age—not because I wanted to be that way but because of a deficiency in adult interaction in my life and depression. By doing what I wanted to do, I caused my mother some upsets, but I stuck to my plan of moving out of her house soon after graduation.

If I'd had an option, I would have chosen to have a guide in life. I'm sure I would have made better choices and stuck to my original plan for success, which was to go to college, major in business, and become an entrepreneur. Unfortunately, it didn't happen that way so my wisdom came from many tough lessons. I learned from experience.

Each incident in your life affords you a decision. You have to choose the direction in which you will travel by acknowledging the potential outcome of that choice. When you make these choices, they dictate your lessons in life.

Let's say you go out drinking with some friends, get arrested for public intoxication and spend the night in jail. Did you make a good decision?

Will you be repeating this incident? The decisions you make and apply will result in wisdom gained or stupidity earned—your choice.

As an adult, one of the most repeated experiences is choosing the same "type" of mate repeatedly and wondering why you experience the same experiences over and over again.

Until you take note of what happened in the relationship that was not good for you, be it a feeling or situation, and correct it, you will continue to attract the same. Repeated experiences afford you the opportunity to correct your errors and love yourself more.

If you have someone in your life that cares enough to steer you in a positive direction, be grateful. Their care may appear to be fussing or "being on your back" all the time but it is done out of love and concern. Taking advice can save you a lot of time when it's genuine and from a person who offers quality advice. You will meet people who are merely opinionated as well as those who have actually walked the walk. Adhere to the information that feels right and logically sound. Try to find a balance between your mind and spirit; logic and feeling.

Pay attention to how you feel.

Make the most of each experience and try to learn the lesson the first time by acknowledging what you did, why and how, the outcome and the effects it had on you, your life, and potentially others in your life. If it is negative, eliminate it from your life. **If the results are positive, then do more of the same.**

AFFIRMATION

I attract positive loving experiences into my life. As I digest each experience, I know and act on that which is good for me. I make better choices each day of my life.

ACTION

- Take your time and weigh all your choices.
- Act on that which is good for you.
- Don't take chances that can be harmful to you.
- Learn from your experiences.

TRUSTING YOUR FEELINGS

Allow your body and spirit to guide you.

As an adult, one day I was in church listening to a message about how every action is either an expression of love or a cry for love. An expression of love is an act that shows love. A cry for love is an outburst that shows the need/desire for love. Towards the end of the sermon, my stomach knotted and hurt so bad, I couldn't stay. I left and as I was driving home, I thought, something is going to happen today. The day resulted in someone acting out in a cry for love. It was full of pain and turmoil. Similar to the pain I felt in my stomach.

Have you ever felt something was going to happen? Has your stomach ever tightened into a knot or you felt butterflies before something major occurred? Have you had a dream that came true? Did you ever see something in your mind and then it came to pass? How many times have you later said, "I knew that was going to happen?"

If you have ever experienced any of these instances, do not ignore them. You have experienced one of the other senses of the body and spirit. The body is super-intelligent and your spirit uses it to direct, instruct and even warn you of potential occurrences in your life. This is intuition, often called the sixth sense. When you acknowledge this sense, your body and spirit will acknowledge you by sharing information.

Pay attention to how you feel in your surroundings. Notice the comfort or discomfort you feel when interacting with others. Allow your body and spirit to guide you to whom and what is right for you.

The next time you hear a little voice in your ear or feel something, don't disregard it. Accept it and stay aware throughout your day to find out why. When you do, appreciate the "warning" and thank your spirit for the guidance it gave. Saying "thank you" makes room for more. **Remember what you don't use, you lose.**

AFFIRMATION

I am in tune with my creator. I am thankful for divine wisdom and guidance. I am in tune with the inner promptings of my body and my soul. I am in tune with my intuition. Thank you body and spirit for guidance, I am continually becoming more intuitive.

ACTION

Pay attention to and acknowledge your intuition. Diary your "intuitive promptings" and what actually happened. Find the pattern or how your intuition informs you. You will be able to discern true promptings versus false ones.

ASKING FOR HELP

Don't let pride keep you from reaching your goals.

If there is never a time in your life when you need help, you will be the exception to the rule. I can personally count several times that I had to call on my family or friends for assistance, not because I wanted to but because I had to.

Pride makes people question whether they should ask for assistance. Pride will make you suffer unnecessarily. I'll give you an example.

I had a friend who was self-sufficient. For a young man, he'd done quite well financially. He made the money but didn't manage the money. He'd saved and invested diligently which allowed him to take off from work for three years. As his money dwindled, he knew he had to go back to work but didn't prepare himself properly so he hit hard times. He didn't have an income but he had people in his life that loved him and desired to help him but he refused. He stressed over how he was going to pay his rent, electric and other bills, all because he was too proud to accept help.

You know yourself and your reputation. Have you been an honest person? Will people believe you when you say you need help or will they think you're crying wolf? See, the same friend I previously mentioned cried wolf an awful lot. He never wanted anyone to know the exact financial position he was in so he'd in one breath tell you he had money and in the next breath say he was flat broke. Be truthful. If you lie, you lose. You lose trust and potential assistance.

Life has its ups and downs. Your choices will always influence your position in life. You have to make good choices. If there comes a time when you haven't made a good choice and you need help, ask for it. The type of people and relationships you have in your life will determine the response you get.

There are those who will *rub* your situation in your face. There are those who will question you as to how you got yourself in this position and want to know how you will get yourself out of it. What will you do to put yourself in a better position or make sure this doesn't happen again? There are those who will empathize, listen and say, "How can I help you?" Understand that no matter which person that you've gone to for help, you do owe them an understanding of where you are. Don't feel offended. Many times this is just a concern for your well-being. By all means do not put yourself in a position where someone is making you feel worse that you already do. Friends and people who really love you won't do this.

The possibility of one day needing someone is a great reason to help others in need and a good reason to not burn bridges.

It is also important to ask the right person for assistance. Think about the person who would have an answer to the problem. Is it a person or an organization you need to contact?

Most importantly, review the situation and what you did to get yourself there. What could you have done differently? What will you do to make sure it doesn't happen again? **Take responsibility and learn your lesson.**

AFFIRMATION
I am thankful for all that I have achieved. I realize the ability to help others is a blessing and each day that I am able, I will.

ACTION

If you ever need assistance, seek the proper resource. If you ask for a loan, repay it. Treat others the same way that you'd wish to be treated if you helped someone.

For the Guys

Notes

GUYS INTRODUCTION

{ *You are the master of your fate.* }

Being a young man in this era is definitely a challenge. Regardless of where you live, be it the inner city or suburbs, life has become increasingly challenging as you deal with avoiding drug dealers, gangs, and even trying to survive on a daily basis; not to mention those without a father or father figure who are trying to learn how to be a man.

I want you to remember and understand that as you are met with daily challenges you are proving your strength, developing yourself and accumulating skills that can either help you or kill you. You don't have to become a negative product of your environment, what someone has thought of you or told you that you are, or anything other than the greatest you that you can be.

As a young man, you have the opportunity to change, be respectful, take care of your body, become a great father and have a legal means of income and success.

Never give up! Never say what you can't do! Remember that all you need to succeed, you already have within.

If you feel no one believes in you, remember there are two people that do, me and you! **Expect great things to occur in your life, act on opportunity and pursue your dreams…achieve!**

BEING A MAN

> *Though your father is who you'd look to for a male role model, don't limit yourself.*

Reflecting on my father in an attempt to figure out if he was a positive role model, I came up with this:

- He was a loving, influential and playful father.
- He was irresponsible in many ways.
- He was not the best husband.
- Overall he gave us love.
- He was not the best example of a positive male role model.

It has been a struggle for my brothers. Their lives have been full of trial and error and self-discovery to make better examples of themselves as fathers and uncles.

Though your father is who you'd look to for a male role model, don't limit yourself. Positive examples of respectful, responsible men are all around you. Being a man does not require you to do illegal things, harm yourself or other people, sleep around, have many women and children, or be abusive in any way.

As a child, your family, environment, and the media dictated your image of what a man is. As an adult, you have the opportunity to define what a man is to you.

If you were fortunate to grow up with your father in your household, think about him. Regardless of the type father he was, he gave you a base to work with. In your father you will see the traits that you admire and dislike. Make the attributes you admire a part of you. Make it a point to deny the attributes you dislike.

Be proactive and become the best you can be.

Life has a way of presenting lessons concerning the very things that we disliked as a child, thus providing us with an opportunity to make a better choice than we witnessed. Change your outlook on negative experiences by acknowledging your growth or lesson and make it a positive. Turn lemons into lemonade.

It's easy to be the victim and blame your actions on not having a father in the household. You're now becoming an adult and part of adulthood is choosing how to react to what's presented to you. Your parents have lived their lives; you have the rest of yours to go. Forget being a victim, be proactive, and become the best you can be.

It is time for you to make choices about your manhood.

- *Mold and shape yourself into the person whom you desire to be.*

It's time out for trying to fit in and allowing your peers to influence you. Don't allow anyone to coax you into doing anything that can harm anyone or put you in jail. You are responsible for you. You have to live your life for the rest of your life. When your friends are no longer around, you have to deal with the effects of your actions.

- *Stand for something.*

If you don't believe in something then you lack passion in your life.

Passion makes people active and progressive. Find your passion.

- *Develop trust in others by keeping your word.*

If nothing else, you have your word. By keeping it, you will develop a good reputation as a man of honor.

- *Set goals for yourself.*

What lifestyle do you desire and what will it take to get it? Start now by learning what really interests you. You have innate talents that you can apply to a career or trade. Decide how you'd like to earn your way. Stand firm on your goals and dreams and complete them.

- *Always have a skill to fall back on in case you're unable to work in the profession of your choice.*

- **Always have legal means to make money.**

- *Respect yourself by respecting others.*

Cussing women, acting loud and obnoxious is not cute and it lowers your respectability.

- *Be responsible.*

No one owes you anything. Make your own way in life. Do not depend on women to take care of you. Men provide for themselves and their families. Everyone needs help once in a while; but never become lazy and dependent upon anyone. Don't cry wolf or abuse anyone's generosity.

- *Accept responsibility for your actions.*

Be able to own up to your mistakes. Don't run from anything in life. For each issue you confront, you lighten the load you have to carry. Finalize events in your life.

- *Express yourself.*

I know you may have grown up thinking a man doesn't cry. Crying and tears are a mode of expression that was given to man to release and relieve himself of the pain he feels inside. To deprive yourself of tears is to take years from your life. Every pain you feel that goes unexpressed is affecting your body. A man who is able to cry is more peaceful because he is not walking around with pent up emotions. It's ok to cry, don't let anyone tell you different.

- *Respect your life and respect your seed.*

By controlling your seed, you control your life. You determine when to have a child versus making a mistake. You control your finances, your time, and your future.

Because you are a man does not mean you have to bed every woman that offers you sex. Men are usually taught to get as much sex as possible. Today you cannot afford to take that risk. Just as a woman should be particular about the man with whom she shares her body, so should you. It should be an honor for you to share your seed with a particular woman. At that point you should both be willing to take responsibility for a child in case she is impregnated.

Consider whether or not you want a family. Take the appropriate steps so that you're prepared. If you are blessed with a child before that time, take care of him or her. Don't run from responsibility.

If you were not raised with a spiritual foundation, seek one for yourself. Do not limit yourself to traditional American religions. Seek the knowledge that feels right to you. **Faith in a higher power can help you through a situation when you can't see your way.**

Never give up your power (will) by allowing anyone to dictate where you go, what you do, how you dress, your dreams, or anything else. **Use your power of choice and always decide what's best for you!**

AFFIRMATION

I know as a child, my environment dictated my perception of life. I am now a man, able to become and accomplish anything I desire. I release the past and accept the now. I am aware and accept all the good that life has to offer. I am honoring my mind, body and spirit by making positive choices.

ACTION

Be proactive about your goals. Make lists and accomplish them. If there are things you don't like about how you grew up or things you want to change about yourself, take them one day at a time and become the man that you'd admire.

Take Care of Your Body

{ *You will only have one body in this lifetime. Take care of it.* }

As a child, I remember my brother would wear the same socks over and over until they became crunchy. As an adult, I've known men who thought it was natural to not wash their feet and have streaks in their underwear. Regardless of what stage of life you are in, this is never acceptable.

Guys tend to become more concerned with their bodies as they mature. As youth, a lot of guys seem to be consumed with the look of their bodies and not the smell.

If you can smell it, and especially if you tried to cover up the funk with cologne or deodorant, everyone else smells it too. FYI, cologne doesn't make it better. Take the time to clean your body. A fresh smelling man is more attractive than a funky one. In addition, please brush your teeth.

Protect your body from STD's by using contraceptives when you're sexually active. Feed your body with supplements such as herbs to keep you strong and remove toxins from your body.

Your body is the house you live in while you're on this planet. How you care for it will dictate how long your house will stand. When you neglect and mistreat it, it starts to fall apart. Peer pressure can influence your experimentation with alcohol or drugs. You don't have to do these things to fit in. Don't let other people take years off your life by trying to please them.

If you begin to drink when you're of age, limit it. If you don't want to, then don't drink. Ask the bartender for an Easy Living or another virgin drink. No one has to know that it's virgin but you and the bartender.

If you started drinking young, ask yourself why? There is an underlying issue to your drinking and you may possibly need help.

Do you smoke? Did it initiate as something "cool" to do? Has it grown to be a full fledged seemingly unbreakable habit? Do you desire to continue smoking? If not, stop.

As you grow older, continue to get a yearly health examination. Though you may feel well, the exam is an opportunity to become aware of potential issues that may affect your overall health.

Learn self-control. You have nothing to prove to anyone at the risk of damaging your body and decreasing your life expectancy. **Live your life so that you can have a life.**

Express Yourself Extend Your Life

> *When men don't express their emotions, they disregard a part of who they are.*

How many times were you told as a little boy that men don't cry, to suck it up, or were you popped upside your head and called a punk or sissy for crying? How many times have you wanted badly to cry but someone else's idea of what a man is got in the way? How many times were you hurt, did people die, you were unhappy, or were scarred emotionally and not one tear fell for fear of being less than a man?

Think about all of the emotions and unshed tears that have gone unexpressed because of fear of someone thinking you're not a man. Think about all the pent-up emotions that you've held in and have not expressed since you were a child. Think about how you felt then and how you feel now.

When men don't express their emotions, they disregard part of who they are; it's locked inside. All the pain, hurt and sadness has to go somewhere. It hides out in different parts of your body. If you stop and think about an incident that really hurt, you will feel that emotion in your body. Anger becomes the acceptable emotion and aggression the alternate expression. For many, sports have become the outlet.

125

Men can literally die of heartache. Heart attacks happen because of stress on the heart. Don't go through life biting your tongue, trying to please, dealing with problems inwardly instead of expressing outwardly. You have a mouth and a voice, a brain, and a heart to express yourself: use them.

Your heart is where your love lives. Have you ever noticed that when you are hurt emotionally, your heart sometimes hurts too? Imagine a 45-year old man who has not cried in years. How is his heart doing?

A friend of mine who is nearly 65 years old grew up with a gang of uncles who told him, "Men don't cry." So guess what? He spent the majority of his life not crying. It wasn't until about 10 years ago that he cried for the first time since his childhood. He had forgotten how to cry. He is now on heart medication and has high blood pressure. When you look at him, you'd think he was the meanest man in the world. His emotions have scarred his face, yet he is one of the kindest men you will ever meet.

Don't end up like him. Express yourself. Even if you cry alone, do it. If you choose to write it out, do it. God doesn't make mistakes. You have tears and intelligence for a reason. **Express yourself and extend your life.**

AFFIRMATION

I am a conscious, caring, expressive being. I safely use the modes of expression given to me by my creator. I am healing and expressing myself daily. I release pain, anger and hurt, from every cell of my being and replace it with love, lightness and ease.

ACTION

Take time daily to write down all the occasions that you felt you needed to cry or express yourself and you didn't. Take each situation and cry or write and live in that moment to release in a safe and healthy way. Clear out the negative feeling as you visualize your cells being washed with love, happiness, and great health.

Are You a Dad?

{ *A father sets the example for his son of what a father is.* }

A young man that thinks being a father is less important based on his mother having raised him "fine" is confused. His mother may have done a great job, but she is not a man and will never be a man. His mother raised him to the best of her abilities.

The number of single-parent households is consistently rising. A large number of children are being raised by one parent, the majority being women, with some to no contact with the other parent.

The dynamics of relationships and the perception of responsibility have greatly changed over the years due to a pattern of irresponsibility concerning children being established and perpetuated. Children are growing up without fathers and have no clue as to the impact that a father could have had on their lives. This leaves young men naïve about manhood and familial responsibility, young women clueless about the dynamics of male-female relationships, and both with self-esteem issues.

A father sets the example for his son of what a father is. Many young men don't have an example to follow because their fathers weren't present in their lives. This leaves them to figure out one of the greatest responsibility they will ever have, raising a child.

With the prospect of becoming a father, a young man will have to decide his place in his child's life. He will use the example set for him and contemplate. If the father wasn't in the household, or the young man doesn't know his father and he thinks his mother raised him *fine*, he may be in denial, angry, or simply doesn't know the difference of having a father present in his life. He may struggle with the importance of having a father. He may want to be there for his child and participate in their raising, depending on his experience as a child. He may fear the fact that he doesn't know how to raise his child or fear being like his father. He may walk away from the situation and repeat his father's mistake. He may take the responsibility honorably and commit to himself and his child to be the best father he can be.

Fear

It is normal for a young man to fear fatherhood due to lack of knowledge or of becoming the same type of father he had. We fear what we don't know or understand. If your fear is from lack of knowledge, know that no child is born with a manual. As a parent, you can read books, you can talk to fathers, and you can dig for as much information on parenting as possible. The most important things you can give your child are love and time.

If your fear is becoming a father like your own, you have some issues that need to be healed. You don't have to become your father, but you do need help. One funny thing about adulthood is that you sometimes find yourself behaving like your parents. It will be important for you to seek counseling to deal with the issues that are affecting you and your opinion of fatherhood so that you can be a better father to your child.

Young men, I pose the questions: who taught you how to tie a tie? Who taught you how to shave? Who taught you about confidence and the strength of a man? Who taught you about working in this world as a man? Who taught you how to shine your shoes? Who taught you how to treat women? Who did you talk to when you had questions about being a man? Who taught you the importance of taking care of your family? Who taught you about taking care of a car? Who taught you how to hoop, play football, or baseball? Who was at your game rooting you on along with the fathers of other boys? How many father-son events did you miss? Those of you whose father isn't present, how many times did you wish for a father?

Committing to yourself and your child to be the best father you can be is one of the greatest gifts you can give to yourself and your child. If you were without a father in your life, think about how you felt. Do you want your child to experience the same pain? If your father was present in your life, think of what you are able to share with your child.

One of the coolest things about life is that we can change what we do not like about our lives or ourselves. If you were unhappy about your treatment as a child, you can change your perspective of parents by being a better parent. You don't have to repeat your parent's actions. Their actions are to be used as a lesson. You can be greater.

Fear is not respect.

I must mention how many men make their children fearful of them by beating/whipping them and think that's respect. Fear is not respect. You don't gain respect by hurting someone. **You gain respect through your actions, tone, and being respectful.** Remember that!

As a father, you can offer your child love that only a father can give, attention, quality time, friendship, and discipline. You can help build your child's self-respect, self-esteem, self-love, confidence, and pride. You can teach them about relationships, self-protection, responsibility, etc. **You can be a role model for your son and set an example of a strong man for your daughter.**

You can teach your daughter about men; what to expect and not allow, demanding respect, spotting "bull hockey", and male-female relationship dynamics.

The attributes I've listed don't cover a third of what you will offer your child. The memories, laughter, happiness, moments shared, discipline, and growth will be reflected upon over a lifetime. **Don't deprive yourself or your child of this wonderful experience.**

AFFIRMATION

I am the best father I can be. I learn and seek out knowledge to help me be the best father I can be. I tap into my inner resources and know that divine love will guide me in making the right decisions for my child.

ACTION

If you are or will be a father, I suggest that you seek out men that have healthy relationships with their children as personal mentors. In addition, there are organizations that help with understanding fatherhood such as Head Start organizations, 100 Black Men, etc.

YOUR PERCEPTION OF WOMEN

> ## *Life on the planet is born of women.*
> Adrienne Rich

Your perception and what you think of women is largely based on your relationships, first with your mother, and then any other women that surrounded you in your youth. Your idea of women has been shaped by the examples you have been shown.

Was your mother the type who baked, cooked, cleaned all day, and may still do your laundry? Maybe your mother was a single parent who worked hard to provide for you. She juggled everything to make sure it was all taken care of. Was she a mother who was always on the go and you rarely spent time with her due to her work, or other things that she felt was a priority? She could have been a drug addict or prostitute and you raised yourself. Alternatively, you didn't have a mother in the picture at all, being raised by whomever loved you that much.

You can pretty much finger your situation or mix and match the examples to create a picture of your mother. Whoever she was, directly relates to what you think of women and how you treat them. It will also dictate the type of woman you run from or are attracted to.

The possibility of you having a mother that you feel could have done a better job is there. If you feel that way, understand that she did the best she could with what she knew. Take into consideration how old your mother was when she had you and her life's circumstances. Remember she too is a product of her environment. Forgive her for her shortcomings.

If you have vowed to not have a woman in your life that is like your mother but that seems to be the only type of women you attract, that's a sign for you. You need to heal from the pain that you still hold concerning your childhood and your mother. These women enter your life for that purpose. Once you don't fear that, and deal with it, then you shouldn't attract them anymore.

If you have the opportunity to talk to your mother, do it. Sit down and calmly talk to her. Ask her the questions that have puzzled you all these years. It may be emotional, but try to remain calm. Get it all out; release everything so that you can move on in your life.

If your mother is not available or unwilling to talk to you, write her a letter. Write every question, thought, or opinion that you may have. If you can mail it to her, do it. If not, address it and seal it as if you were and put it away. You have sealed the pain within the envelope and time will heal you.

If you had a mother who was everything you could have asked for then you are blessed. Be grateful. You need to know that you can't expect a woman to fill your mother's shoes. It will be slightly difficult to find a woman who will do everything your mother did and live her life too. Your mother's life as a mother was her motherhood.

In any situation, do not take out your fear, anger, or expectations on anyone. That is something you need to deal with. Abuse is unacceptable in any form, mental, verbal, emotional, or physical.

Heal by releasing; learn by recognizing who your mother is or was to you.

AFFIRMATION

I understand that we are all here to learn. I appreciate my mother for giving me life. I forgive my mother for each and every action that I disagreed with. I understand that she was who she was supposed to be, fulfilling her role in the lessons I must learn in this lifetime. I release the pain, anger, or other ill feeling and replace them with peace, love, and happiness.

ACTION

Forgiveness is very important in your life. Though we don't understand everything we experience, nothing happens without reason. If you live in the past, you are not present and enjoying what the present has to offer.

Forgive. Write it out, talk it out, cry it out, or if you're able to, ask questions to get understanding. When you're finished, forgive and release. Let go.

SOMETHINGS YOU SHOULD KNOW ABOUT WOMEN

If you're real with yourself, then you're able to be real with her.

You have so much of your life ahead of you and I assure you that your experiences are not in vain.

Trying to understand the opposite sex can be a struggle. As a young man, it is important for you to understand that many women are being raised by single parents and are watching women take on the typical male responsibilities of a man to try to balance their households. With this, young women are crossing the boundaries of womanhood and stepping on men's toes unconsciously.

Many women are raised watching their mothers being the breadwinner, protecting the family, putting bass in her voice to provoke action and taking on the chores normally done by men. When a woman has herself to depend on to take care of her family, it's hard for her to let go of the steering wheel and let you drive. She needs to know you will be there. Instead of criticizing and condemning her, step up and show her she doesn't have to do it alone.

Some men are insecure within themselves so they are intimidated by resourceful women. Don't be. Appreciate the fact that she can change a tire, change oil, drill holes, hang paintings, and will kill bugs. These attributes among others will come in handy. It should tell you that if you marry this woman and you become impaired, she will be able to take care of you and the rest of the family.

Many young ladies may:

- Be either conservative or promiscuous. Promiscuity comes either from the relationships she saw her mother have or she equates sex with love.

- Be dependent or independent.

- Think cursing or hitting is an expression of love. You have an opportunity to teach her differently.

- Not know how to cook or lack maternal instincts because her mother may have worked all the time to make ends meet.

Before you give up on a particular woman, learn her history, reflect on yours, and if she is worth it, work with her. Allow her to be a woman and teach her to allow you to be a man.

When building your relationship, learn about her, ask questions, and listen. Learn about her childhood, her dreams, and goals. Find out who raised her. What does she wish she could change about her life? Was her father around? What is important to her? What does she want to change about herself? What are her faults? Learn as much as possible. Everyone has dysfunctions they have to deal with. The quicker you find out the truth and get to know the real person, the quicker you'll know if you want to stick around.

The following are some things you should know about women:

- ***Women desire respect, appreciation, love and honesty.***

Women desire strong, respectable men who show they care.

- ***Innately, women are caretakers.***

Women enjoy taking care of men, especially when they show appreciation. Saying thank you goes a long way. If she does something nice for you, think about her occasionally and do the same. If she cleans the house, don't dirty it up.

- *Reciprocate.*

That means to take it upon you to do something for her as well. Relationships should not be tit for tat. What you do does not have to immediately follow what she does. Just don't forget about her and make her a priority in your life.

- *Contrary to what some may believe or have grown up around, women do not appreciate being called profane names.*

- *Women should always be held in high regard.*

Chivalry is not dead.

If you encounter a woman that doesn't respect herself, you then have the opportunity to school her on how special a woman is.

Ways to be chivalrous:

- Acknowledge her.

- Pick her up on time.

- Call if you're going to be late, can't make it, or just to say, "I was thinking of you".

- Open doors, including car doors.

- Assist her with her coat.

- Assist her with seating by pulling her chair out.

- Honesty is the best policy. Tell the truth. By telling the truth, your heart and mind will rest and so will hers.

Communication

- *Talk to her.*

Men seem to go through life a lot more carefree than women. However, women have to know if you care, love them, and where you want the relationship to go. Women suffer a lot of broken hearts, mainly because of dishonesty from men who think that trying to be a player is cool. Players don't get caught so I guess that there is probably not one successful player on this planet. Women are gifted with this wonderful thing called intuition. Men have it too; women seem to use it more.

- *If you act responsibly and define the relationship you desire to have, you can alleviate a lot of problems.*

When you take the time to talk, you give the woman an option in the situation. Be honest with your desires. If you don't want to be committed, say it. You'd be surprised. She'll probably go along with the idea. You can't have double standards though. Whatever the situation, you need to express it to her.

- *If you really care about someone, let her know.*

Tell her without her having to ask. She won't ask as much if you tell her sometimes. Women need confirmation.

Your actions will speak louder than words.

- *Be more than just talk.*

So you say you love her. When you don't call, don't show up for a date, forget to pick her up, don't spend time with her, etc., it shows her that you are all talk. These actions do not dictate love. You are using the word "love" loosely. Love shows in your words and actions. She should know that she matters and is important to you. She should be a priority in your life. Let her know that she is special. It's the little things that count.

- *Treat the woman in your life the same way you desire her to treat you.*

Don't keep her hanging on if you don't want her. Don't keep her around because she buys you things or gives you money. Be a man and get your own. Don't tell her you love her when you're really just infatuated or trying to block her from dating others. Don't mistreat or embarrass her.

Be her friend first. Most importantly, be real. If you're real with yourself, then you're able to be real with her.

137

AFFIRMATION

I am aware and in tune with my spirit. I attract positive, loving women into my life. I am respectful, honest and loving in my relationship. I understand that my words and actions must match. I care for my mate's heart as if it were my own.

ACTION

Be honest. Honesty goes a long way. Be kind with people's hearts and know that each experience you have with someone will leave either a positive or a negative impact.

Relationships

__Notes__

RELATIONSHIPS INTRODUCTION

The most enjoyable and hurtful experiences in life will be obtained through your relationships.

The relationships that you yourself decide upon and cultivate early in life begin with friendship. Friendships usually occur after a favorable impression is made upon you. Relationships can be more fulfilling by being aware that relationships are a way for you to learn and grow. Everyone enters your life for a reason.

In your relating, remember that you can't change anyone. In order for anyone to change, they must have desire and will to take action. Pay attention to those with whom you interact. Learn their behavior and trust them to be themselves. No doubt you will encounter liars. Everyone lies here or there, but be especially watchful of those that make it a habit or lie without regard to others feelings.

Forgive often to rid yourself of stress, anger and unhappiness. Realize that at some point in all our lives, we will experience rejection. I know it doesn't feel good, but everything happens for a reason.

Make a habit of telling the truth. If you tell the truth, you never have to try to remember the lie you told and to whom.

Learn what is important to you in relationships. When you are in the midst of a healthy relationship, absorb the moment. Attempt to make a positive impact by setting good examples in every relationship you have.

To establish a meaningful relationship, you must make deposits in the love bank in order to receive a comparable return. Love is real. Never confuse it with rejection. Date, date, date, and take your time doing it.

Don't rush love, allow yourself to grow into it. Marriage is a commitment and is not to be played with. Take it seriously. Death is a part of life. **Live life; love it, relate, and ride it 'til the wheels fall off.**

FRIENDSHIP

{ *Friends are assets.* }

I had just moved to a new neighborhood and I met a girl named Michelle who was about my age. We went to the park and as we rode the swings she asked, "Do you want to be best friends?" I replied, "Okay," and 20+ years later, she is still one of my best friends. Friendships don't usually happen like this, but this one did. Though we've had fights and gotten angry with one another from time to time, those times have been few and far between. We've even lost contact a few times, but we always know how to find one another. She has been there for me through thick and thin. She has been my friend.

Certain words are used loosely. Friend would be one of them and love would be the other. A friend is a person who you can trust. You have mutual respect for one another. They accept you for who you are and they don't try to change you. They can fuss you out when you're wrong and you know they do it because they care. A friend is someone who has your back. A friend will help you grow as a person. They share their lives and whatever else they have to offer with you. They don't judge or condemn you; they try to make things better. Friends don't use you and aren't in your life simply for what they can gain. They don't run away when the chips are down. Friends are very special people and they don't come around too often. So, when you get one, hold on to him or her. Friends are valuable assets in life.

When you are blessed with someone in your life that cares about you just because you're you, cherish the relationship. When you can express anything to this person and they don't judge you, cherish it. When you can be an a**, and they understand that you're just having a bad day, cherish it.

Don't ruin a friendship over petty things like arguments, egos, he says/she says, or anything else. **Cherish your friend because they don't come a dime a dozen.**

AFFIRMATION

I attract friends in the truest essence of the word. My friends and I love one another and cherish our relationship. We honor and respect the bond we have. We grow together and share divine love.

ACTION

Be choosy with the people you allow into your life and your surroundings. Get to know people before inviting them into your personal space. Believe them when they show you who they are. Make good choices – making sure the person is trustworthy and has your best interest in mind.

FIRST IMPRESSIONS

The first impression can get you in the door, but the lasting impression will decide your future.

If a person walked up to you and said, "Hi, I noticed you across the room. You look like you are well off. What kind of car do you drive? How much money do you make? You have to make over $70,000 and at least drive a Benz or a Beemer to get to know me. So what's up?" What would be your first impression?

If you were a hiring manager and a young lady came in wearing heavy makeup, a mini skirt, stiletto pumps, a shiny halter-top, a wig that looked like a dead cat, and she wouldn't stop popping her gum throughout the interview, what would be your first impression?

If a guy wearing casual clothing walked up to you and said, "Hello, I'm new in town and I need directions. Can you tell me where the art museum is?" What would be your first impression?

How many times have you heard, "Make a good first impression?" A good impression means being on your best behavior and could entail wearing your best clothes and speaking appropriately for the particular situation. An impression is important because it's a person's initial summation of who you are.

In relationships, your introduction, attire, and initial conversation will assist another in judging whether they want to get better acquainted.

In business, punctuality, attire, and articulation are important. These show how you will conduct yourself as a businessperson. These effects will make or break your chances of getting a job or promotion.

Tips on making a first good impression:

- Say "Hello" instead of a corny line.
- Look people in their eyes when conversing.
- Shake hands firmly, not too hard and not too soft.
- Respect others.
- Don't tell lies attempting to impress someone.
- Dress appropriately for whatever the situation.
- Practice good hygiene.
- If you're ever uncertain about what is "appropriate", ask someone who has experience.
- Be punctual.
- Carry breath mints or freshener and use it.
- Be yourself…appropriately.

EVERYONE ENTERS YOUR LIFE FOR A REASON

Each person is in your life to make an exchange with you.

I was once in a relationship with someone who was much too playful for my taste. He was never serious when necessary. Everything was a joke. Even children would tire of his antics. This guy just could not understand that I wanted him to be more serious so we could better our lives together.

At times I enjoyed his playing. When I chose to, in his company, I could freely be the silliest person in the world. One day I realized that I often walked around unaware that I was frowning. Therefore, I learned that we were there to teach each other traits that we both needed to work on. He needed to be more serious about his achievements, and I needed to loosen up.

It took me time to learn this because I was too busy being angry with him for not being serious when necessary. I finally looked at myself one day and realized that I couldn't change others. I asked myself, "Are you getting your lesson?"

He was in my life to show me balance. It's okay to be serious, but you also need laughter and lightheartedness. So I now try to laugh and play more. After all, you only live once.

Each person is in your life to make an exchange. You have something to learn from one another. The relationship or association you have may not always be pleasant but you will find a lesson in it. If you learn it, you won't have to repeat it. That is gaining wisdom.

Why this relationship with this person?

When you find yourself in a relationship that's testing who you are, your strength, knowledge, or what you stand for, you may want to reflect. Ask yourself what you are getting out of the situation.

One example is someone who always ruffles your feathers. Don't you wonder why this is happening? Well, pay close attention. Look in the mirror. You see your reflection, right? Now pretend that the person that ruffles your feathers is the reflection in the mirror. Take a good look at that person. What are the qualities that you dislike or like about this person? Are they qualities that you have sometimes displayed and now realize that they are unattractive? Are they qualities you wished you had? Are they traits that you need to work on? Pay attention, take note, and get your lesson.

Another example; let's say you're a generous person and the other person is selfish. What you would need to acknowledge is two things. They may be there to teach you that it's okay to be selfish as long as you're not hurting others. It's also good to be selfish in the sense that you realize that you have to take care of self first. You are also there to share and teach that person that it's okay to give.

These examples are very small compared to the experiences you may encounter. However, they do demonstrate the small lessons in life that ultimately **develop our character.**

The "better way" to utilize a relationship is to take each situation that causes a disagreement – the times your feelings get hurt, whenever someone magnifies one of your traits, or anything that makes you reflect on yourself or that person – and be proactive about changing what you can to become a better person. Also be aware that the other person may be projecting what they dislike about themselves. You know yourself and if you're honest you'll know the difference.

Finally, pay attention. Realize that no one is perfect and we are all playing our roles to assist one another with development. You have free will to accept or reject any situation you encounter. Never keep people in your life that cause you pain or detract from your happiness or self-respect. **If the good doesn't outweigh the bad, your ultimate lesson is using the power of choice.**

AFFIRMATION

I am receptive and open to change. I acknowledge and learn from each life lesson and make appropriate changes to better myself and elevate my consciousness.

ACTION

If you have past experiences that you think about often, take time to review those relationships to discover your lesson. Pay attention to current relationships and how they affect you. Do your relationships bring you joy or stress?

Remember some relationships are there to simply test whether or not you will protect yourself by letting go.

Some relationships are there for you to develop. Unhappiness is always a cue to make a change.

YOU CAN'T CHANGE ANYONE

It is not your job to change anyone.

I had a couple of boyfriends who just didn't seem to have it all. I thought if I changed the way they dressed, certain of their mannerisms, enhanced their personalities, and exposed them to new foods, arts, or places; I could mold them into the man I desired. Not! No matter how I tried, they wouldn't change. They wound up with a better wardrobe and a few new experiences but who they were initially remained the same. I couldn't make myself a man.

I have been a party to the theory that I can change someone. I have wasted time, energy, and money trying to make myself a man. Women are notorious for doing this because of our desire to help or to make things better. Why shouldn't you try to help Joe Blow become a better person? It is not your job! Each person will develop in his or her own time through life experiences, including the relationship a person has with you.

Some older men and women try to change people as well. They may find someone less experienced whom they can manipulate and attempt to make him or her into the perfect mate for them. This is usually about control. The older adult can't deal with a mate their age so they go after someone young and naïve. Hopefully in this situation, the young adult gathers experience and realizes he or she has free will. Not all May-December relationships (those with a large age gap) are bad; some are actually genuine. Not all of them are based on control. You will recognize if it is a control issue based on how your mate treats you, how much they're trying to change you, and what they accept about you.

When a person tries to change someone, they are not looking at what's in front of their face. They are looking at the potential, their desires, and the possibilities. Sometimes people take on this chore because they find someone with some of the qualities they desire their mate to have and they figure if they just fine-tune the person, they'll have the perfect match. Wrong!

It is not and never will be your job to change someone. If you are doing this, you are wasting your time. You may be filling a space with someone who is not necessarily the right person for you or deflecting to not deal with addressing personal concerns.

No one is perfect. Though you may find some traits unappealing, accept them as being part of that person. If you're just attracted to the outer appearance and not the inner person, don't put yourself or that person through unnecessary problems because they aren't who you want them to be.

If someone is meant to be with you, it won't be necessary for you to make him or her into whom you desire him or her to be. That person will come prepackaged. Maybe you should **take some time to work on yourself and allow time to take its course.**

AFFIRMATION

Everything is in divine order. I accept and understand I can't change people. I know people develop in their own time.

ACTION

If you notice that you're focused on changing someone, redirect your focus and take the opportunity to change something about yourself.

TRUST PEOPLE TO BE THEMSELVES!

A person will be who they are no matter what.

I observed a then boyfriend of mine as he often told people what they wanted to hear and misled people to get what he wanted. He didn't think of the repercussions that would affect his reputation. He only thought of the moment.

One day, he came to my home, full of enthusiasm and passion, swept me into his arms, laid a kiss on me, and said he wanted to make things work. He wanted to commit so that we could work on getting married.

My first clue that something wasn't right was that I felt nothing when he kissed me. The second was that he was having financial difficulty, had been evicted from two apartments, and was currently living in less than adequate digs.

Being myself, I considered the fact that we had a child on the way. I allowed him to move in my home, only for him to confess a year later that marriage wasn't his intent. He had done to me what I had watched him do to others.

You meet someone and like their first impression and decide to get better acquainted. They appear to be a great person with few flaws. After a few days, weeks, or months, you notice something else. All the wonderful qualities are changing as the real person emerges. You're looking for the person you met, but that person only makes special appearances once in a blue moon. At this point, do you try to figure out who this person really is or where the other person went? Alternatively, do you accept this person for who they are at this time?

A person will be who they are no matter what. They can pretend to be someone else for only so long.

We often expect others to live up to whom we thought they were, who they presented themselves to be, or who we desire them to be. Who we thought they were is typically a combination of whom they presented themselves as being and our efforts to make them into who we desire them to be.

Points to remember:

- Everyone is on his or her best behavior when you first meet (trying to make a good first impression).

- Pay attention to everything about them to avoid the "I thoughts." A person can hide who they really are for only so long.

- Always remember you can't change anyone! If you are trying to help them, they must be willing to change themselves. Everyone has their own path and will develop in their own time.

- Trust people to be themselves, the person you have grown to know. If they desire to change, they will. It just may not be when you want them to.

> ## Look at what's right in your face.

To cut to the chase about people, ask them to tell you all their uglies. The things they know they want to change or aren't proud of and determine if you can deal with it. Are you willing to be patient and allow them to develop in their time?

To trust people to be themselves and be able to use it to your benefit, you have to look at everything that person has shown you in the time that you have known one another.

Using the information you've learned about a person is to:

1. Acknowledge who the person is.

2. Decide whether their presence in your life benefits you or are they taking up space.

3. Decide if you're willing to accept them and their behavior.

4. Place them in or out of your life and leave them there.

Trust will be a factor in every relationship you have.

Trust is the basis upon which you decide whom you accept in your life, what type of relationships you have, and their longevity. When trusting people to be themselves, you only have to worry about trusting one person…yourself! You have to trust yourself to guide you about where this person stands in your life.

- If a person is a liar, recognize it, acknowledge it, and trust them to lie to you again.

- If a person is a great business partner, trust their business acumen.

- If a person is a thief, trust them to steal.

- If a person is someone you can depend on, trust him or her to be dependable.

- If you're in a relationship and your mate cheats on you, trust them to do it again.

- If a person constantly tells you that they have a certain belief about something, trust them to act on it.

When you trust people to be who they are, you get to the purpose of the relationship. You can apply this information to all relationships. You will waste less time and have fewer hurt feelings because you are using facts, information based on what you have observed from your experiences with a particular person. Forget about who they were when you first met. Forget about who you hoped they would become. Look at what's right in front of your face. **Trust yourself to do what's right for you and actually do it!**

AFFIRMATION

I am aware. I am honest with myself. I honor my inner promptings. I set aside my desires and recognize people for who they are. I pay attention to how I feel when I'm in their presence. I make choices that are good for me.

ACTION

If you recognize certain traits about a person that you don't care for, be honest with yourself. Make a conscious effort to not fool yourself into thinking they're other than who they are. See the person for who they are at this present moment without anticipation of change.

FORGIVENESS

Forgive to create peace in your life.

Forgiveness is the ability to absolve a person of what you may consider to be a wrongdoing, by way of releasing any "bad" feeling or emotions of a situation, thus freeing yourself of the hurt that is detracting from the happiness of your being.

While preparing to hang wallpaper at my mother's home, my nieces and sons were playing in the den. They were well-behaved children so it wasn't unusual for them to play alone.

My niece came from the den and announced that my two-year-old son had fallen out of the window. Of course, we adults just knew we'd heard wrong so we questioned the other children. Without hesitation, they all confirmed that he had fallen.

My spirit was ahead of my body as I ran barefoot down concrete stairs with visions of my baby lying on the ground pulsating in my head.

I picked up his lifeless body and began talking to him and trying to keep him awake as I yelled to his father to hurry.

Fortunately, the hospital was less than five minutes away. We spent the evening in the hospital praying, crying, trying to be strong, and being questioned by the police as they tried to decide whether to press charges for child neglect.

My son was blessed. We took him home and stayed up all night to keep an eye on his swollen head, which resembled a melon. The mental agony I suffered I would wish on no one. I spent the night wondering if my son would live to see another day.

The next day I had to deal with my family, who obviously didn't know how to react to the situation. During an unrelated business meeting, I had to see my sister and her daughter who had stood my son in the window and caused his fall.

Months and years passed, yet my sister never apologized. To my knowledge, my niece was never reprimanded. As time passed, I had to forgive my niece, who was only a child. I had to dig deep to forgive my sister, who never stepped up to take responsibility by apologizing for her child's actions. I forgave them because holding on to the pain and anger only caused me more pain, which was not good for my health or my relationship with my family.

Unhealthy non-expression can ruin relationships of all kinds. Think about any unresolved situation that has caused you pain. Focus on how your body feels and how your emotions change. You are harboring this energy. If you are aware of a situation that you have created that has caused someone else pain, think about the luggage they're carrying as well.

- *Why should you forgive?*

To create peace in your life and anyone else involved.

- *Who should you forgive?*

You should forgive anyone and everyone. Start by forgiving yourself.

- *When should you forgive?*

You should forgive as often and early as possible but the sooner, the better. Do not harbor ill feelings. The longer you hold onto something, the longer it will have an affect on you and your mental, physical, and spiritual well-being. Don't procrastinate due to fear.

- *How do you forgive?*
  1. You forgive by processing the situation to get an understanding of what happened.
  2. Release the emotions you feel by expressing them in a healthy manner.
  3. Calm yourself and make a complete release of what happened.
  4. If necessary, utter the words, "I forgive you", to yourself or others.

- *Listen to what the person has to say if they have chosen to apologize.*

Realize that it takes a lot to admit a wrongdoing. If they thought enough of you to take the time to apologize, hear them and express, if you feel it necessary, how they've hurt you (in a civilized manner). Heal yourself and that person by saying thank you. Thank you for thinking enough of me to apologize.

- *If someone doesn't immediately apologize, you can contact him or her and ask to express how you've been hurt.*

In your expression, you can ask for an apology and depending on the character of that person, they may or may not apologize.

- *The apology is not that important; your sense of well-being is.*

What is most important is the opportunity to express your feelings. This should provide a sense of relief for you.

- *Don't confront the issue with the "expectation" of an apology or your ideal outcome.*

Express for the purpose of releasing pain and allowing yourself to move on. No one owes you anything. Don't create additional pain through expectation.

- *If you'd rather avoid confrontation, you can use your journal to release your feelings.*

In your journal, make a list of all the people you need to forgive from childhood to adulthood.

Because that negative energy has taken up space and you're getting ready to release it, you'll create a void that needs to be filled. Write next to the person what you would like to fill that space with. It can be mental, physical, spiritual, or material.

Address one person at a time. Write the person as if you're talking to them. The best thing about journaling is that you don't have to hold back, let it all out!

When you're done, read it aloud with feeling and emphasis and finish it off with an affirmation. "I forgive _____ for _____. I release the pain and _____. I forgive myself for harboring these feelings. I am grateful for the healing that is taking place in my body, mind, and spirit right now. I now fill this void with _____."

If you truly release, there is a great possibility that the void will be filled with what you desire. It worked for me. At any rate, **what's most important is the healing has taken place.**

AFFIRMATION

I forgive myself for what I've allowed to affect me negatively. I will make better choices by learning from my experiences. I forgive those that have harmed or offended me. I understand that though an experience may not be favorable, it has occurred for a reason.

I accept my responsibility in the situation. I actively love myself by making positive choices.

ACTION

Forgive as soon as possible.

REJECTION

It is rejection, not love that causes hurt. Change is constant.

Oxford University Press defines rejection as reject>verb 1. To refuse to consider or agree to 2. Fail to show deep affection or concern for

One of the most common and devastating forms of rejection is rejection from a loved one. When you experience rejection while loving, you blame love. Love is not the cause of the pain.

Rejection in any form is devastating be it a job, school or friend. Anything you desire but don't receive, that you have an expectation for, results in the feeling of rejection.

I had a friend that treated his mate horribly. She bent over backwards for him. She had flaws, but to him she was just about everything he needed. He dated other women, wasn't affectionate, and was verbally abusive. She loved him and tried to work things out.

One day after being strung along for so long, she got tired. She asked his intent. Not only was he not in a hurry to pursue anything permanent, he said he considered himself single.

At that point she dropped him and his shenanigans like a hot potato. He thought she'd come back. After all, she'd threatened this action before. This time, his face was broken because she was finished.

She wouldn't see, talk, or spend time with him. She began dating someone else. He freaked out. He didn't like being rejected.

If someone said to you, "I don't want to be with you," "You're fired," "Buy your own food," "No, you can't drive my car," what single word would describe how you felt? Did rejected come to mind?

Rejection is not discussed and is rarely used by young adults to describe their feelings, especially during young adulthood when it's prevalent. Here is the beginning of the idea that love hurts; rejection has not been acknowledged or used to define emotions when there is a loss or non-acceptance.

Rejection is experienced in a variety of circumstances outside of personal relationships. It begins at home, then on the playground, and continues.

Rejection occurs at work, on the street, in school – it's everywhere. You may not get the job though it seemed perfect for you. You may not get accepted to the school you desired to attend. You may have a credit application rejected. You may have family reject you. Not only will you be rejected, you will reject.

Don't confuse rejection with love. Rejection can be when you love someone and they don't agree with your desires. You're hurting because you're being rejected. Not being accepted hurts, not love. It hurts, but in time you will get over it.

For men, rejection occurs more often. Women reject men daily. Why? Men are the suitors. They initiate a courtship and from the first "hello" they are being judged.

Men, because a woman doesn't desire to be with you or she isn't accommodating to your approach, don't take it as a negative. Just as you sized her up and decided that you were interested in her, she is allowed to choose as well.

Another point: a woman will often not converse if she's approached in a distasteful manner or quoted a lame line. A simple "hello" will take you much further than something rude or corny.

Don't allow rejection to make you bitter. Instead of approaching a woman with a fantasy, approach her as if you're trying to make a friend. If you treat the situation in this manner, you will be less apt to be disappointed with the outcome or take a blow to your self-esteem or confidence.

Young ladies, rejection can be painful because of women's desire of acceptance and willingness to nurture just about anything and anyone. Everyone has a right to choose. Even if you feel you're the most beautiful or loving person in the world, you may not be right for whomever.

> **Everyone has a right to choose.**

Recognize that men are put on the chopping block more often than women. Each time a man approaches you, he has built up the courage to say hello and is hoping for a positive response.

Reflect on how you feel when you're rejected. It's not a good feeling. So the next time someone approaches you in a respectful manner, instead of ignoring them, turning up your nose, being rude, or saying something mean, realize he has feelings just like you. By being mean, you can damage their confidence and self-esteem. A simple "hello" will do and a gentle letdown is sufficient if you're not interested. Always use discretion and protect yourself if you don't feel comfortable.

If you are rejected, say NEXT! There is always a more suitable person or situation for you and your life! **Know that what is for you is just that; for you.**

Dealing with rejection

From childhood up, we all learn that being accepted is good – it's approval. Many of us often take extra steps to do what makes others happy and when things don't work out the way we expect, we take it personally. The questions begin. What could I have done differently? What did I do wrong? Why does this hurt so?

Rejection is not easy and I don't know a sure fire way to immediately relieve the disappointment or pain associated with it. What I can say is that when you are secure in yourself and don't take peoples' decisions personally you will suffer less from rejection. In addition, as you elevate in consciousness and realize that people are constantly changing and making choices conducive for themselves that you have absolutely nothing to do with, you will feel less or no rejection at all. It takes time and understanding.

Know that the right people, job, car, relationship for you will appear in your life exactly when they're supposed to. So if you're job hunting and feeling discouraged, don't worry or be disappointed; you just haven't made it to the right interview yet.

If you've just ended a relationship or people are flowing in and out of your life, it is time for change and growth. They served their purpose in your life. Allow the change, don't fight it. **Know that life has something better in store for you.**

AFFIRMATION

My life is constantly flowing and changing. As I mature and grow, life provides me with the perfect opportunities and lessons for me to become greater. I accept change and the wonderful possibilities to come.

ACTION

When faced with rejection, don't get down on yourself. Realize that situation is no longer the right opportunity for you but a new one is on the way.

TELLING THE TRUTH

> *Challenge yourself to be a better person.*

I knew a guy who lied just about all the time. He would lie about you to another person in your presence. I believe he had a problem dealing with himself and reality, so he fantasized. His lies caused him to lose many friends who could have helped him tremendously throughout his life. He lied so much that his family didn't want to be bothered with him.

What happens when you tell a lie? You have to remember the lie you told. It's possible that you'll tell another lie to cover one lie and another to cover that lie. If more than one person is involved, you may get yourself in a bunch of mess that could have been avoided by telling the truth.

Why do people lie? People lie because they:
- Don't like to take responsibility for their actions
- Have mental illness
- Fear hurting someone's feelings
- Are still living in their past and have a fear of being reprimanded
- Are selfish and don't care how they affect others.

What does a lie really do for you? What will it do for your reputation when the truth comes out? How does it affect the development of your relationships?

Lies shatter trust, respect, reputations and relationships. People are involved and are emotional beings. When the truth is found out, expect a response that will not be favorable for you.

If you lie often, you need to get to the root of the problem. Are you afraid of hurting people, getting hurt, or both? You have to decipher what incident in your life has caused you to develop this pattern. Did your parents advise you to tell the truth and you wouldn't get in trouble? When you told them the truth, did they keep their word or respond by giving you a serious whipping?

If you don't tell the truth and you are conscious of it, you may beat yourself up over the guilt or question why you told that lie. Avoid it by being honest.

The truth can hurt. However, **by telling the truth, you can save yourself and the other person time and worry.** I have this rule that I stick by. If someone is bold enough to ask the question, then they deserve the truth; an honest answer. This keeps you honest and forces you to think about the things you do. You will think about the possible outcomes of situations and make better decisions. Ultimately, it's not just a decision you're making for you. It's a decision that is going to affect others as well.

We don't desire to cause pain but we increase the depth of the pain by lying. By speaking the truth, we have the opportunity to deal with the situation, clear the air, and move on. The longer the lies are drawn out, the harder it is for someone to believe you. Free yourself from all the garbage that comes with lies. Challenge yourself to be a better person. **The truth will truly set you free.**

> **AFFIRMATION**
>
> I am present. I am aware. I am not fearful of the truth. I understand that telling the truth is healing, empowering, and honest. I am an honest person.

ACTION

Pay attention to your conversations. Learn what triggers your lying. Are you protecting yourself from something? Are you trying to impress someone? What is your trigger? When you know the trigger, and there may be more than one, go backwards in your history and figure out why you began this pattern. Address it by first being honest with yourself. Realize that every time you've lied to others you've also lied to yourself.

From now on, when you find yourself beginning or even thinking of telling a lie, stop yourself immediately. Regroup and tell the truth. Then pat yourself on the back ... Good Job!

Tip: If you find you are an extremely imaginative person, start writing the stories you wish to tell. You may one day be a best selling author.

TIPS FOR A SUCCESSFUL RELATIONSHIP

Piglet sidled up to Pooh from behind. "Pooh!" he whispered. "Yes, Piglet?" "Nothing," said Piglet, taking Pooh's paw. "I just wanted to be sure of you." ~A.A. Milne

I was twelve years old and one night my mom, dad and I were watching television in their bedroom. I was absolutely enjoying the quality time with my parents. My mother had setting rollers in her hair made of hard plastic. She had chosen to not sit under the dryer but to allow her hair to air-dry overnight. It was often painful to sleep in those rollers unless you slept "pretty" meaning you folded your arms and rested your face on your arms to avoid your head touching the bed, which would cause pressure and pain.

As we watched television, my father proceeded to pick up a newspaper, roll it up, and hit my mother in the head over and over again. He paused only to tell me to get out. I left the room and sat on the stairs. My siblings noticed me crying and asked why. I shared what had happened.

Another instance, my family was returning from an outing. As we entered the doors to the apartment building, I witnessed my father smack my mother's behind in a flirtatious manner and my mother giggled approvingly.

Those are two examples of what some may witness and process mentally in the pursuit of trying to understand what is and isn't acceptable in a relationship. As young adults, we begin to gather all the experiences and try to place them as to what we desire and don't.

What I witnessed and thought to be a loving relationship, I later realized to be an abusive relationship with love as an underlying factor.

As an adult, I had to sort through everything. I firmly committed to not being involved in an abusive relationship. I focused on the hitting aspect and wound up experiencing mental, emotional and verbal abuse.

After developing myself, I realized what I'd experienced. I was later blessed to have someone in my life that felt the same about developing a healthy relationship. It was an extreme learning process – lots of pain and recognition, but I learned, successful/healthy relationships are possible.

Generally, when we think of a relationship we think of a husband and wife or a boyfriend and girlfriend, which are a couple of the meaningful relationships we will have in our lives. For each person with whom you interact, there is potential for a relationship of some type. We spend our lives relating to one another and we build our relationships based on how we relate.

Relationships can sometimes be very complex to maintain. However, there are a few simple rules that we can apply to ensure that we have done our best to make our relationships of any kind be a success.

- *Be honest with yourself about why you have the relationship you're having and why this person is in your life.*
- *Tell the truth to yourself and the other person.*
- *Continue striving to become a great communicator in your relationships.*

This means learning to listen and paying attention to what people are saying to you. Speak and express your feelings after the other person finishes expressing theirs.

- *Don't be afraid to say what's on your mind.*

Explain to them that your intent is not to hurt or harm but to only be truthful and honest.

- *Follow the golden rule. Do unto others as you wish them to do unto you.*

If everyone followed this rule, the world would be a better place. If you keep this in mind, you will be more thoughtful of others' feeling and how your actions will affect them. Treat people the way you want them to treat you.

- *Always respect another's right to their opinion, their option to change or to choose again.*

As much as we'd like things to go our way all the time, it just doesn't happen that way. We change on a daily basis and what may have been right for you today may be wrong for you tomorrow. Each person has to guide his or her life in the way that's best for him or her. Respect that and you will respect yourself.

Expression is the way to keep any relationship healthy. If a relationship doesn't work out on one level, you may find another level that best suits the both of you.

Just because two people disagree doesn't mean they have to end any type of relationship. Learn to agree to disagree. Respect each other's feelings, opinions, expression, and emotions and you should have a relationship that lasts as long as you both desire.

Remain an individual. Never get so engrossed in someone's life, problems, or personal issues that you end up neglecting yourself.

AFFIRMATION

I attract and am involved in healthy, positive relationships. I communicate in an honest and healthy manner. I respect others as they respect me.

ACTION

As you relate, stay aware of your interactions and make sure they are healthy and positive.

THE LOVE BANK

Love is a wise investment. Therefore, make wise choices with it.

As a teen I was so naïve that I gave of myself, money, and time to make others happy as an expression of my love. I desired love and thought if I showed people love, they'd reciprocate.

Love is the most compelling feeling. Everyone wants to be loved and will spend the majority of their lives seeking or attempting to understand love. Many people will do things in the name of love, yet they do not understand the difference between infatuation, actions done based on the desire to be loved, and love itself.

There are people in this world who prey on others' weaknesses. These people will take your kindness for granted or will outright use you and take everything that you are willing to give.

You're not obligated to give of yourself, your body, your money, or anything else because they say they love you. Innately, women are caretakers and should monitor how much of themselves they share. Not only men, but people will use this knowledge to their advantage. Many times, when a woman thinks a man loves her and will possibly commit, she sees this as a green light to open up and share. Young men should be cautious as well because some women do and will prey on nice men or men with low self-esteem and use them until the well runs dry.

Some people will say whatever they need to say and behave however they need in order to get what they want. **Sincerity is shown through a person's actions.**

Instead of relying on the word love or someone saying they're committed to you, rely on the love bank. The love bank works like any other bank; a person must make a deposit in order to make a withdrawal. Their deposit can be time, loyalty, friendship, appreciation, affection, and commitment when shown through their actions and not just muttering words.

Put aside their having said, "I love you" and check their balance in the love bank. What has this person done for you in your life that enables them to make a financial, physical, or mental withdrawal? Check their balance against their request; does it equate? Has this man actually been a man in your life? When you call on him, does he help? Does he treat you like a lady? Does he spend quality time with you? Does he let you know that you're important in his life? Does this woman allow you to be a man? Does she respect you? Does she extend herself to you or is it a one-way street? **Check their actions and you'll know if they have insufficient funds or if they're allowed a withdrawal.**

LOVE

Love doesn't have special requirements. It just is.

As children, our jobs were to observe our surroundings and learn. If you were to reflect on your childhood, what examples of love were you shown? The first relationship you will probably reflect on is your parents' relationship; how they loved one another. If not that, then your relationship with your parents; how they loved you.

Your first definition of love is learned through your familial relations; the degree of affection expressed, your way of interacting, and how you express care for one another. As you develop as an adult, you will have the opportunity to refine your definition of love through new relationships. By expressing love as you know, you'll learn through trial and error which expression is right for you. A great example of love is the unconditional love that a child expresses for his parents.

Love is not about being beaten, abused, talked down to, being forced to do things you're uncomfortable with, having sex against your will, being used or manipulated, being made to feel ashamed, inadequate, or threatened with death.

Sex does not equal love. The greatest love does not require sex. The simple fact that another complements your life and brings you that much joy is enough.

Have you ever heard the expression "love hurts?" Love doesn't hurt; rejection and expectations are the culprits that are often confused with love. The phrase "love hurts" should be changed to "loneliness and disappointment hurts."

When someone tells you, "I don't love you anymore" or "I don't want you in my life," or begins a new chapter that doesn't include you, rejection causes you pain. Love isn't to blame; it's the feeling of being undesired or unaccepted. People want acceptance, which leads to love, and when it is taken away they feel love caused it.

Love is unconditional acceptance of people in our lives. When love is present, there aren't stipulations or a tit-for-tat exchange. Every gift, hug, chore, or favor is done because of a desire to share yourself and your abilities with someone. Love is compassion, warmth, a listening ear, a kind word, a tear, a smile, and a hug. Love can motivate, arouse, and give you courage.

Don't ever confuse the scars and wounds of rejection and disappointment with love. Free yourself of the notion that love causes pain and you free yourself to love freely. Acknowledge each experience for what it is.

If you feel pain, ask yourself, "What is happening to me that I feel is undesirable? What is being taken away from or not being given to me? Am I upset because I can't control the situation?" Acknowledging your feelings will allow you to get to the root emotion and from there you can be real with yourself and understand that love is not the offender. Accept the rejection and/or disappointment. Own it as being an expression of the pain that you feel. Use helpful ways of expressing your pain by crying, writing, talking, or any other creative mode of expression. Release this pain from your body and move on.

Do whatever you do from your heart. Realize a person's actions will differ from what you may expect; people change just as you do. What you know about a person today may be a little different tomorrow.

Rejection is a part of life. We will all experience it. When it happens, it's for a reason. You're making room for something greater to occur in your life. It may hurt, but time will heal the wound. **Know this and you will know that love will touch you again.**

"Love is patient, love is kind. It does not envy, it does not boast, it is not proud. It is not rude, it is not self-seeking, it is not easily angered, and it keeps no record of wrongs. Love does not delight in evil but rejoices with the truth. It always protects, always trusts, always hopes, and always preserves."

-- 1 Corinthians 13:4-7

DATING

Date, date, and date some more!

I wish I had known when I was in my twenties how important dating is. I was always one to start seeing a guy and the next thing I knew I was in a full-fledged relationship. I strongly recommend that young men and women should date, date, and date some more. Through dating, you learn your likes and dislikes. You will have experiences that show you with whom you are compatible and the qualities you desire in a mate.

Dating is taking time to experience and learn about the person with whom you're spending your time. Dating does not mean you're committed to one person; you're leaving yourself open to see other people. The problem-free way to do this is to let everyone know that you're not interested in a serious commitment.

Being upfront about your dating habits will lead to less heartache and give you freedom of choice. **Take your time, enjoy life, and settle down when you're ready.**

Points to remember:

1. Dating doesn't equal promiscuity. You're not obligated to have sex with anyone.

2. Always protect yourself sexually.

3. Tongue kissing is very intimate – eliminate it to avoid creating a close bond with someone.

4. Do not give keys to your apartment or vehicle to anyone especially if you're seeing other people.

5. Be honest and when you're ready to date exclusively tell everyone you were dating that you've committed to a serious relationship.

GROWING IN LOVE

> **Don't use the word "love" loosely. This word changes lives!**

I remember when I thought I was in love with someone. It was funny because I thought I was in love after only a couple of months Yes, I cared for him but I was not in love with him. I was caught up in the fact that I had finally met someone with whom I clicked.

The term "falling in love" is used to describe the moment a person realizes how deeply they feel for someone. Take a moment and think about the word falling. When someone falls it usually results in feeling pain.

Falling in love is losing control of your feelings and before you know it your feelings have surpassed "like". But, are you really in love or are you still infatuated with a person who is still doing their best "first impression?" You get a rush of excitement when you see or talk to that person. They make you smile, your palms sweat, and your your heart goes pitter pat. All of the emotions are from the newness and infatuation in a relationship.

Loving relationships grow like a plant being nourished by being watered, placed in adequate sunlight, pruned, and having its beauty acknowledged. In the loving relationship you water it by feeding it with dedication and time. You prune the relationship by working through disagreements and compromise so that it may continue to grow in a healthy manner. You acknowledge the beauty of the relationship with affection, attention, kindness and commitment.

Growing in love comes in time. As an older gentleman, once told me, "You may love your partner, but the growing in love comes when you go through years together. It's the years of learning one another that test the strength and endurance of your relationship, the years when you learn that this person is really in your corner. It's when you know that this person is truly with you when you suffer and triumph together and no matter what you are still together."

By growing in love, there is a steady pace which can result in fruitful development of the relationship. You may love someone and even feel that you can't do without them. You'll really know when it's love when you dedicate your time and energy to learning one another and exploring the possibilities of the relationship. When you're interested in your personal development and growth (even spiritual development) is when the growing in love starts. It comes with trust, commitment, time, and energy. It comes with knowing that this person is really for you and is willing to grow with you and learn you because you're just that special to them.

Before you tell someone that you're in love with him or her, take your time. Love takes time. **Be sure that you're sure.**

MARRIAGE

Take your commitment seriously.

Marriage! When you choose this road, make sure that your heart, mind, and body are ready. Everything changes when you join your life with another.

I knew of a couple that met, got engaged in three months, and married a few months later. They both assumed the other had money based on appearances and got their cars repossessed.

As they began to learn one another, they each realized they had different ideals. He came to the conclusion that she was too snobbish and materialistic. She came to the conclusion that she did not desire to have children with him. Their learning process continued and they eventually learned the reasons why they couldn't make it as a couple; which was what they should have done before making the commitment.

The divorce rate in the United States is 50%. Marriage isn't what it once was. Years ago, people married for various reasons including, love, pregnancy, and stability. One consistency was the fact that they honored their vows. Many couples are entering marriage with the thought, "If it doesn't work out, I'll just get a divorce" versus, "I know with marriage comes challenges and I am willing to work."

More marriages are failing now because they are rushed. Some people marry with a fairy tale fantasy that everything is supposed to be perfect all the time. They don't discuss important issues such as finances, credit, goals, family, and history. In addition, there is also the major issue of having to deal with a spouse's previous relationships that won't fade away because of the permanent attachment-of children.

It is unfortunate that the sanctity of marriage has been reduced to a fly-by-night commitment. Marriage is a commitment that requires the dedication of two people. They must be dedicated to their family.

- *Before getting married, be sure that your reasons are the right reasons.*

The person you marry should be a complement to you. They should have your best interest in mind, understand you and allow you to be an individual while you also operate together as one. This person should be a plus in your life and you should be the same.

- *Be careful about to whom and when you choose to marry.*

Timing is important. Don't let fear be your motivation. If someone loves you, they will acknowledge and respect your desires. Take your commitment seriously.

- *Be sure that you are ready to commit.*

The best thing you can do for yourself and your mate is to take your time to get to know one another before you get married.

- *Ask questions before you propose or accept a proposal such as:*

1. How do they feel about family? Is it important?
2. Do they want children, if so, what are their ideals about raising them?
3. Is education important?
4. Where do they want to live?
5. What are they good at and what household chores would they be responsible for?

6. Are they set in "special roles" meaning is a woman supposed to **be** at home barefoot and pregnant? Is the man supposed to go to work, come home, pop a beer open, sit in his favorite chair and rub his belly while being waited on hand and foot?

7. What is their financial standing?

8. How is their credit?

9. What are their goals?

10. What are their plans concerning retirement?

11. Are they religious? If so, do they feel the whole family has to practice the same religion?

12. Are the open-minded?

13. Are they clean?

14. What are their strengths and weaknesses?

The questions can go on and on. Make sure that you're sure!

Tips for a successful marriage

1. Whatever your faith is, incorporate it into your relationship.

2. Great mates find what they lack in one another; the complement. Know your limits. Allow your mate to complement you; by filling in the blanks when you don't know the answer, when you fall short, they pick up.

3. Communicate by listening, ask questions if you don't understand, and respond. Respect one another during conversation by not over talking or discounting your mate's feelings.

4. Express you love. Sex is not the only expression of love. Nurture your relationship by spending quality time with one another. Continue doing whatever you did to deserve this person. Remember little things mean a lot and will confirm your love without you having to say, "I love you." Write love notes, send flowers, run a bath, call your mate at work to say "Hi", or do that special something that you know your mate loves.

5. Respect your relationship. Never allow anyone to dictate how much

time you should spend with your mate. Don't allow temptation or any other excuse to be your logic for bringing a third person into your relationship. Infidelity is a huge impediment in any relationship.

6. Share the responsibilities of the household. Do whatever chores you agree on.

7. Teach your mate what pleases or makes you happy.

8. Financial stress is the detriment of many relationships. Discuss your finances, create a budget, and uphold your end of the bargain. If you spouse makes more money than you, don't take that as a blow to your pride. Contribute what you can. Plan your family's future.

9. Put the shoe on your foot sometimes. Take time to consider your mate's daily experiences, responsibilities and stresses before you make accusations or assumptions if they are not in a good mood.

10. Remember your mate was an individual before you married. It is likely they will still have interests outside your marriage to include their hobbies and friends. Don't smother your mate and allow them to be themselves. Allow them space and use the space they afford you.

11. Be supportive of your mate's dreams, goals, and accomplishments. Motivate and help when you can. Never degrade your mate in any fashion.

12. Be honest, real, and respectful. Treat your mate, and their heart, the same way you'd want them to treat you.

13. Men and women don't be abusive in any manner. **Respect begets respect.**

When Love Isn't Enough

> *Whatever you do, don't lose yourself in the process of helping someone else.*

I had a friend, whom I loved dearly, who was going through a very stressful time. Because I loved him, I chose to be supportive by being there when he needed me. I listened to him, comforted him, advised him, laughed with him, and gave him my time and resources. I loved him but that wasn't enough.

Of all the things I did for him, I couldn't take away his pain, stress, anger, or worry. I couldn't give him peace, a week in which he slept through the night every night. I couldn't restore his faith, ability to trust or love. Of all that I was to him, my love wasn't enough.

There may come a time in your life where your concern and compassion for someone overwhelms you so much that you do everything in your power to help a person because you love them. I did. I wouldn't walk away because I've always felt that you shouldn't leave your friends when they're down. After all, I'd want someone by my side supporting me if needed support.

Sometimes it gets to a point that your lesson is done and whatever lesson that person has to learn no longer includes your participation.

You've completed your part. What you gave or offered is no longer needed and they have to continue on their path without you. They have to find their peace alone. They have to love themselves. That's what will take them to where they need to be.

If you experience this, there is a lesson in it for you as well. Free those you love and free yourself by trusting your creator. Turn their well-being over to your creator. Know that you've done all you could. It's not your path to change someone. First a person must desire change and then initiate it.

In my opinion, angels are not all mysterious creatures flying around. We are one another's angels. We touch and bless each other's lives with a smile, a kind word, money, a meal, or whatever we are to do at that time. Angels perform acts of kindness. You were an angel to your friend for the time you were needed. Remember everything happens with reason. **Never stop being compassionate to others.**

You may think about your loved one often. If it consumes you try this:

1. Take in that moment and give it your attention and close it with an affirmation such as, I release and let go of _____. I have completed my lesson and freely place your well-being in the hands of the Creator.

2. Write it out. Express whatever you need to express.

3. Busy yourself. Exercise, dance, or do whatever creative outlet you may enjoy.

DEATH

Rejoice and remember the good times.

Death is a somber time. We can no longer see, touch, or hear the deceased. No matter when it comes, it is always a harsh reality when someone you care for is no longer here.

You experience so many emotions when someone dies. One minute you're smiling or laughing as you remember the person; the next minute you're crying because you're angry or sad because they're no longer with you.

No matter how or when it happens, death can be surreal. Your loved one may be gone, but you are still here and have the rest of your life to live. With their passing, they have given you an experience that became a part of who you are.

One beautiful thing we're left with is their memory. We can remember the moments we shared, their smiles and laughter. We can rejoice in who they were, how they touched our lives, and keep them alive in our hearts.

One day you may have to soothe or comfort someone who is in a similar situation. One day you may be able to say to someone, "You will be okay."

If you believe in reincarnation, perhaps your souls will meet again!

Death and family

Losing a parent is devastating. It feels as if you have lost a part of you. Your guide has left you to find your own way. You can no longer turn to them just to say, "Hey, I love you," or "Mama, give me your recipe for carrot cake," or "Daddy, how do you know when your transmission is going bad?"

When you lose a parent, you lose a friend. As we grow up, we love our parents, then hate them, then we understand them, love them, and they become our friends.

Mothers and fathers are irreplaceable. They each play a major role in your development. Losing either creates a void that can never be filled. Only life's lessons will attempt to give you the knowledge and wisdom that could have been shared with you.

A person, who loses a parent, especially at an early age, has to tap into their inner strength. Remember what your parent admired or loved about you. Use that as a source of strength and love. Remember their faces and the laughter you shared. Their presence is forever with you because you were born from their energy.

Sudden death

I had a friend who for some reason I became extremely close to in a very short time. In a matter of months, we had bonded as if we had known one another for years.

One day upon arriving at work, I was greeted with the news that my friend had committed suicide by jumping from a forty-eight-story building. Mind you, I had just seen my friend four days before.

I had experienced death before in my family, but this was the most disturbing because of the way he died and the surprise of it.

I experienced many emotions very quickly. I was angry with him for leaving that way. I was sad because I felt like his work here wasn't complete. I wished I could have helped him, especially since he had called before he committed suicide and I wasn't able to accept his call at that time. I felt like if I had taken the call maybe he would still be here. I was surprised by the length of time that his death affected me. It was worsened by the constant conversations I overheard at work. I cried a lot, talked to him, and then eventually let him go. He is now a memory of a very loving and creative person whom I wish I'd had in my life longer.

Denial

You must confront your emotions. The person is gone but your life is continuing. Denying that your loved one has passed is playing a fool's game with yourself. You must see the reality.

As much as we wish we could all live forever, that's just not reality for the physical form. Death is a part of life. If you deny that a loved one has passed, you will feel as if you're continually being stabbed in the heart by looking for them to be there when you need to talk, need a hug, want to crack a joke, talk about what happened today. Don't torture yourself. Yes, it will take time for their passing to sink in. You must accept the fact that they no longer exist physically.

I recall flipping through my phone book and coming across my grandmother's phone number. I was ready to dial when I remembered she died two years before. I'd been unable to attend the funeral. Part of me had not accepted that she was gone because I did not have the opportunity to say good-bye. I didn't see her in the casket. I didn't cry. I didn't mourn. My last memory of her was seeing her resting in bed. I had to once again tell myself that Grandmama is dead. She passed away. She won't make homemade rolls. You can't hear her say "Yello" when she answers the telephone. You can't hear her play the piano anymore nor can you get a sloppy Grandmama kiss.

Although my grandmother died, I can still smell and taste her rolls. I can hear her voice. I hear her playing the piano and I feel her kisses. I keep my Grandmama alive in my heart. Her spirit lives in me because she is a part of me.

Accept the passing of your loved ones. Accept the fact that they aren't there physically. If you are lucky enough to have pictures or videos, look at those each time you need to visit with them. Remember their smile, their smell, their favorite cigar, or their funny dance. Remember all the things that made you love that person. Hold them close to you forever.

Mourning

There is no designated time for mourning or grief. Several factors will affect how you deal with the death of a loved one: the timing, your relationship to the person, whether you have accepted the death, whether you are allowing yourself to grieve, and whether you are running away from the pain.

Mourning is natural and healthy. It's okay. We love and hurt when we feel a loss. We hurt because we know our loved one is irreplaceable. Fortunately, we have several release mechanisms to help us deal with the pain.

- *Crying is a great release.*

Cry as often as necessary.

- *Talk it out.*

Talk to a friend or family member about how you feel.

- *Write them a letter.*

Write to express anger if you feel anger. Write to tell your loved one about your day. Write to forgive or be forgiven. Write to say I wish you were here. Use that blank sheet of paper as your sounding board. Have your private conversation with your loved one so that you may come to terms with their passing. Express all that you wish you could have each time it comes to mind.

- *Dialog.*

If you need to have actual dialog, put a picture of them in a chair or in front of you on a table and talk it out. Tell them how much you miss them or why you hurt. Whatever comes to mind that you need to express, say it.

In order for you to heal and come to terms with their passing, you must express all the sorrow, pain, and anger, or whatever emotion necessary for you to go on with your life without regrets, doubts, or judgments.

If you take the time to address your grief, the memories of your loved one can become more pleasant than painful. You can rejoice in his or her life instead of their leaving this earth. Your pain may never completely disappear because those persons occupied a space in your life and were dear to you. However, **you can now smile about who they were to you, how they made your life better, and what you have learned and are able to share because of your having known them.**

Sex & Parenting

Sex & Parenting Introduction

{ *Your choices affect others.* }

As a teen, I'd heard many of my friends talk about sex. I really thought the girls were fast because sex was the last thing on my mind until a boy brought it to the forefront. Since there was minimal conversation in my household about life, period, I read books to learn about my body and sex. Guidance would have made a serious difference at this point in my life.

Now as a parent, I have spoken to my children since they were each five years old on how the body works and gradually increased their knowledge as they've gotten older. I've informed my children because if I didn't the world would. I've shared information such as the fact that sex in not to be played with. Sex does not equal love but can be an expression of love. Respect and always protect your body. It is an honor for anyone that you choose to share your body. Do your best to wait until you are married before you have sex. The best protection is abstinence.

Sex invokes curiosity, breaks hearts, creates bonds, creates life, and can cause lifelong illness or death. Sex equals responsibility. Before having sex, be sure that you're ready. Don't allow anyone to force or manipulate you into having sex.

Homosexuality, "being gay", is a sexual preference. What goes on in your personal life is your business. It is not necessary to broadcast your sexual preference. **Be yourself, be safe, and seek positive role models.**

Sex and children

Birth control and contraceptives are important to prevent pregnancy and disease. Before becoming sexually active, educate yourself. If you and your partner become pregnant, share the process of making the decision that is in the best interest of all involved, including the baby.

Abortion is an option and the action can scar you emotionally, physically, and mentally. Abortion can also provide another chance, opportunity, and peace. There are alternatives to abortion. Choose what's best for all involved.

Having children with someone that you don't plan on sharing the duration of your life can place you in the Baby's Daddy – Baby's Mama Syndrome. Choose your partner wisely and try to maintain a healthy relationship for the child's sake.

Having children is not the end of your life. You can still accomplish your goals. Support systems are important. If you don't have one, create it.

Take care of your baby. Choose relationships and whom you allow around your children carefully. If you ever become a step-parent, remember you are a complement to the family. Complement them and allow them to complement you.

Sex and parenting are significant acts, especially since your choices affect other's lives. Take this seriously.

SEX

> *Treat Your Body With Respect!*

As a teenager, I had a persuasive and aggressive boyfriend. He was also an opportunist who took full advantage of my depression as he convinced, rather, laid a guilt trip on me about having sex. I made up my mind. I went to his house after school one day and we had sex which was quite painful and took only a few minutes. After it was over, I jumped up and went off. I hit, cussed, fussed, and asked him, "This is what you bugged me about?" I had been under the impression that sex was to be a wonderful experience.

He later convinced me to do it again. I went to his house and we proceeded without protection. He was no expert at withdrawal so lo' and behold, I became pregnant.

When you engage in sex, you must be able to accept the responsibility of the action. Sex is a beautiful act and is even more enjoyable when experienced by two responsible people in a responsible relationship such as marriage. For some reason, men are perpetuating the idea that you have to be rough or pound a woman to be "doing your job." It's not about that. Sex doesn't require and isn't a contest to do or withstand aggressive pounding actions with our bodies. Be aware that a woman's body is precious and can be damaged during sex.

People like to express themselves in many ways sexually. Take your time and treat your body with respect by not allowing people to do any and everything to you. If it doesn't feel good or is morally wrong, don't allow it or stop and tell your partner how you feel.

The best protection is abstinence.

Having sex now is like playing Russian roulette. There are so many diseases, including some that are deadly, that you have to be extremely careful. When sexually active, you have to protect yourself from contracting STD's, death, and pregnancy. In addition to HIV/AIDS, Syphilis and Gonorrhea are also widely spread. If left untreated, you can wind up blind, or unable to have children, among other things. What about Herpes? One unprotected encounter and you have a disease that subjects you to painful breakouts for life. There's Herpes Simplex I, which are cold sores, and can develop into Herpes Simplex II (genital herpes), which is contracted through oral sex. Herpes Simplex II is also spread through intercourse.

"Trich"monasis, Chlamydia, and bacterial infections can travel and cause PID (pelvic inflammatory disease), which can leave women sterile. Men can carry these diseases, spread them, and not know it. Some diseases are discreet in women as well. Pay close attention to your body and if you notice any change in scent, discharge, pain or itching, see a doctor. Men, don't be afraid to go to the doctor. If certain diseases are left untreated, you can also become sterile.

HPV or human papillomavirus is the most common sexually transmitted infection. You can't see it so there is often no indication you have it. It can cause diseases such as warts and even more serious, cancer. There is now, however, a vaccine available. In most cases, the body will naturally clear itself of the disease within two years.

The best protection is abstinence, but how many people are going to abstain from sex their entire life? Therefore, the next best thing to do is to maintain a monogamous relationship with a trustworthy individual.

Establish an understanding with your partner that you prefer to be sexually active with them only and you'd like reciprocity.

You may have a partner who agrees to be monogamous, but we are human and subject to error. Before engaging in intercourse, you both should be tested for STD's, HIV/AIDS. There is no guarantee that your partner will forever be monogamous and not be tempted to experience sex with other people. Protect yourself to avoid STD'S by using a male condom. The other methods of birth control complement the male condom by preventing pregnancy. The various methods are listed in the contraceptive chart.

When you are sexually active, you are affecting your life, your partner's, potentially a child, and any partner you and your partner may have in the future. **Act responsibly** and enjoy your life without any unnecessary upsets.

Remember:

- Never do anything you're uncomfortable with.
- Never use sex as a way to receive love. Having sex with someone won't make them love you and it definitely won't make them stay in a relationship with you.
- Always respect yourself and your partner. Don't frivolously share your body.
- Cleanliness. Always keep your sex organs clean. Avoid any contact with feces or secretions from the anus with the vagina. This can cause serious infection.
- Protection. Use it to avoid pregnancy or contracting an STD including AIDS or HIV.
- Act responsibly for you and your partner. Be honest if you're not monogamous.
- Don't have sex with a person you can't see yourself having children with.
- Remember you don't owe anyone sex because they take you out.
- Remain aware when you're out. Guard your drink to reduce the

possibility of being drugged and possibly raped.

- Avoid videotaping and photos that may haunt you later in life.

HIV & AIDS

You can't tell if a person is HIV positive by looking at them.

I'm not sure if you read the chapter that mentioned my childhood friend who was given a laced marijuana joint and became mentally ill as a result. This same person, due to his mental illness also became a male prostitute and was the first person that I have known to contract HIV and later die of AIDS. This happened back in the 80's when AIDS had just hit the scene. Who would have thought that it would come to our neighborhood?

Some of the people that grew up in the 80's had contracted HIV and had children. Their children were born with HIV and are part of the population of young adults now, currently dealing with sexuality and whether to be honest about their condition. Be aware of this before you decide to be intimate with someone.

Important definitions

Immunodeficiency: when the immune system has a decreased ability or inability to fight infectious disease

Immune system: the system in the body that protects you from disease

Immuno-compromised: a term used to describe a person whose immune system is compromised which leaves them susceptible to opportunistic infections

Opportunistic infections: infections caused by germs that would not cause disease in a healthy immune system. Examples of these infections are Pneumonia and Tuberculosis.

HIV is the precursor to AIDS. HIV is a virus that is passed from person to person when infected blood, semen, vaginal secretions, come in contact with another persons mucous membranes or open wound. Mucous membranes are found in the vagina, penis, rectum, eyes, nose, and mouth.

HIV is contracted through sexual contact with a HIV positive person. It is passed through the vagina, penis, rectum (butt), or mouth. It is also passed through sharing of needles or through breastfeeding.

You DO NOT contract HIV or AIDS from shaking hands, hugging, doorknobs, toilet seats, food, or from a peck on the cheek.

HIV symptoms

HIV symptoms are similar to those experienced with other ailments and may remind you of a cold. Some may or may not experience symptoms during the initial onset. Symptoms may include fever, fatigue, rash, swollen lymph nodes, or sore throat.

> **YOU CAN'T TELL IF A PERSON IS HIV POSITIVE BY LOOKING AT THEM.**

HIV test

If you feel you may have contracted the disease, the HIV test will not work until the body had built antibodies which are your body's way of fighting off disease. The antibodies are detectable from two weeks to six months after the disease has been contracted.

HIV/AIDS test can be taken anonymously. You can go to various centers in your city and be tested for free. Please contact your local public health department for resources.

AIDS or Auto Immune Deficiency Syndrome

If left untreated, HIV progresses, the immune system becomes weaker and progresses to AIDS. At this point the body is contracting various infections and having difficulty fighting them off. Opportunistic infections also take their shot at the immune system as well making the body weaker and weaker. You'll often hear about persons with AIDS dying of pneumonia.

Statistics

(These statistics are from the Center For Disease Control)

Young people with HIV/AIDS in 2004

- An estimated 4,883 young people received a diagnosis of HIV infection or AIDS, representing about 13% of the persons given a diagnosis during that year.

- African Americans were disproportionately affected by HIV infection; accounting for 55% of all HIV infections reported among persons aged 13–24.

- Young men who have sex with men (MSM), especially those of minority races or ethnicities, were at high risk for HIV infection. In the 7 cities that participated in CDC's Young Men's Survey during 1994–1998, 14% of African American MSM and 7% of Hispanic MSM aged 15–22 were infected with HIV.

HIV/AIDS in 2005

- Blacks accounted for 49% of the new HIV/AIDS cases.

- Of all black men living with AIDS, primary transmission was from men having sex with men, followed by injection drug use (sharing needles) and high-risk (unprotected) heterosexual contact.

- Of all black women living with HIV/AIDS, primary transmission was from high-risk heterosexual contact, followed by injection drug use.

- Half of the youth with AIDS are Black.

- Whites follow Blacks with 31% of the new HIV/AIDS cases.

- Hispanics account for 18% of new HIV/AIDS cases.

- Asian/Pacific Islanders and American Indian/Alaska Native are 1% each of new HIV/AIDS cases.

Many people don't know they have HIV and are spreading it because they don't get tested. Many women are contracting the diseases due to men bringing it home. Many men choose to be closet gays; sleeping with men discreetly and unprotected, on the "down low", hence the moniker "down low brothers." These men fail to discuss their sexual preference with the women in their lives or use the women as a cover for their homosexuality because of fear or shame. Fear of losing the woman or feeling shameful that they have desires to be with men. Other men satisfy their sexual needs in prison and are released and infect their wives or girlfriends.

Women

There are some women sleeping with men unprotected and are spreading the disease as well. Black women are the fastest growing population with HIV/AIDS. If not watched, Black people will eliminate themselves as a race.

It is a woman's responsibility to protect herself. Many unsuspecting women are married to men that contract the disease. Sexual HIV/AIDS awareness has to be brought to a new level. This means that you must take extra precautions before becoming sexually active with someone and continue to be tested each year.

Women, if you are sleeping with men unprotected, you heighten your risks of contracting HIV/AIDS. In addition, you may be spreading it to your husband or married men who in turn take the disease home to their wives.

Awareness

It is very important to stay aware of what is happening in your community and trust no one to decide whether you live or die. Before you become intimate with someone, question them. Take it to another level and have them prove to you through an HIV/AIDS test that they are not a carrier.

This may seem drastic or extreme. In order to protect yourself, these are the measures you want to take. Yes you can use a condom but condoms break. The spermicide in the condom may kill sperm but it doesn't kill AIDS. If this is your mode of protection, have your partner layer the condoms, putting on 2-3 at one time.

None of the birth control products on the market actually kill AIDS. Condoms are the best protection, next to abstinence.

Avoid exchanging any bodily fluids to include, blood, saliva, or fluids from the penis or vagina. In addition, do not have oral sex with anyone if you do not know their current medical history. Not only can you contract HIV/AIDS, you can contract other STD's through your mouth. Do not take those chances.

Men

Young men, if you have a desire to be with a man, be upfront with the women in your life or don't involve them at all. Being gay and ostracized by your family and community can be painful but don't use another life to cover your own. If you are sexually active with men, protect yourself. Get tested every six months.

Sign of the times

If there was ever a time and reason for couples to be monogamous, it is now. As you grow and develop, be aware that although that face may be beautiful and handsome, they may actually be walking death. Are you ready to die? Are you ready to risk your life just for pleasure? Is it worth it?

Notes

Homosexuality- Being Gay

{ *You have to be you.* }

I was exposed to the gay lifestyle in my childhood. My uncle is gay. He is the sweetest guy and I am grateful that our family has never passed judgment on his sexuality because he has so much to offer as a human being.

If you feel or believe that you're gay, don't be ashamed. There are attributes that were innate within you when you are born. This is maybe one of them. On all the talk shows I've seen or conversations I've heard, it has been expressed that each person who is gay has known they were gay as a child.

There are some people that have been sexually abused by the same sex that "become" gay because it is the only sexual experience they're accustomed to. Some are traumatized to the extent they are unwilling to believe they are heterosexual.

For those of you that are unsure about your sexual preference, seek out a counselor that can help you heal and walk through the self-discovery process.

Many sexual predators will brainwash you into thinking what they did to you is right or is the right way of doing things. Think about how you felt before the abuse occurred. Try to remember how you felt about the opposite sex. That may give you an idea of your true nature. I know several people that have been sexually abused who learned that they are attracted to the opposite sex.

"Gay" is actually a sexual preference. Your sexual preference is your business. "Coming out" may provide a relief to you because it lets everyone know to whom your attraction is directed. But if you are a teenager and still in school, be careful about speaking about your sexual preference.

Children can be cruel and mean. Many don't care how their actions affect the next person. Being gay is still not well accepted in society. To announce you're gay in a school environment is to set yourself up for disrespect, abuse, and unhappiness.

People have a tendency to shun what they're unfamiliar with or afraid of. Maintain peace in your life by not being flamboyant, attracting negative attention, or imitating what you feel "gay" is.

There are many successful businessmen and women who are gay and no one would know unless they were told. They realize "gay" is a sexual preference. It does not mean that you have to be a spectacle. Respect yourself and respect others. Look for role models to pattern yourself after.

Though your parents or society may not approve, you have to be you. You may lose friends and family because of their closed minds, but your real friends and family will develop as you meet people. To deny who you are only creates problems for you.

Instead of trying to shun homosexuality, perhaps people should consider this theory, which is strictly my opinion.

When we enter our bodies, we are either a masculine or feminine energy. I believe that spirit is energy. When a person dies, energy leaves the body and returns to the original source until returning to this reality. Each spirit is developing to the highest level of consciousness it can obtain. To get there, the spirit must experience on earth what it needs to elevate in consciousness. The experiences can be learned by being "gay": having a masculine energy in a feminine body or a feminine energy in a masculine body.

Now there are those of you that say it's a choice to be gay. Well, I can vibe on that because our lives are full of choices. If a child or person learned only one lifestyle through what they have been shown or taught, then, yes, they can change their desire for same sex interaction; they can be healed. I say healed because they do have to actually heal from the experience and learn other options.

> Every creation is an aspect or attribute of God.

Now some of you say that being gay is sacrilegious and goes against what God intended. Who really knows what God intended? Did you have a conversation with God or are you relying on what man has told you? Remember, everything, every creation is of the Creator. Every creation is an aspect or attribute of God.

In my opinion, the parts do work better with a man and a woman. But whose business is it what goes on in the privacy of others' bedrooms?

Remember that people are here to learn what they need to elevate their consciousness. Perhaps people who choose to be gay need to understand that lifestyle. Maybe they won't want to repeat it in their next existence. Maybe it's an experience for someone who disliked gay people.

Whatever it may be, it's your life. Live it, learn it, be it.

BIRTH CONTROL

Most birth control only prevents pregnancy but not the spread of infectious disease.

The first birth control I had was the Pill. The doctor never explained to me how they worked. I just read the accompanying literature and hid them from my mother.

She later asked me if I had and was I taking the pills. I told her yes, but I got the feeling that she didn't want me taking them or, more accurately, she didn't want me having sex. This was another of those times when communication could have made a difference.

I stopped taking the pills partly because of her reaction and partly because they didn't make me feel very good. The latter caused me to dislike anything that altered nature's process. Therefore, I have used other birth control methods.

I wanted to be married before I had children. Through circumstance and choice, I have given birth to three sons out of wedlock. The importance of family – a mother and father raising their children together – was never discussed nor was the importance of keeping your legs closed and experiencing life before having children ever mentioned to me. If you got pregnant, you decided to have the child or an abortion. My mother was initially pro-life, but I guess her view may have become slightly slanted.

Young ladies, whichever way you decide to protect your body, do it consistently. Live your life and be in a committed relationship before taking on the responsibility of having children. Ultimately, you are responsible for that potential life.

Young men, there are several methods of birth control you can use as well, including a natural herb called Neem. Become aware of your choices and make them. Do not blame a young lady if she decides to have a child. She can't do it without your sperm.

If you don't use protection and birth control, the risks you take are:

- Getting a STD that may be incurable or deadly.
- The possibility of having an abortion, which can affect your ability to have children in the future.
- Having a child you're not ready for
- Having to deal with a "baby's daddy or mama," child support court, and an attachment to a man or woman for the rest of your life.

Females, if you make a mistake, the same day or next day, get the morning after pill and take it.

Men and women, it is imperative that you visit a doctor and discuss which method is best for you.

While contraceptives can help prevent unwanted pregnancies, the majority won't protect you from sexually transmitted diseases. The only protections from STD's are abstinence and condoms. There are male and female condoms. You can increase their effectiveness by using a spermicide.

If you're unable to find a suitable commercial contraceptive, visit a naturopathic or homeopathic doctor. They can assist you in choosing natural methods of birth control that aren't harmful to your body.

Birth Control Guide

Method	Number of preg-nancies expected per 100 women	How to use it	Some Risks
Sterilization Surgery for Women	1	One-time procedure; nothing to do or remember	• Pain • Bleeding • Infection or other complications after surgery • Ectopic (tubal) pregnancy
Surgical Sterilization Implant for Women	1	One-time procedure; nothing to do or remember	• Mild to moderate pain after insertion • Ectopic (tubal) pregnancy
Sterilization Surgery for Men	1	One-time procedure; nothing to do or remember	• Pain • Bleeding • Infection
Implantable Rod	1	One-time procedure; nothing to do or remember	• Acne • Hair loss • Weight gain • Headache • Cysts of the ovaries • Upset stomach • Mood changes • Dizziness • Depression • Sore breasts
IUD	1	One-time procedure; nothing to do or remember	• Cramps• Bleeding• Lower interest in sexual activity • Pelvic inflammatory disease• Changes in your periods • Tear or hole in the uterus• Infertility
Shot/Injection	1	Need a shot every 3 months	• Bone loss • Bleeding between periods • Weight gain • Breast tenderness • Headaches
Oral Contraceptives (Combined Pill) "The Pill"	5	Must swallow a pill every day	• Dizziness • High blood pressure • Nausea • Blood clots • Changes in your cycle (period) • Heart attack • Changes in mood • Strokes • Weight gain
Oral Contraceptives (Progestin-only) "The Pill"	5	Must swallow a pill every day	• Irregular bleeding • Weight gain • Breast tenderness
Oral Contraceptives-Extended/Continuous Use "The Pill"	5	Must swallow a pill every day	• Risks are similar to other oral contraceptives • Bleeding • Spotting between periods

Patch	5	Must wear a patch every day	• Exposure to higher average levels of estrogen than most oral contraceptives
Vaginal Contraceptive Ring	5	Must leave ring in every day for 3 weeks	• Vaginal discharge • Swelling of the vagina • Irritation • Similar to oral contraceptives
Male Condom	11-16	Must use every time you have sex; requires partner's cooperation. Except for abstinence, latex condoms are the best protection against HIV/AIDS and other STDs	• Allergic reactions
Diaphragm with Spermicide	15	Must use every time you have sex	• Irritation • Allergic reactions • Urinary tract infection • Toxic shock
Sponge with Spermicide	16-32	Must use every time you have sex	• Irritation • Allergic reactions • Hard time removing • Toxic shock
Cervical Cap with Spermicide	17-23	Must use every time you have sex	• Irritation • Allergic reactions • Abnormal Pap test • Toxic shock
Female Condom	20	Must use every time you have sex May give some protection against STDs	• Irritation • Allergic reactions
Spermicide	30	Must use every time you have sex	• Irritation • Allergic reactions • Urinary tract infection

This information was provided by the FDA Office of Women's Health

There are options to commercial birth control methods. Herbal and natural birth control methods are available. A web site that offers additional information is located at: www.sisterzeus.com.

PREGNANCY

> *Preparation allows you to be fully conscious and ready to be the best parent you can be.*

I discovered I was pregnant with my last son when I purchased a pregnancy test and tested positive after missing my cycle. I didn't have to wait three minutes. The results were immediate. I was undeniably pregnant.

I went through the ups and downs of deciding whether or not to have the baby. Finally, one day I decided that no matter what, I was keeping my baby.

During my first ultrasound, I asked the doctor if it was a boy or girl. He consulted the nurse saying, "Nurse, what do you think?" She replied, "I don't know Doc, I think it's a boy." I shrieked, "No! It's a girl. I want a girl. Look again!" The doctor looked and said, "Either this is a boy or that's the biggest clitoris I've ever seen."

I cried all the way home and the next two days. I accepted the fact that I was having another boy and went back to being happy about having my baby.

I enjoyed each kick, flip, and turn. I enjoyed seeing his feet, fingers, elbows and head move beneath my skin. Incredibly, I had been blessed to carry and feel a life grow inside me.

Though the pregnancy was emotionally difficult at times, my baby – the little life growing inside me – made me smile each day as I watched my belly grow.

The U.S. Department of Health and Human Services concluded that between 2005-06 the birth rate for teenagers 15-19 rose 3 percent. This follows a 14 year downward trend in which birth rates fell by 34 percent from its peak in 1991.

Unmarried childbearing reached a new record high in 2006 rising nearly 8 percent, a 20 percent increase since 2002. The biggest jump was between unmarried women 25-29.

It is important that you make every effort to control when you bring a life into the world. Do it when you are fully prepared. If you happen to have brought a life into the world and you weren't ready, it's okay. That soul was ready and it came in divine time.

Your life can be less complicated when you are prepared to have a child. By waiting until you are more mentally, physically, spiritually, and financially prepared, you don't have to deal with the regrets that begin with "if I could have," "if I should have," "if I would have" and the struggle of trying to figure out how to financially support the baby. Preparation allows you to be fully conscious and ready to be the best parent you can be. Experience life and become an adult before having a child. There are far too many children raising children.

Experience life before having children.

If you, like me, didn't afford yourself the opportunity to not have children at a young age, there's still hope. There may be things you have to rearrange or delay in your life. You have to take care of the ultimate responsibility in your life; the life of your child.

Recommendations:

- Never have sex with a person unless you can envision you and that person acting responsibly, no matter what the outcome.

- Take full responsibility for your actions. You can't place blame on someone when you had equal control. A man has the option to wear a condom or two and a woman has several methods of birth control available to her.

Women, you are the most important party to the act because without a doubt you will have the responsibilities below.

You:

- May have a life growing inside you
- Have to agonize over whether or not you will keep your child
- Are ultimately responsible for the upkeep and upbringing of the child
- Will stay up late for feedings, sickness, or any other problem
- Are the one whose life will be altered, your freedom hindered
- Will for the next 18 to 21 years have to prepare your child to be self-sufficient
- Will possibly have to put your dreams on hold
- Should take the lead in protecting yourself and your life "time" by using some form of contraceptive until you are ready for a child. Save your life, save time, enjoy you!

Men, don't think with your little head; think with the big one. What are you really doing here? Are you wearing a hat? Do you really want to have a child now? Is it worth the risk? Have you considered the young lady's life and how a child will impact her? Do you want to pay child support? Consider how you were raised. How do you want to raise your child? When you have a child, you are bonded and bound to have the child's mother in your life for the rest of your life. You will have to deal with her and her personality. No quickie is worth impacting your life, that of your sex partner or a child if you don't intend to be there. Act responsibly for the both of you. Become a father and not a "Baby's Daddy".

We're having a baby, so what now?

Congratulations! You're having a baby. I hope you were ready, but if you weren't, join the masses. Babies seem to have a way of getting here on their own time, not on ours. Perhaps it's all about them.

If you found out through a pregnancy test from the store, you need to make a doctor's appointment immediately. Visit the doctor for confirmation and begin your prenatal visits. If you're choosing to not have this child, you should read the topics concerning abortions and adoption. The remainder of this section is for those desiring to have their child.

Women:

Pay close attention to your doctor's orders. If yours is not considered a special or high-risk pregnancy, then consider the following suggestions.

1. Keep yourself pretty. There are going to be a lot of days that you don't feel so good or you feel fat. It's part of pregnancy. Take the time to pamper yourself by taking long baths, doing your hair, touching up your makeup, or buying yourself pretty maternity outfits.

2. Exercise. Buy a prenatal exercise video, go for walks, or get in the pool. Stay active to help eliminate excessive weight gain. Exercising helps the body and makes labor easier.

3. Spend time with supportive people. Keep yourself surrounded with positive energy. It keeps your spirits up and helps to have a happy pregnancy.

4. Read to your baby and play music. It will soothe both of you.

5. Eat plenty of vegetables and fruits. These foods are alkaline and are in harmony with our bodies. They also supply the nutrients most needed by our bodies and babies.

6. Take your prenatal supplements. Whatever the baby needs will be taken from your body and leave you nutrient deficient if you don't take your vitamins or supplements.

7. Stay peaceful. Avoid arguing, confrontation, cussing or being loud. Think about what that energy feels like. It isn't very positive. You want to stay positive for your baby.

8. Interact with the baby's father if you have a good relationship.

Incorporate him into the pregnancy. Allow him to help you. Allow him to accompany you to the doctor, hear the baby's heartbeat, and feel the baby's movements.

9. If you have morning sickness, buy yourself some pregnancy tea or ginger ale and crackers. It will be your best friend throughout your pregnancy. Drink it everyday to help get rid of the nauseous feeling.

Men, congratulations, you're having a baby! Supporting your partner at this time is very important. Her attitude may fluctuate. She may seem a little crazy at times, but she isn't. Just imagine what it would be like to have a baby growing inside you, another being living in your body, altering your body, your hormones, everything. This baby makes her sick, can put her in pain, alter her sleep habits, and she gets kicked. Just think; this pregnant woman is expected to continue with her life, working, cleaning, possibly even taking care of you or other children, all while a life is growing inside her.

If a woman has decided to have a child that you fathered, she has given you the greatest gift and compliment you could ever receive in your lifetime; to have your offspring brought to life. She has made a sacrifice. Did you know that each time a woman has a child she risks her life to do so?

From the point of conception, a woman is connected with her child. She feels the progression of development of her child. However, this is your pregnancy, too. **You can be connected as well by being an active participant in the pregnancy.**

1. Help her.

2. Sympathize with her. Every day will not be a good day for her.

3. Compliment her. Don't make jokes about her body or the way she looks. Treat her to a day at the salon. Take her to buy an outfit.

4. **Go for a walk with her.**

5. Take her to the park and relax on a blanket; play music the three of you can enjoy.

6. Don't argue with her. Remain peaceful.

7. Make sure she has everything she needs: food, vitamin supplements, clothes, etc.

8. If you have other children, help her with them. Keep the house clean.

9. Go to the doctor with her. Listen to your baby's heartbeat, see the ultrasound, and feel the baby kick.

10. Talk to your baby, it can hear you. Read the baby a book.

11. Rub her stomach. You soothe her and the baby at the same time.

12. Be present during the delivery.

ABORTION

Sex = Responsibility

On my second attempt at having sex, I became pregnant. When I became aware of the pregnancy I told my mother. She wanted me to keep the child and I was adamant about not doing so. Eventually it was agreed upon that I'd have an abortion.

I went to the abortion clinic and the doctor was sadistic. I think he hated his job but for some reason he continued to do it. That's the only excuse I can give him for purposely hurting me and fussing me out as he performed the abortion.

After leaving the operating room, I was taken to recovery. There, along with many other girls, I witnessed girls crying and moaning from pain. I was convinced this man purposely hurt everyone. That clinic was later closed and he was arrested.

Sex=Responsibility. Don't put yourself in a situation that you're not ready to make a life or death decision about. Ladies, taking the time to learn your cycle will undoubtedly save you some heartache. More women than we could possibly imagine have had abortions for various reasons.

Having sex, intercourse, making love, is a huge responsibility. If you are not ready to handle the possibilities, either don't do it or protect yourself. You cannot depend on what someone else is going to do. **Women:** do not depend on a condom, it may break. **Men:** don't believe that she can't make a mistake and miss taking that pill. Be responsible for yourself and your actions. It's better to be safe than sorry.

Abortion is the extraction of a fetus from a woman's womb. Abortions are risky and often traumatic, leaving scars internally, emotionally, and mentally. No one feels good about having to eliminate a life. No woman is excited about going through the abortion procedure.

To gain insight on what happens during an abortion, read on; the system may vary slightly bur it's pretty much the same. Someone takes your information, you make a payment, have tests performed, and have a seat. They move you along, and you get closer and closer to the procedure room. The last and final thing you will remember if you're having full anesthesia is the anesthesia.

If you're not fortunate enough to afford the full anesthetic and receive a local instead (basically a shot in your cervix to numb you), I sympathize with you. With this procedure, you feel everything and you may even see some things as well. The doctor uses surgical tools to open the cervix to gain access to your uterus to dissect the baby, suction and scrape your uterus.

With either procedure, when you're done, you have to face it. I don't care how happy you are that the situation is over, you still feel pain knowing that you had to get rid of a life.

Try to understand what can really happen before you act carelessly. Think about the sexual act and if it's really worth being irresponsible.

For the young men out there, consider yourself lucky that you don't have to bear the responsibility of carrying a life and possibly experiencing the procedure of someone opening your insides and removing a life. **If you really respect the female body and the person you are intimate with, think for the both of you.** Use the larger brain in your body. Be responsible for you, your life, hers and that fetus. Abortions are not an easy thing to deal with. If you have any emotional ties with the woman, I know it's not easy for you either. Be careful and save yourself undue stress and strain in all ways.

If you had sex and the condom broke or you have a concern that pregnancy may occur, see a doctor or call a pharmacy so the female can take the morning after pill.

Circumstances may occur in your life that will make having an abortion necessary. Rape, incest, medical reasons, finances, etc. may play a role in the decision you have to make. Take the time to think about which option is best for you. How will a child change your life? How will your current circumstances affect the child? **Follow the logic of your mind and your heart and make a balanced, informed decision.**

ABORTION ALTERNATIVES/ ADOPTION

Always do what is best for you and your baby.

Choosing whether or not to have a child can be scary. Choosing whether to keep a child or give it up for adoption can be equally as taxing. With each decision we make, we alter our lives and have to live with that decision. Children are life changing. Once you go there, there's is no return. You are forever a mother or father.

Children who are placed for adoption usually wonder who their birth parents are. You can practically expect someone to appear on your doorstep years later asking, "Are you my mother or father?"

Ask yourself these questions:

1. Do you have a job? Are you able to get a job now? If not, how will you support your baby?

2. What is your living situation? Can you afford rent? Will you be able to pay rent when the baby gets here? Are you in school and will you have to postpone your education?

3. Will the father be a participant? Will he help you raise the child and with finances? Be careful, I can testify that he may say he will and won't; look at his history with keeping his word and what type

of father he had. If he chooses not to offer support, can you and your baby survive?

If you're undecided about having an abortion, you do have options. If you just had sex and are concerned about pregnancy, consider using the morning after pill; obtainable from the pharmacy or a doctor.

You can keep the child and raise him or her yourself no matter what age you are. However, having support when you have children is a plus. Look at your support base. Who is willing to help you when you need them? Even if your support base is weak, you can still have a child and be okay.

The federal government does offer limited assistance. They will provide medical insurance for you throughout the pregnancy and the baby after it's born. When the baby is born, the government will assist you with returning to school, finding a job, making daycare or childcare payments, and obtaining child support.

You can opt to have your child placed for adoption. Choosing adoption can be great for you and your child when you choose to do so of your own free will. Many parents choose to place their child for adoption due to their inability to adequately care for the child and in hopes that the child will be able to have a better life.

Something to keep in mind is the fact that many children will never be adopted. They will grow up in foster homes or group homes until they are released for the independent living program when they are in their late teens. The older a child becomes, the harder it is to place them in an adoptive home.

A positive aspect is that a child who is adopted is wanted. The people choosing to adopt have various reasons for adopting including inability to conceive, the desire to help, to be a parent, etc. They are willing to take on the responsibility of raising a child and giving it all the love and support they are capable of giving.

Choosing to place your child for adoption gives you a chance to continue your life and your child an opportunity to have a stable, loving family. You may even be able to have a relationship with the child and adoptive parents. You might also consider allowing the child's father to raise the child.

Consider adoption a real option if you're not sure about keeping your child or having an abortion. Many people desire to have children and may be willing to adopt your child. **Whatever the case, always do what's best for you and your baby.**

If you need help or counseling to make a decision, please consult the reference section.

How many births do you know of that were planned versus the number that just happened? More unexpected births occur due to irresponsibility

BABY'S MAMA -BABY'S DADDY SYNDROME

Your actions are impacting your child for the rest of their life right now.

or accidents. Turn on the television and, in the course of a week, you will see at least two talk shows on "Who's My Baby's Daddy?"

I have three sons with three different fathers. I always thought I would have a husband and then children. That wish vanished when I was 19 years old and decided to have my first son even though I had just ended the relationship with his father.

Not one of my children was planned. I weighed my heart with my spirit and did what I felt was right. I made a choice to have and keep my children. I accepted the responsibility and was willing to work around parenthood to achieve my goals. I was blessed to have had the skills to support my children without depending on their fathers.

Single parenting has not been a bed of roses for me. I have to deal with child support, custody battles, paternity tests, and irresponsible selfish men; all while sacrificing myself to make sure my children have a happy life. This is the hardest job in the world. I am raising three men. I am a woman who has to fill in the gaps caused by fathers who don't participate in their sons' lives.

The fear in some men is so great it's unreal. Some of them say they're not ready to have a child, but aren't doing anything to prevent impregnating anyone. Some get angry with the women for being compassionate, caring, and loving – probably the same traits that attracted him to her in the first place.

Stepping up

Young men need to realize that it takes two to make a child. When you have intercourse with someone, you should be ready to accept responsibility for whatever the outcome may be. Sleep only with the woman with whom you have a relationship or you feel confident you can get along with if you should have a child; preferably the person to whom you are married.

Now that you're old enough to have a child, you must consider factors such as are you mature enough to be responsible for a child? Have you graduated from school? Do you have a job? Are you financially secure? What are your dreams? Do you realize that a child is demanding of you and your time? Will you be a deadbeat dad or will you be what you consider the ideal father? Money is not all a child needs. It takes two people to make a child for a reason. A child's growth and development is enhanced when he or she has two active parents in his or her life. Protect yourself and your time by acting responsibly.

Young ladies, understand that you aren't obligated to share any part of your body to earn love because someone took you out, because you think they're cute, or for whatever other reason you may have for being sexually active. Women have the greatest responsibility and decisions to make. Women decide with whom and when a life is born. Women decide with whom they want to mate. The problem I see is that there are too many young ladies having sex with multiple partners, not using protection, and not knowing who the father is. I've seen men acknowledged as being the father and they're not. Why are you not respecting your bodies enough to even know – if you were to get pregnant – who your child's father would be? Close your legs – take it from me. I never questioned who my sons' fathers were because I only had one partner at a time.

223

Before you have sex with any man, you should ask yourself if you can see yourself having a child with him. Is he responsible? Does he have job skills and a job? How will I support this child if he chooses to not participate? Take precautions for your body. Don't depend on him or his condom. Ultimately, if he chooses to not be a part of the baby's life he will continue on with his life and his freedom and you will be the one at home with the baby, trying to get him to visit, pay child support, or be a real father to your child. Do you really want to be bothered with this? More than anything, this situation causes you pain. You will blame yourself for the mistake of ever being involved with this guy, let alone getting pregnant.

When you choose to have a child and become a single parent, realize that your life will never be the same. You will have to divide your time and your child receives the majority of it. All your efforts from that point on will be to secure you and your child's lives.

To prevent your becoming a part of the Baby's Daddy – Baby's Mama Syndrome:

- Abstain.

- Protect yourself even when your partner is protected.

- Have sex only when you're old enough to be responsible for the outcome.

- Remember your goals and dreams in life. Do they include having a child on your hip? You can achieve your goals faster without the responsibility of children.

- Get married first!

- Have sex with the person with whom you actually have a strong relationship and can see having a child with, preferably you husband or wife.

- Remember that it only takes once.

- Ask yourself is this one night stand really worth it?

- Love yourself enough to manage your life.

If you do decide to have a child or children as I did, know that your life continues. The goals you set can still be achieved. The dreams you have can still be realized. It may take more time to get there, but you can do it. Children are blessings. They bring you joy and unconditional love but don't have a child to get love when you're a child yourself. Children can't replace the love of our parents or mates.

Be prepared for your life to come to a screeching halt and begin again. It's a new and different life. There are now lives involved. You must plan for you and your baby.

Ladies or men, whoever is the custodial parent, gets child support. You may say you don't need it; you may not, but the child does. Extra money never hurt anyone. It costs over $100,000 to raise a child. To the parent who doesn't have the child, pay child support and, equally important, spend time with your child. You have something to offer this child that only you can give.

I have shared my life with you to let you know that the situation isn't unfamiliar. I have chosen my life path and I accept responsibility for my children. I just hope that this epidemic slows or stops because there are so many children missing out on having two parents. Remember you always have a choice in your life for as long as you live. Choose the "Best Male (or Female) Bird."

To give you some insight on what conflicts arise when parents have children out of wedlock, read on.

The custodial parent (the child/children live with) argues:

- When are you going to spend time with your child?

- Why are you so inconsistent with visitation? When you say you're coming over you need to come.

- Don't make empty promises to our child.

- Can you help with the payment for daycare/aftercare? Can you at least pickup our child from school and bring him home?

- You're not there when I need you. When I'm up or at the hospital due to our child being sick, you're no where around.

- I need some time for myself. (The non-custodial parent usually

225

starts an argument to get out of keeping the child).

- You're so self-absorbed that you don't see how you're affecting your child.

- A child needs a mother and a father. I can't teach my son to be a man or vice versa.

- Why do you argue to avoid paying child support?

(Child support is a contribution to the upkeep and wellbeing of your child. Child support pays for food, clothing, medicine, fuel, gas, electricity, daycare/aftercare, extracurricular activities, etc. The amount of money the custodial parent gets for child support will never be enough to compensate them for their time and their attempt to fill the absent parent's shoes. Absent parents need to not/stop think(ing) that the money they give is going to the custodian's pocket. The money is supposed to give the child the necessities as if the household were a two-parent household.)

Non-custodial parent's argument:

- He/she (meaning the custodial parent) is trying to control me.

- He/she just wants the money for themselves.

- I don't have time to go over there.

- I don't want to keep the kids for the summer. That's too much work.

It is important for non-custodial parents to understand the situation is not a matter of control. It's a matter of consideration, appreciation, and love. Consider the fact that the custodial parent has the child 24/7. Appreciate the dedication/commitment he/she has shown your child. Express love to your child by being there. Never use a disagreement you may have with the custodial parent as an excuse for not showing up to pickup your child, not buying pampers, medicine or anything else.

The money you give will never compensate the custodial parent for time, delay of attaining their goals, loss of sleep, level of stress, and compensating for your absence. Remember, you are free at all times; they have to make arrangements to do anything the desire.

People make time for what's important to them.
What is important to you?

Keeping the children for 60-90 days out of 365 is nothing. You should gladly accept the opportunity to bond with your child(ren). Spending this time will help you appreciate what the custodial parent goes through on a daily basis. Maybe you will say "thank you."

No one can ever replace you. **You have something to share with your child that no one else can give.**

GROWING UP IN A SINGLE PARENT HOUSEHOLD

Break the cycle of single parenting by marrying before having children.

Single parent households seem to be the norm these days. With the rate of divorce at 50% and the number of children being born out of wedlock steadily increasing, growing up in a home without a father or mother present is likely.

As a single parent raising three males, I must say that it is not the easiest endeavor in the world. As a mother, I have to control over-pampering, maintain a certain amount of sternness (to maintain respect), and love them enough for two people.

As a woman and a mother, I felt I could do it all and that not having their fathers present didn't really matter. Then one day, my ten-year-old came to me and said, "Mama, I feel like I'm missing out on learning about being a man." He was approaching a time in his life when he was having questions about his feelings and his body that he didn't want to discuss with me.

When he told me that, I hurt because for once my son desired something I couldn't give him. I am not a man. Therefore, I began to look for alternatives such as Boy Scouts and sporting activities. Yes, these activities gave my son the opportunity to exert masculinity, but he was still missing male companionship.

I was blessed to have my father in the household for a portion of my life. I suffered, however, when I needed him the most; to help me define my relationships (how to relate to men). I'm sure if he were present to educate me on men, how they think, the games some of them play, what to expect, and what not to put up with, my life would have definitely been different.

Living in a household with one parent and siblings, you don't necessarily get all the attention you feel you need. You also spend more time with yourself or friends to fill the void of what's missing at home.

Subconsciously we tend to draw to us what we lack. Pay attention to the way you relate to people. Watch to see if you are trying to fill the void of a mother or father in your relationships. If you find yourself encountering the same situations, there's something there for you to learn.

Your parents may not have been there for you all the times you needed or thought they should have been. However, they did the best they could with the knowledge they had at that time.

You are at a point in your life where you must make decisions about your life. If you are interested in having children, reflect on your life and what you felt was missing. Promise yourself that you will make well thought-out decisions when it comes to procreating. Make your life easier and balance your child's life by having a two-parent home or a partner who takes parenting seriously. If you have children, give them everything you felt was needed by you.

Reflect on your parent(s) to help you understand them and what they went through to raise you. I had to do this as a result of being embittered with my mother.

I thought about how my mother and I counted pennies to buy food when the shelves were bare and she was a day away from payday. She'd ride her bike across town to borrow money to make it through to the next week. Though she struggled financially, she kept a roof over our head, clothes on our backs and we never went hungry. Our lights were never off. She made it a point to buy a house for us to live in. She did this with minimal support from my father. We finally stopped moving around when she became head of household. Though she didn't spend a lot of time with her children, we were never worried about finances or having a place to live. Reflect and maybe you will develop a new appreciation for your parent.

Use the wisdom you've gained from having lived in a single parent household. Break the cycle by marrying, staying committed and giving your child the opportunity to experience a balance of male and female parental love.

HAVING CHILDREN IS NOT THE END OF YOUR LIFE

> *Children are gifts.*

After graduating high school, I wanted to attend college but didn't have the support of my parent nor the knowledge to enroll alone. Therefore, I got a job. My immediate goal was to move out of my mother's house, and that's what I did.

I never knew that my twenties should have been years of self-discovery, freedom, and fun. I didn't get that far. On my 20th birthday, I was pregnant with my first son. I decided to have my child after flashbacks of an abortion I'd had as a teenager. The doctor hurt me purposely as he fussed at me about how it didn't make any sense and how I should be ashamed. I thought about all the women and girls bleeding and moaning in their beds. I decided that I would not experience that trauma again. I accepted my son and the changes that would occur in my life. I knew my life wasn't over. But I didn't know or realize how much having a child would impact my development, my freedom, or my life in general.

If a child has chosen you to be his or her parent, consider yourself special. Having children is something you can only understand by having them. Children are gifts. They help you develop into someone you had no idea existed. They help you to stretch your imagination, explore life,

231

do things you wished you could have done as a child, and parent like you probably imagined but never knew it would be quite that way.

Having children is something you want to be prepared for; however, life sometimes throws us a curve ball. It really isn't the end of your life. Your life is just different than your peers. You have a responsibility other than yourself.

Do not give up on life, education, or enjoying life. You still have every opportunity that you've always had. You just have to plan for life's events now.

No matter your age, you can always go to school. There are programs that assist young parents, those who can't afford sitters or who just need help; period. See the reference section.

Take advantage of everything that life has to offer you. Utilize every community or government program that will assist you to prosper. Never say, "I can't because I have a child." Remove that from your vocabulary. You can achieve whatever you desire. The same way you have dedicated yourself to your child, dedicate yourself to you! You can do it!

Never look at the parenting experience as a burden, regardless of your circumstance. Welcome it with open arms. Focus on the positive. Enjoy your child. You will be a greater person when it's all done. **You're already equipped with what the child desires most … love.**

BABY CARE

> *Every child begins the world again.*
> Henry David Thoreau

Nine months is ¾ of a year. That's quite a while to anticipate an arrival. Quite enough time to learn about the bundle of joy that will arrive expecting you to sustain its life.

For nine months I read as much as I could. I reflected on babies I had baby-sat. I thought about how I would love and take care of my baby.

When he arrived, after a nineteen-hour labor it was time to use everything I'd read and learned. Baby care isn't easy. A lot of what you learn to do is from instinct and guidance. The best thing you can do for you and your baby is to attend a parenting class, ask questions of parents, lean on family members, and read as much as possible.

A child is the most precious gift and the greatest responsibility you will have in your lifetime. Having your first child can be intimidating. Like all species, we have innate knowledge of what is needed to care for our offspring.

Babies' communication

Babies come into the world helpless. They have a natural response to suckle their mother's breast for nourishment and they cry to tell you when something is wrong. As a parent, you have to take the time to learn your baby, the way they cry and for what reason.

Crying is the only form of communication they know at first. Don't get angry when you hear them cry. Find the reason and fix it.

If your baby cries:

- Check his diaper.
- Is he sleepy?
- Is he teething?
- Is he hungry?
- Is he feeling well?

Your answer should be one of the above. Once you eliminate the discomfort, you should have a happy baby again.

Nurturing your baby

Humans love the touch and affection of another human, feeling wanted, loved and cared for. Take the time to cuddle, hug, rock, sing to, and play with your baby. Remember that your baby was in a very safe and constricted environment before being born. Swaddle your baby in a blanket by wrapping the baby comfortably to help him feel safe and to help ease the transition from the womb to the world. This helps your baby to continue feeling the love and the warmth he felt inside you. Allow your baby to listen to your heartbeat and voice. That is what he heard while he was in utero.

Music

Music can stimulate the mind, feelings, and emotions. Pay attention to the types of music you listen to. You know the difference between what creates a peaceful or aggressive feeling in your environment. Choose peaceful music for your baby, such as jazz or classical music, to create a peaceful environment.

Stimulate your child's mind

You child learns by mimicking you, your sounds and your actions. Start teaching your child early.

- Teach him colors by pointing to them and saying the names.
- Sing the alphabet often.
- Count and show him pictures of the numbers.

(Mothers, don't be upset or offended when your baby says Dada first. The sound is easier for a baby to make.)

- Read to him.
- Use flash cards for words and colors.
- Buy him musical instruments. Color and paint with him.
- Never forget to praise your child for their efforts.
- Show him various modes of expression. Expression opens children's minds and helps them to explore themselves.

Listen. Nuture. Stimulate. Feed. Love.

Foods

The earth offers us everything our bodies need. Many of us have gotten away from what's natural and know little about natural foods due to the American way of instant food. What could be more instant than fruit, a salad, or raw vegetables? Fruits, vegetables, grains, and legumes are nutritionally sound and supply the body with what it needs. These foods energize the body instead of making it sluggish. Feed the baby what he is able to digest at the appropriate time. If you're interested in healthier eating, visit the library or a bookstore and purchase a book on how to make baby food.

Artificial drinks and aids with heavy food coloring and sugar are not nutritional for your baby. Feed your baby real juice, and choose the juice that is appropriate for his age.

Breastfeeding

Humans are the only species that allow their young to drink milk from another species. Could you imagine yourself sucking the breast of a cow for nourishment? God doesn't make mistakes. Women are equipped with the necessary tools to supply their baby with the proper nutrients. The first milk is colostrum, which strengthens the baby's immune system. Breast milk changes as the child grows older to accommodate the child's needs.

Many mothers choose to not breastfeed because of vanity and the desire to keep perky breasts. I had a friend who once told me, "Girl, I wouldn't want no baby hanging on my titty." Some women can't take the initial discomfort when the baby suckles, which dissipates in a relatively short time. Some think it's normal to not nurse because that's what everyone else in the family did. Some don't like the fact that the baby has a greater dependency on them because they are the food supply. Do you think you would produce milk if it wasn't necessary?

Nursing is a beautiful choice. Breastfed children and their mothers have a special bond. While breastfeeding, they are in tune with one another. The mother knows when the baby wakes or is hungry. Mothers are signaled through the breast. Breastfeeding provides the baby with milk that is easily digested. Breastfeeding is economical. It doesn't cost you anything and you don't have to worry about fixing a bottle in the middle of the night. Breastfed babies are said to have fewer ailments, earaches, and skin rashes. They also tend to excel academically.

Water

Water is not a sole source of nutrition for a baby but it is needed. Water supplies minerals and is a conduit for nutrients to be carried through the body. Don't use water as a substitute for milk but do give your baby water.

Many doctors say that "there is water in the milk" you give your baby. The baby milk that babies drink often causes congestion, gas, and constipation. Water will move the congestion and help the baby to move his/her bowels and decrease gas. A little water a day will help alleviate a lot of discomfort.

A healthy baby is a happy baby!

STEP-PARENTING

{ *A step-parent is a blessing as they are the missing piece to the puzzle.* }

Step-parenting occurs more often as the number of children being born out of wedlock and the divorce rate increases. To be a stepparent requires patience. You must be patient with the child(ren), your mate, and the ex-spouse.

A few tips when entering a family:

1. Don't enter trying to be the forceful disciplinarian, whipping and punishing. These are not your children.

2. Demand respect but not with the threat of physical harm. There is a difference between respect and fear.

3. Do get to know the children and the inner-workings of the family.

4. By gaining respect, you also gain love. Do this by establishing a line of communication and interaction with the children. The children have to get accustomed to another adult telling them what to do and being around all the time.

5. Include the children in activities and even spend some one-on-one time with them.

6. Be sure that this is what you want to do. Children are impressionable. Your presence will affect their perception of relationships and what is considered healthy.

7. If the children are standoffish, give them time. You may experience some friction. They may not attach easily because they are trying to figure out if you're going to be around.

8. Don't rush to meet the children and become a part of their lives until your relationship is solid.

9. Don't forget to spend quality time with your mate.

10. Don't buy the children's love. Allow them to appreciate you for who you are. Anything extra is a bonus.

Every relationship will not require outside help. But if you really desire the relationship, you may even consider family counseling or support groups.

Any person who loves enough to take on a family is special. Being a step-parent requires a person to open their heart and mind and forget about stereotypes and society. Accept the family by not throwing in their faces all that you've done. **Remember, every interaction that the children witness or are a part of will influence their lives. Always leave a positive impression.**

Health

HEALTH INTRODUCTION

Caring for self is threefold. You must care for the mind, body and spirit.

When people think about health, the first thought is of the body. Is my body healthy? The body is the ultimate concern because many don't think about the fact that the mind, body and spirit all work together and the health of the mind and spirit can directly affect the health of the body through stress, worry, or lack of a spiritual foundation.

Good health is not only obtained through proper diet and exercise but also through care of the mind – emotions and feelings and stress level; and spirit – development of a spiritual foundation. Emotional stress and strain can adversely affect the body. By being grounded spiritually you can better manage life events that can affect your emotional health thus positively affecting your physical health.

Many times we take our bodies for granted. Be appreciative of the mobility and health you have. You only get one pair of feet so take care of them; they are your transportation. Luckily, you get two sets of teeth; take care of them. It's not cute having to take your teeth out at night and sit them in a glass.

Did you know that medicines are derived from herbs? Herbs are wonderful. Familiarize yourself with them as way to promote healing and not mask symptoms. Keep active. Exercise, walk, do something. Drink water. The body is mostly composed of water. Water is a beautiful thing. Learn your body. Keep your body clean, inside and out.

Protecting our bodies includes protecting our minds and spirits from abuse, which is not only physical but can be mental and emotional as well. If you experience any feeling that doesn't bring you joy, question it. Never stay in an abusive relationship. If you ever feel the need to resort to alcohol or drugs to escape, get help. Find the root of the problem so you can heal. Preferably, don't go there, talk to someone first. Your life is important. Don't throw it away. Talk to someone. Depression is real. If you ever feel down and it seems as if it won't go away, seek help. **Take care of your body, mind, and spirit. You only have one you.**

HEALTHCARE

Pay for insurance now or pay a higher cost later.

There is a lot of discussion about the lack of and affordability of healthcare in the United States. A visit to the doctor without insurance can cost well over $100. If you have insurance the cost is greatly reduced to your office co-pay which averages around $20.

If you need medicine, it can range from a few to several hundred dollars depending on the prescription. But with insurance you pay either your prescription co-pay which averages $15, or a percentage of the cost of the medicine.

If you have to visit an emergency room, it can be as low as $250 or as high as several thousands depending on your ailment or injury. With insurance, the initial visit to the emergency can be as low as $50.

If you are admitted to the hospital, my, my, my; the expenses are over the top. Did you know many people without insurance refinance their homes or take out loans to pay their medical bills? If you have insurance you are responsible for a deductible. For example, you may have a $10,000 hospital bill but only be responsible for paying $2,000.

So now, you get to tell me, do you need health insurance? A benefit of being a child, you can be covered by your parent's insurance up to age 25 if you meet the insurance company's qualifications. Usually you have to be unmarried and attending school if you're over twenty one.

If you are no longer in school and living with your parents, it is important to inquire about benefits when seeking employment. Insurance is an important part of your benefits package. When asking about benefits, be sure to ask if benefits start on day one.

Your insurance cost is greatly reduced when purchased through an employer because insurance companies give employers group rates.

If for some reason your job doesn't offer benefits and you're no longer eligible for coverage on your parent's policy, I suggest you go online and do a search on health insurance companies that offer insurance directly to consumers. The premium will be higher than employer group rates but as least you will be covered.

When shopping for insurance, think of your budget. Find the best policy with most coverage that you can afford. Be aware that your plan selection will affect your out of pocket expense. The health insurance companies will offer two plans, HMO or PPO. HMO or Health Maintenance Organization is a managed care organization where its member physicians treat patients at an agreed upon rate. A PPO is a Preferred Provider Organization that has an agreement with the insurance company but the rates for this plan are often higher. Having a PPO plan allows you to go "out-of-network", meaning you can go to any doctor you choose. Before you choose this route, check to see if your doctor is listed as an HMO provider.

Consider all of this information when making your health insurance decisions.

DENTAL HYGIENE

No pain, no gain.

My most memorable dental issue was having an abscess/ infection that caused the whole left side of my face to swell. The pain was so intense that it traveled through my body and made my left arm numb. All this pain was accompanied by headaches that would not go away. The pain laughed at the hydrocodone and acetaminophen. I suffered until the dentist's office open. That was my lesson on the importance of taking care of my teeth.

Your teeth are valuable assets. A smile and fresh breath go a long way. If we ate properly (consumed fewer sugars and processed foods) and brushed and flossed properly, we would have fewer problems with our teeth.

Decay is caused by food (sugars) sticking to your teeth and bacterial buildup that gradually eats away at the enamel of your teeth to create holes, or cavities.

We should heed the commercials we see about going to the dentist for preventative maintenance and getting an exam and cleaning. We need a dentist to clean our teeth because tartar buildup and stains are difficult to remove. The less time we spend brushing and visiting the dentist, the more likely we are to need fillings, root canals or even dentures.

Properly brushing your teeth includes using back and forth and circular motions. Brush all sides of your teeth and your gum line.

Floss your teeth as well to remove plaque and food from between your teeth that your toothbrush can't reach.

Signs that you need to see a dentist are:

- Bleeding gums
- Halitosis-very bad breath
- Sensitivity to cold or hot temperatures when eating or drinking
- Inflamed or swollen gums
- Teeth that are loose
- Pain in your teeth or gums

The idea of going to see a dentist can be scary. Many dentists have made their area of expertise "painless dentistry." Remember, however, no pain, no gain. **Save your teeth!**

FOOTCARE

Feet are the original mode of transportation. They need tuneups too!

Footcare is not just a female thing. Manicured feet are happy feet on men and women. Men, please eliminate the thought that pedicures are a girl thing and, no, stinky feet are not the "norm" for men. Though women may not voice it, most women like a man who takes care of himself from his head to and including his feet. Here are a few tips on foot care.

Wash them. Believe it or not, there are people who don't wash their feet. I don't know if it's pure laziness or what. Then they wonder why their feet are darker than the rest of their bodies, their feet are hard, or their toenails are dark and coated with cuticle. Be sure to wash in between your toes as well; toe jam stinks!

You have to cut your toenails. Clip them straight across and file them to keep them even and to smooth rough edges.

If you have excess cuticle (skin growing onto your toenails), use cuticle remover to soften them and push your skin back with a cuticle stick.

For the excess skin, get a white block and buff the skin gently off your toenail or use a cuticle cutter to remove excess cuticle.

If your feet are rough on the bottom, it's from the buildup of dead skin.

Purchase a pumice stone (a gray stone) from a local drug store. A pumice stone removes dead skin from the feet. Soak your feet in the bathtub and after the skin softens, rub the stone on your feet to remove the dead skin. Don't be rough. If you have excessive skin, don't go overboard. You can take away too much skin, which will make your feet sensitive and painful to walk on.

You can also purchase a foot scrub which is a cream with granules to help remove dead skin and soften your feet overall. Use before the pumice stone.

Personally, once my feet are dry, I like to take a white block and smooth any rough skin on the heels of my feet.

Rub lotion on your feet to moisturize them. If you plan to polish your nails, wipe them off with a cotton swab soaked in polish remover first to remove the lotion. This helps the polish to last longer.

If you have a problem with your feet, such as athlete's foot, see a doctor. If you prefer using a natural remedy, tea tree oil would be a great choice. You can purchase tea tree oil from a health food store. Rub it on your clean feet, put on a pair of clean white socks, and sleep in them. This should help them to heal. Repeat this process for as long as necessary. While using the tea tree oil, avoid wearing the same shoes you have been wearing because they have the fungus in them. Don't wear the same socks more than once without washing them. Spray the insides of the shoes containing the fungus with a disinfectant spray and replace the footpads.

If you have nail fungus, see a doctor. Purchase a fungus treatment for minor cases or have your doctor prescribe treatment. Fungus is more common in women who have artificial nails. Water or other substances being trapped beneath the artificial nail allows fungus to grow. In this case, the artificial nails must be removed. The fungus, if yellow or light green and on the surface of the nail bed, may be filed away gently. It should still be treated with a fungus medication. For other fungus problems, see your doctor; follow the instructions of the medication given.

If you have corns, don't cut them off with scissors, knives, or clippers.

Purchase patches that will soften and remove them. In addition, you can use a scrub such as St. Ives Apricot Scrub to soften and remove them or a pumice stone. Stop buying shoes that don't fit. Treat yourself to some decent shoes even if they are a little more expensive.

Take care of your feet. You only get one pair. Plus you'll get to wear your sandals with pride.

HERBS

> *Herbs...the original medicine.*

Did you know that many medicines that man comes up with are derivatives of herbs? Hundreds and hundreds of herbs grow on this planet. Man discovers additional curative properties of various herbs daily. I will cover a few of today's most popular herbs. (This information is not meant as a diagnosis or a suggestion of treatment. Please seek guidance from a doctor).

Immune system

- **Echinacea**: Effective in eliminating colds or flu at the onset and easing some symptoms once the illness has set in. It is a blood purifier. It stimulates the immune system and acts as an antibiotic by promoting T-cell growth (the germ-fighting cell).

- **Garlic**:   A household seasoning which enhances the immune system. It acts as an antibiotic as well. Garlic aids in the fight against colds, flu's, and viruses. It enhances the immune system and can be used against some sexually transmitted diseases.

- **Golden Seal**: Acts as an antibiotic and strengthens the immune system. Useful for menstrual disorders and the prostrate gland.

Can be used to fight Candida or Trichmonasis through vaginal douching.

- **Red Clover**: Stimulates the immune system to remove toxins. Acts as an antibiotic and fights cancer. Calms nervousness.
- **Capsicum (Red Pepper)**: Increases blood circulation. Boosts any herb taken by helping it to reach the blood stream more quickly.

Mental

- **Kava Kava**: Reduces stress by relaxing the central nervous system. Is useful in alleviating insomnia.
- **Gingko**: Increases circulation to the brain. Improves memory. Alleviates circulatory problems. Improves hearing and protects eyesight. Helpful in reversing Alzheimer's disease.

Nerves

- **Chamomile**: Relaxes the body. Promotes restful sleep. Calms nervousness. Reduces or eliminates cramping.

Laxatives

Helps facilitate or ease bowel movements. Natural laxatives include:

- Prune juice
- Buckthorn Bark tea

Be cautious in your use of laxatives. Some can be habit-forming.

Women

- **Red Raspberry**: Acts as an overall tonic for the female reproductive system. It is great for nausea in pregnant women and can be used throughout pregnancy. It is used as an aid for decreasing the menstrual flow and reducing or eliminating pain during menstruation.
- **Ginger**: Eases menstrual cramping. Reduces hot flashes. Reduces morning sickness and mucus. Great for digestion and motion sickness.

- **Wild Yam**: Used by the body to create testosterone and estrogen. Helps to balance hormones. Helps to prevent abdominal cramping and miscarriage. Reduces pain in pregnancy.

- **Pau d' Arco**: Can help prevent or eliminate intestinal or vaginal candidiasis (yeast infection). Dissolves tumors of all kinds. Can cause remission in various cancers. Strengthens the immune system. To ease or eliminate vaginal candidiasis, soak a tampon in the tea. Insert and continually replace until the symptoms subside. You can also use Pau d' Arco as a douche.

- **Uva Ursi**: Used for kidney and bladder infections. Tones the urinary passages. Useful in healing the prostrate. Strengthens the kidneys and bladder. Can be used as a douche for vaginal infections. Can be added to a sitz bath following childbirth to reduce inflammation or infection.

- **Dong Quai (Angelica)**: Balances female hormones. Strengthens female organs. Regulates menstrual flow. Useful in treating PMS and menopause. DO NOT TAKE DURING PREGNANCY. Treats anemia. Has been known to increase breast size in some women.

Men

- **Saw Palmetto**: Tones the male reproductive organs. Used to treat/reduce enlarged prostrate glands. Strengthens the urinary organs.

- **Ho Shou Wu**: Preserves natural hair color. Strengthens the body. Increases energy.

- **Ginseng**: Increases testosterone. Energizes the body.

- **Pumpkin Seed**: (needs to be eaten raw) Stimulates male hormone production. Used to treat enlarged prostrate glands.

THE IMPORTANCE OF EXERCISE

> ### Be active now so you can be active later!

As a teen, I considered myself to be active. I would ride my bike, walk, dance, or whatever else floated my boat at the time. When I became sixteen, I got a car. The walking and bike riding which helped me to stay in shape stopped.

As you age, your body changes. If you don't keep active, you're apt to keep on weight in places you didn't notice before.

As the saying goes; what you don't use you lose. I think it's true but should include a note that says what you don't take care of you lose as well. When you look at all the people with ailments in this country and how we treat our bodies, it's no wonder that stuff starts falling apart as we get older.

Exercise is important because it keeps our bodies limber, minerals and fluids don't stagnate and reduces stress. The more you exercise, the more the body effectively processes nutrients and waste.

Exercising helps the body to eliminate waste and unnecessary fats from the body. It builds the body, strengthens its structure, and helps it to function better.

You don't have to train for the Olympics or become a body builder; just give your body some extra cardiovascular activity. You can walk or run a mile or two each day. Ride a bike. Go swimming. Take a dance class. Use a workout video. Light weight lifting will tone your body, build your muscles, and strengthen you. Be sure that you are active everyday and committed to moving parts of your body that you don't normally move.

Exercise is also a great stress reliever. I enjoy running. I'm not sure how it happens, but by the time I'm done with my workout, whatever was bothering me isn't there anymore.

If you're trying to lose weight and have excess fat on you, eliminate or reduce your carbohydrates so the body doesn't store them as fat. Your body will use the already stored fat for energy. Gradually introduce carbohydrates back into your diet.

If you haven't exercised in a while, start slowly. Gradually increase your workout and you will notice a change in your body. Exercise is a good thing. **Be active now so you can be active later!**

WEIGHT LOSS/WEIGHT GAIN

Weight loss or gain can be indicative of highs or lows in one's life.

My weight has fluctuated drastically in my lifetime. I was active as a teen. I walked or rode my bike a lot. I love nature so I was often outside enjoying it. As I got older, gained more responsibilities, and began to stress, I gained weight.

The most I've weighed as an adult is 225lbs. I was absolutely shocked when I got on the scale to see that I had crossed over 200lbs. I thought this would never be me. But, I also stated that I didn't understand how people let themselves go and get to that point. Life has a way of allowing you to experience that which you don't understand.

Obesity runs in my family on my mother's side, but I have always been the smallest female in my immediate family. I've always loved the ability to walk in a store and purchase clothes without trying them on. I was in shape and whether the clothes would fit was never a thought.

At 225lbs, I was not accustomed to the weight. I didn't know the tricks and trades of looking cute nor did I want to learn. I wanted to lose weight. My state of mind at that time didn't allow me to immediately lose weight.

People gain and lose weight for different reasons. Right now I am not focusing on diets or fads. I'm speaking of life issues that affect your attitude (happiness, depression, or sadness) and will cause your weight to fluctuate.

When I am in deep thought, I want something to chew on. Even though I am not hungry and I know that I don't really want whatever I am eating, I will snack. Food is often emotionally comforting. If you can't control what is happening in your life, you can at least control what you eat. What causes me to gain weight is that I will usually get stressed, snack, and won't move. I feel like I need to be still so therefore I am sedentary and gain weight because I am not burning calories.

Weight loss

When weight loss is not due to proper nutrition or an intentional act to get to a healthy weight, it is often caused by stress, medical issues, or trying to fit in.

I know someone who would purposely gag herself after her meals to regurgitate so she wouldn't gain weight. She was also verbally and emotionally abused about her weight. I have also worked with young ladies who will not eat for fear of gaining weight. People who lose weight in this manner are creating health issues and need to seek professional help.

Common reasons for people not maintaining proper weight include:

- They grew up in a household where there wasn't an emphasis on healthy eating
- Stress or unhappiness
- Medical or health issues
- Unwillingness to exercise
- Thinking that just because their family is overweight, they're supposed to be overweight too
- Trying to fit in or being self-conscious about their weight

Losing weight in a healthy manner is possible. It comes with self dedication which requires you loving yourself enough to take time for yourself. You have to change your eating habits, exercise, and reduce the stress in your life.

Go to the doctor and tell them your desires. If you are really overweight, you want to make sure you aren't doing anything to harm your health. In addition you may request a body mass index or BMI which will tell you the percentage of fat versus muscle. You can also learn the ideal weight for your body frame. This is a good start.

If your health insurance will pay for an appointment with a nutritionist, I suggest that you take advantage of it. You can learn proper nutrition and how to change your diet.

If you don't have access to a doctor and nutritionist you may want to try a few of the suggestions below. **(This information is not to be taken as medical advice).**

1. Eliminate sugar from your diet.
2. Eliminate white flour products.
3. Go for a walk everyday for at least twenty minutes gradually increasing to as long as you can.
4. Drink lots of water.
5. Eliminate soda and coffee.
6. Eliminate alcoholic beverages.
7. Do not eat while watching television.
8. Make sure you eat breakfast.
9. Eat vegetables.
10. Eat three small healthy snacks during the day.
11. Eat balanced meals and stop eating at least two hours before you go to bed.
12. Eliminate stress or negative people.
13. Don't discuss what you are doing with anyone. If you do, your life change becomes a challenge.

14. Incorporate weights into your exercise regime. Light weights will tone, heavier weights are used for strength.

15. You may want to try protein drinks. Protein is harder to digest and the body will burn fat as it digests it.

Men will lose weight quicker than women. Women, be aware that you may not see results for close to two weeks. Also be aware that each month as your body goes through hormonal changes, you may gain weight and then lose it after your menstrual cycle. **Be patient with yourself and don't set unrealistic goals.**

THE IMPORTANCE OF WATER

> ## 60-70% of the body's composition is water.

Our bodies are composed mostly of water. The average person doesn't consume the suggested eight 8-ounce glasses of water per day and we wonder why we are such a sickly society. Water not only keeps the body hydrated, it allows our cells to communicate with one another. It conducts energy and it cleanses our bodies on the inside.

Water:

- Hydrates the body and conducts energy
- Helps to cleanse and remove toxic waste from the body
- Helps to transport nourishment
- Reduces weight and promotes clear skin
- Keeps us alive

Drink at least eight 8-ounce glasses of water each day. If you have to flavor it with a little lemon, that's fine. **Replenish your body's water supply and help your body to remain healthy.**

FEMALE REPRODUCTIVE ORGANS

Take care of your body and it will take care of you.

The female reproductive organs are commonly referred to as the "vagina"; however, they actually include several organs such as the fallopian tubes, uterus, ovaries, the vaginal canal, and the cervix.

Ovaries are where eggs are produced and stored until they are released for fertilization.

The fallopian tubes are the canals through which eggs travel from the ovaries and where sperm will travel to meet the egg.

The uterus is the area that nourishes an unborn fetus until its birth. The uterine walls store nutrients for the fetus. If no fetus is present, the uterine lining sheds and the unfertilized egg is released from the body, which is menstruation.

The cervix is located at the very back of the vaginal canal. It is a part of the uterus and acts as a barrier between the vaginal canal and the interior of the uterus. It has a tiny hole, which allows for minimal passage of fluids. During menstruation and birth, it expands to accommodate the excretions.

The vaginal canal is the area from which menstruation flows, babies are birthed, and the penis is inserted during intercourse.

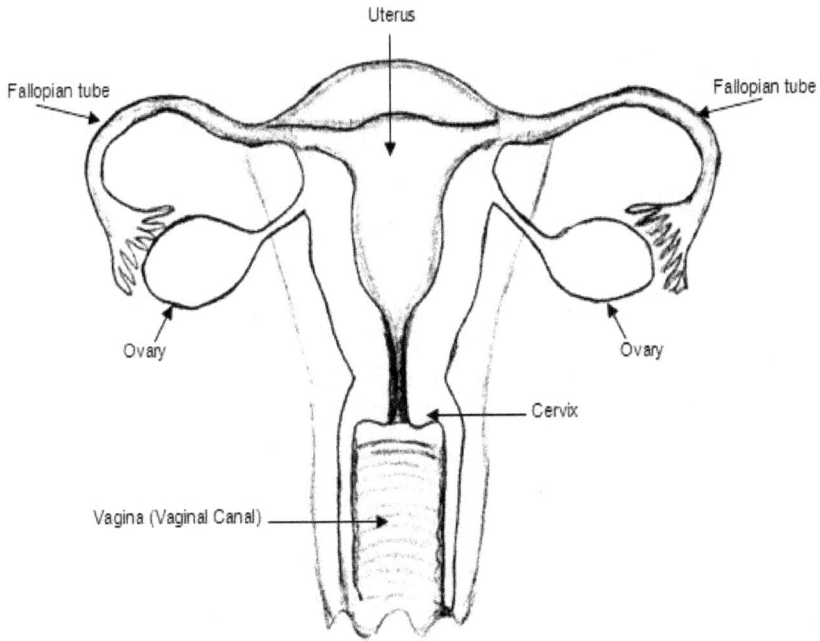

BREAST SELF EXAM

Men and women are susceptible to breast cancer.

Far too often breast cancer has gone undetected until it has become a critical situation. Be proactive about your health by doing a breast self-exam every month. The exam should be performed each month about five to seven days after the beginning of your period. If you don't have periods, choose the same day for each month.

Examine yourself by standing in front of the mirror with your breast exposed. Raise your arms above your head and look for any changes in your skin and the size and shape of your breast. Squeeze your nipples to check for discharge.

Next, while lying down, place a pillow under your right shoulder, and place your right hand behind your head. Using the three middle fingers of your left hand, feel around your right breast and armpit from the collarbone to the bra line, using circular motions and light to medium pressure. Do the same for the left breast. If you prefer, you can perform this exam in the shower while your hands are soapy.

If you notice any changes, consult a doctor.

MALE REPRODUCTIVE ORGANS

Protect your man parts. What you do with them can alter the course of your life.

Before you ever ask a woman to give you a baby boy or girl, understand that that's a request she should be asking you. Men walk around under the assumption that women decide the sex of a baby. The fact is that women carry the X chromosome only. Men carry X and Y. Two X chromosomes, one from the man and one from the woman will make a girl. A X from a woman and a Y from a man will make a boy.

In the male reproduction system, there's a lot going on. The system is like a fine-tuned machine. In the testes, testicles or "balls", sperm is created. Once created, the sperm travels to the epididymis to mature.

Matured sperm travel through a tube called the vas deferens to the seminal vesicle where semen is added. The semen acts as a carrier. This sperm and semen combination travels through the prostrate gland to the urethra through which ejaculation occurs.

Men have the ability to produce billions of sperm. There are millions of sperm in a single ejaculation. The body releases so many because of the distance they have to travel to finally reach and successfully fertilize an egg.

The female vaginal canal is an unfriendly environment for sperm. To aid in their transportation, the female body produces lubricants that assist the semen with travel.

Sperm can live in a woman's body for up to seven days. Remember this information before you choose to not wear protection during intercourse and never blame a woman for not having the boy or girl you wanted should you decide to have children.

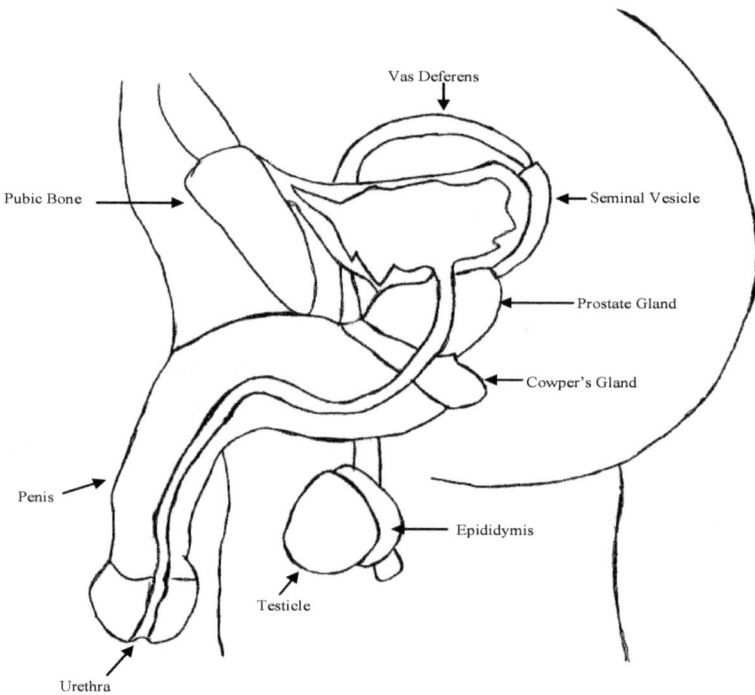

VINEGAR BATH

Whoever thought something stinky can make you smell so good!

Okay, I know it sounds stinky and you're probably saying "Yuck, there is no way I'm taking a bath in vinegar." If you have ever had that not-so-fresh feeling, do you know what it's caused by? By the time you've finished reading, you'll be taking a vinegar bath.

When our bodies emit various odors, it's because the pH balance of our bodies have changed. Our bodies are releasing toxins that have built up in our systems through the skin by means of sweating. The pores in our skin allow our bodies to cleanse. The body is a large house for those little cells that we must keep clean.

The perfect pH (balance of acidity and alkalinity) for the body is 7.0. Vinegar assists the body with returning the skin to its normal pH therefore ridding it of the various scents emitted through the cleansing that has taken place.

You know how it is when a woman sweats... you know, down there. It can become quite smelly; so bad, in fact, that she may try to run from herself. This does not have to be. It's not "natural".

The vagina does carry a unique scent that is quite distinguishable.

265

The vagina's scent is affected by what you eat, how often you move your bowels, your hygiene, and your activities. This scent can be maintained by paying attention to your body.

Men, rid your body of odors by taking a vinegar bath. This bath is great. Yes, women do have womanly odors because our bodies are constantly cleaning. However, men, your scrotum does get sweaty and stinky and yes women can smell it. In addition, for those of you that are uncircumcised, you have a special situation. You secrete a lubricant called smega beneath your foreskin that can carry an odor the same way a woman's secretions can carry an odor. You need to take time to clean yourself, by pulling the foreskin back on your penis and washing it. Also, when you're in your vinegar bath, pull the foreskin back and allow your penis to soak in the water to neutralize the scent.

My mother told me that for each meal that enters your body, another meal should be exiting. When you don't move your bowels properly, your body is stagnated with toxic waste. If the stuff isn't coming out through your bowels, then all this dead matter has to escape in some other way. What's on the inner reflects on the outer. Remember that.

If you do not smell fresh, check your activities – all of them, including sex. When you have sex, you carry your partner's fluids until you discharge them. If you've noticed an odd smell after intercourse, you'll love the vinegar bath. It really helps to get rid of their scent.

To really appreciate the benefits of a vinegar bath, you should make sure your bowels are flowing properly by taking a laxative or eating prunes (whatever will make you have a good movement). Then bathe and learn what your "natural" scent is. This way you'll know when your body is out of whack.

MENTAL, EMOTIONAL, VERBAL, AND PHYSICAL ABUSE

Love is not painful!
This is a subsection addressing various abuses.

I was once very proud to say that a man had never laid his hands on me. I did eventually experience physical abuse as I was "man-handled." He didn't stop at physical abuse.

Mentally, he degraded me. He took the least happy or proud aspects of my life and threw them in my face to purposely make me feel bad. He'd gained access to this information by telling me he wanted to "help me" understands some things about my life. He left me sad, nervous, and shamed.

I'd experienced emotional abuse from him and a few other people. Abusive people do things without consideration of how it will affect you. Verbal, mental, and physical abuse affects your emotions. Your emotions affect your health, attitude, and ability to function.

People who inflict others with pain are in pain themselves. They are abusive because they are unhappy and insecure. They pour out of them what they feel on the inside and because you are in their presence you get the brunt of everything that is hurting them.

If you are experiencing this, you deserve better. If you remain involved with people that treat you badly ask yourself why? Understand they are in your life for a reason. Did you get your lesson yet?

A person will act out in an abusive manner for various reasons. Life circumstances – what they have seen, how they grew up – can cause a person to act or react to situations in a manner that not only hurts them but others who may be involved.

Abuse does not equal love.

No one is deserving of any kind of abuse. Love is peaceful and gives a good feeling. Abuse causes pain, bruises, illness, or death, which does not equal love.

Mental, verbal, emotional, and physical abuses are perpetrated by choice. Any action that a person can consciously stop or not do at all has occurred because they chose it. Some people have a misunderstanding of what love is and actually feel that they are expressing love through their abusive actions. Either it's a learned action or a response to how they feel about themselves.

An example of a learned action would be the child who grows up in a household where he/she is beaten every day for speaking at what his/her father felt was the wrong time. The child learns that they take a chance of being hit each time they speak. The child realizes that the less he/she speaks, the less he/she is beaten and not speaking to someone equals love.

In another example, a girl is molested by her father who tells her that he does this because he loves her. Her rationalization is he will love me more if I perform the sexual acts and I will also get attention. She grows up and performs sexual acts with boys and men because that's the way she's learned to get love and attention. She's not having sex to please herself; it's simply to get love in the way she knows how.

On the flip side are children who watch their mothers or fathers being cursed and beaten on a daily basis. The children know only that a man and a wife are to express love to one another and this must be the way to do it. The son grows up beating and cursing women and the daughter gets in abusive relationships because this is what they've learned about love. They may feel in their hearts that this is wrong but they have been conditioned to act otherwise, especially if they never see the abused parent leave the situation or the abuser change his or her actions.

All types of abuse, mental, physical, verbal, sexual, and emotional are carried for a lifetime by the abuser and their victim. Many wonder why they do what they do but fail to seek the root of the problem and correct it. Why do they act or react they way they do? Why do they process their thoughts and feelings towards others in that manner? Why do they accept it as their lives, their realities?

The repetitiveness of these actions have been embedded into their being and without a conscious effort to change, the abuse travels from generation to generation until someone takes a moment to learn what true expression of love is.

Love is not painful. If someone hits you, degrades you, or abuses you in any way and then tells you, "I love you", think again and get out.

True expressions of love entail affection, care, peace, happiness, and enjoyment. If you don't feel this and fear outweighs any feeling you have for this person, it's time to choose again. If anyone makes you feel bad about yourself or they raise their hand to strike you even once, it's time to choose again. Abuse doesn't disappear and it is not your responsibility to make the abuser a better person. Each time the abuser strikes out, the abuser will be more abusive.

When you leave, leave for good. If you call the police but return to the abuser, the police will think you're crying wolf and be less apt to believe you really want help.

Gain your power and self-respect by making a critical choice that may very well save your life; love yourself first. There are many resources available such as shelters and counselors that can be accessed by a phone call. Many shelters are safe havens that the abuser wouldn't know about. Please, if you are in an abusive situation, get out while you still have a chance. **The chain can be broken and lives can be changed.**

ALCOHOLISM

Impairment can begin with one drink.

I grew up seeing adults drinking liquor and beer at parties. People in my neighborhood would kick back with a beer or liquor, and the bums would be outside the liquor store before it opened, waiting to get a swig.

As I grew older, I experimented with different drinks to learn my tolerance and what I did and didn't like. I was always concerned about being drunk so I always minimized how much I drank.

I rarely drink. It's not because I don't like the taste but because frequent consumption or overindulgence of anything can be addictive and is not good for your body. In addition, you're not in full control of your actions when intoxicated and you can be taken advantage of. This is especially dangerous for young ladies.

When drinking, pay attention to the frequency and the reason. Are you drinking socially? Are you sad or upset and trying to drown your sorrows? Is it a habit to have a drink to wind down at the end of the day? Are you doing it to fit in? As a child, did you see people drinking to deal with their problems?

Drinking alcohol as an outlet or to escape your problems can cause addiction. Drinking is not necessary to enjoy yourself. If you drink to fit in, order a non-alcoholic drink.

- ***Limit your consumption to stay in control.***

- ***Don't drive drunk.***

Always appoint a designated driver.

- ***Don't leave your drink unattended.***

There are insensitive people who will "slip you a mickey", a mind-altering drug or GhB- the date rape drug.

- ***Practice moderate alcohol consumption.***

Up to two drinks per day for men and one drink per day for women and older people is not harmful for most adults.

A standard drink is one 12-ounce bottle of beer or wine cooler, one 5-ounce glass of wine, or 1.5 ounces of 80-proof distilled spirits.

Currently, nearly 14 million Americans abuse alcohol or are alcoholic. Alcohol abuse is serious and can cause serious health problems such as various cancers, liver cirrhosis, and fetal alcohol syndrome during pregnancy.

Alcoholism is a disease with the following symptoms: strong cravings for alcohol, loss of self control concerning alcohol intake, withdrawal symptoms including the shakes, nausea, sweating, or the need for increased amounts of alcohol to get high.

If you have ever been criticized about drinking, felt guilty or that you should cut down, or needed a drink the first thing in the morning, there is a problem. If alcohol affects your relationships, health or job, there is a problem.

The first step to getting help is realizing and admitting you have a problem. This is not the easiest thing to do, but don't wait on something tragic or life threatening to occur before you to seek help. Visit your doctor and express your concerns. You may also contact Alcoholics Anonymous or other support organizations.

Your blood alcohol percentage is based on your weight and alcohol consumption. Depending on your weight, impairment can begin with one drink. The more you drink your blood alcohol percentage increases. As it increases your driving skills are affected and the chance of possible criminal penalties increase. Women have a tendency to have a higher blood alcohol level though they may weigh the same as a man.

Remember you have nothing to prove to anyone. Don't over do it.

DRUG ABUSE

Identify the pain; stop the abuse.

With my own eyes, I have witnessed children living on the street and starving, babies abandoned, babies deformed and addicted to crack, people dying, neighborhoods deteriorating, possessions stolen, and families torn apart – because of someone's drug addiction. I have been a victim of drug abusers. I have been stolen from on more than one occasion. I have lost friends, and I've had to try to help relatives, children at the time, to heal from their experiences of having a drug abuser as a parent.

Drugs affect everyone on some level or another. I'm sure each of you reading this book knows a friend, family member, or someone who has used drugs.

People who use drugs do so because they don't want to face reality. They indulge to take their minds off what is plaguing them, to escape responsibility, and avoid dealing with self.

All it takes is one hit and you can be addicted. Before you indulge, read about the effects drugs have on the body. Reflect on the people you know who are on drugs and how they have affected their lives.

Ask yourself, is that what you want to become? Is it a chance you want to take? Love yourself enough to say no. If you are currently on drugs or are thinking of starting and need help or just want to talk to someone, refer to the reference section for support, counselors, or rehab centers.

People don't plan to get addicted to drugs. The initial thought is probably to "get away"; to stop thinking about what is going on. That one swallow, snort, injection, or inhalation can spiral your life out of control.

It may seem the problems won't end, things are getting worse, or there isn't a way out. There is. Just when things get their worst, you're about to have a breakthrough. You're experiencing the negative or bad so you will appreciate the good when it comes. Hold on. **Your Creator doesn't give you anymore than you can handle. If you need someone to talk to someone, call a helpline, reach out to a friend or family members. Whatever you do, don't do drugs. It will take you somewhere you don't want to be.**

RAPE

Rape is forcibly having sexual intercourse with someone against his or her will.

(This information was complied by RAINN; RAINN is a national sexual assault assistance program dedicated to helping victims of sexual assault. RAINN The National Sexual Assault Hotline 24/7 free confidential: 1-800-656-HOPE).

- Every two minutes, someone in the U.S. is sexually assaulted

- College age women are four times more likely to be sexually assaulted.

- In 1999, one in every ten rape victims was male. [1999 NCVS]

- 60% of sexual assaults are not reported to the police

- Approximately 73% of rape victims know their assailants.

- About four out of ten sexual assaults take place at the victim's own home. Two in ten take place in the home of a friend, neighbor or relative. One in ten takes place outside, away from home. About one in 12 takes place in a parking garage.

- More than half of all rape/sexual assault incidents were reported

by victims to have occurred within one mile of their home or at their home.

- **43% of rapes occur between 6 p.m. and midnight. 24% occur between midnight and 6 am. The other 33% take place between 6 a.m. and 6 p.m.**

I got involved with a male friend with whom I should never have been involved. We had intercourse a few times, each with our own reasons. I did not agree with the relationship so I told him we had to end it. He did not want to but he decreased his pursuit.

NO means NO!

One day he decided to visit, which wasn't abnormal. I let him in and went back to my bedroom to continue reading a book. He entered my room and we chatted briefly before he pinned me down and proceeded to attack me. Although I said stop countless times, he continued. He began telling me that he wanted me to have his baby. While fully clothed, he raped me. He pushed my shorts to one side and entered me. I told him repeatedly to stop and that he was raping me. He continued until he had an orgasm, fastened his pants and left.

I was confused and did not know what to do. I spoke to a friend who guided me in calling the police. I received death threats from this man and decided not to pursue the case because I knew that he was capable of carrying it through. I later learned from the police that I was not the only woman who had filed a complaint and dropped it. You never know what people are capable of. He was someone I knew and he violated me.

No means no! It does not matter if you are male or female, no means no! Women get raped and men get raped as well.

Rape is forcibly having sexual intercourse with someone against his or her will. Many rape victims know their attackers and the assault may possibly be prevented.

Young ladies, I know that you are becoming aware of your bodies, what men like, and how to use your womanly wiles to get what you want. There is a time and place for everything. You can't tease men and not expect a reaction. You may not know what type of environment a young man grew up in or what he may think is the norm for expressing care or love. Protect yourself by not playing games – ever! Do not leave room for a mistake or give someone the opportunity to take advantage of you by sending mixed signals. This gives them the justification in their mind to commit the act of rape. Do not put yourself through this unnecessary experience.

Men, I know that you are interested in and excited about the female body. Your hormones are raging and, yes, women do sometimes play games that will get you aroused. The best way to protect youself is to never force yourself on anyone. Never assume anyone wanted it. Maybe she did, but if she didn't consent, you just committed rape.

Think about the consequences. There will be many women that will be more than willing to have intercourse with you.

Protect yourself:

- When drinking, don't leave your drink unattended. GhB (the date rape drug) is discreetly mixed in a potential victim's drink.

- Don't send mixed messages. If you're not interested, be firm in your statements and actions.

- Don't travel alone at night.

- If attacked, try to get away if you feel it's the right way to proceed.

- Draw attention to yourself.

- Don't allow strangers into your car or home. Lock your doors.

- If you feel uncomfortable in any situation, leave.

- Take a self-defense class.

- If you're raped, write down (if you can) the perpetrator's identifying marks, height, weight, clothing, shoes, vehicle and license plate number.

- Scratch the rapist to get a DNA sample.

Call the police, give a description of the attacker, and see a doctor immediately. Depending on where you live, the morning after pill may be available to prevent pregnancy, and you may receive medication to prevent contraction of some STD's.

This traumatic experience may jeopardize your future relationships, feelings of safety or your ability to trust. Please don't shelter yourself. You don't have to be ashamed. It's not your fault. You were forced. Accept all the support you can get. If necessary, seek counseling. Speak to a rape victim hotline, or utilize other resources.

With regard to prosecution, you must do what you feel is best for you and your ability to have closure on the situation.

Your goal is to heal and not blame yourself. Take the necessary steps that are right for you.

SMOKING

{ *Each day you make a choice to decelerate or accelerate your eventual death.* }

I can't tell you the appeal of smoking. It stinks, causes bad breath, causes throat, mouth, and lung cancer, premature aging, ugly lips, sickly babies, and death. Your voice changes, you can't breathe properly, your skin wrinkles, and you smell like an ashtray; all for what?

Ask a smoker and they'll tell you it calms their nerves, helps them think, and they know it's bad for their health.

Cigarettes contain an addictive drug called nicotine. An ex-smoker once told me, when trying to quit, it's not the nicotine that causes you to continue smoking. Nicotine is out of your system in seventy-two hours. It depends on the strength of your mind.

Smoking not only affects your health but others in your presence when you're smoking. First and second hand smoke cause aliments and diseases such as bronchitis, asthma, pneumonia, and cancer.

A friend's boyfriend is a nonsmoker and is currently suffering from lung cancer today because his mother smoked around him as he grew up. If you smoke, you need to self analyze and figure out why. Next, you need to confront the reason. If it's from boredom, get active. If it's from habit,

279

break it. It takes twenty-one days to make or break a habit. If it's because smoking soothes your nerves, find out what triggers you and learn how to address your problems. Whatever the reason, you have to get control of you and stop harming yourself and possibly others.

Reasons to quit:

- Become healthier. Nonsmokers are healthier than smokers.
- Save money. Depending on your habit, you could save hundreds of dollars each year.
- Have fresher smelling breath, clothing, and air in you home and car.
- Reduce you risks of getting cancer.
- Reduce the risks of causing someone you love to die or get ill.

Quitting is not necessarily easy but here are a few tips:

- Take high doses of vitamin C (about 3000 to 5000 milligrams per day) during the first three days.
- Chew gum or drink water when you feel the urge to smoke.
- Seek homeopathic or naturopathic remedies.
- Try herbal supplements.
- Fill the time that you used to smoke with something productive.
- Remember the reasons you decided to quit.

SUICIDE

Reach out; save your own or someone else's life.

As a teenager, after my father's death I thought of committing suicide. I felt alone, very depressed, and disappointed in myself. I was doing things that I knew my father wouldn't approve of. I didn't have anyone to talk to and I was ashamed and scared of being judged. I figured the easiest way out would be to commit suicide. I attempted to take some pills but couldn't do it.

As an adult, I had a co-worker that I befriended. We bonded fairly quickly and everyone knew how close we were. He left the company we worked for but later came back to fill in for someone. He was a very spiritual person and often helped others with his gift of prophesy. He stopped by my office to talk and seemed a bit disturbed as he began to tell me about the various things he had visualized and the fact that it was troubling him that he couldn't help those he saw in his visions.

One Friday afternoon he called me at work but I was speaking on another line and didn't answer the call. As I looked at the phone, for a second I thought, "I'd better answer that call." I didn't know his number by heart so I couldn't call him back.

On Monday morning, I received an unusual call from a co-worker asking if I was on my way in to work. I replied, "Yes, what's up?" She told me she'd see me when I got there. When I got to work, I was greeted by some of my coworkers describing how my friend was working on one of the tallest buildings in downtown Dallas, removed his harness, and jumped, falling to his death.

Following this event, even still to this day I ask myself what would have happened if I had answered the phone when he called. If you ever know someone who is troubled, answer the phone, you may save a life.

If you feel suicidal, before you attempt to kill yourself, talk to someone. Yes, it may seem that you have nothing to live for, but if you can hold on, get some support and help, you will be alright. Your circumstances may be more extreme than mine were, but there is a light at the end of the tunnel.

Support groups are available. You can speak to counselors anonymously about rape, incest, drug addiction, alcoholism, binge eating, anorexia, depression, or any other problem you may have and they will be able to refer you to someone or help you themselves.

Please, before you attempt to end your life, talk to someone. Reach out to a friend or family member or call a hotline.

DEPRESSION

You are not alone.

In any given one-year period, 9.5 percent of the population, or about 18.8 million American adults, suffer from a depressive illness. The economic cost for this disorder is high, but the cost in human suffering cannot be estimated. Depressive illnesses often interfere with normal functioning and cause pain and suffering not only to those who have a disorder, but also to those who care about them. Serious depression can destroy family life as well as the life of the ill person. But much of this suffering is unnecessary.

Everyone experiences a form of depression at some point in his or her life. Now that I look back, I have experienced it on more than one occasion, once due to my father's death, after childbirth, and during different stressful times in my life. Thankfully, I was able to get over the depression and go forward in my life.

I had an opportunity to take a close up look at depression as a serious illness as my friend suffered greatly on a daily basis. She was affected mentally, emotionally, and physically as this illness manifested itself.

Depression can sneak up on you and before you know it, you are in a very dark place possibly wanting to be alone, fearing interaction with other people, having thoughts that no one loves you, feeling worthless, lack of energy, thinking of suicide, having insomnia, having a lack of desire to do things you once loved, etc. These are just a few indications.

Depression will affect your family and work relationships and friendships. It can take a toll on everyone, especially when undiagnosed.

Many women seek treatment but men have a tendency to think that what they are experiencing is stress and a part of life. If you are a man, and are experiencing any of the previously mention indications, please seek help. Everyone knows you're strong and will not think any less of you as a man.

There are different types of depression that will range from periodic to long term. Whatever the length of time it lingers, there is a mental and emotional healing that needs to take place. Whatever the prevalent issue, seek forgiveness of yourself and anyone else involved. Medicine or herbal supplements can help to balance the body chemicals, but the problem will linger as long as you don't confront the issues.

Everyone needs help at some point in his or her life.

MENTAL ILLNESS

Seek help early.

I was first exposed to mental illness when a neighborhood friend was given a marijuana joint that was laced. He smoked it and lost his mind. He thought he was a genie at times and could change his eye color. I remember seeing him walk by my house as I stood in the doorway and I said, "Hello Dan." He turned to me and said, "My name isn't Dan. I'm the purple genie." He folded his arms one on top of the other, without turning, moved his head from side to side, and made a popping sound with his tongue and said, "Would you like to make a wish?" I smiled and said, "Okay. I wish I had ten dollars." He said, "Okay." He then made the popping sound with his tongue, stepped back, extended his arms and pointed his fingers at me, and said, "How about ten thousand years in HELL!" He made motions and sounds like he was a machine gun, which was supposed to be him shooting electricity at me. I ran in the house and he left.

The second occurrence was when my sister in-law returned home from overseas. She was a totally different person than she was prior to going overseas. She came home paranoid, afraid, and very nervous.

My third experience was with one of my son's great aunts. She wore a

285

trench coat year round and carried her personal belongs in a brown paper sack of with edges that she meticulously rolled. She often walked around talking to herself and was unapproachable. The family shuffled her from home to home as each person tired of her presence.

The next experience outweighs anything I'd ever experienced. I dated someone that was mentally ill. He was a sweet person and had you met him, he would have charmed the socks off you. I saw signs that something was wrong with him but often concluded that he was behaving in a particular manner because of stressful circumstances. The next few years proved me wrong.

He became paranoid and believed he was part of a secret organization among other things. When you have someone in your life that is mentally ill, it wears on you mentally as well. I never cried so much in my life. I gained weight and lost a lot of hair. I watched as my best friend, my sweetie began to deteriorate. He became mean, aggressive, and abusive – mentally, physically, and emotionally. This combined with paranoid delusions and drug abuse made life very difficult and unpredictable. I never knew what I was going to get. He would change as fast as you could flick a light switch on and off.

Mental illness affects the ill person, their family, and their ability to function in society. The hard part is getting the mentally ill person to understand and/or admit they are ill. Depending on their illness, they may believe you're working against them. They sometimes strike out at the people they're closest to in abusive manners, verbally and physically. They eventually may not be able to work because of lack of focus or other issues.

There are many types of mental illness such as depression, bipolar disorder, schizophrenia and more.

The symptoms of mental illness will vary from illness to illness. Some symptoms to keep in mind are:

- Being withdrawn
- Excessive weight gain or loss
- Extremely happy then extremely sad

- Participation is destructive or risky behavior
- Lack of interest in things they usually enjoy
- Seclusion
- Abusing alcohol or drugs
- Delusional
- Hearing voices
- Paranoia

Coping with mental illness

Do not blame yourself or remain in denial if you feel something just isn't right about yourself. Seek assistance from your doctor, state mental illness insurance company, county hospital, or mental illness helpline.

Many illnesses can be controlled or maintained but first you have to admit you have a problem and be willing to be treated. Mental illness is not something to be embarrassed about. There are many successful people who suffer from mental illness and are able to function after being treated. When you are treated, you should begin to feel progressively better. You'd actually be amazed at the number of people who have a mental illness who work, have successful relationships, and are happy.

Coping when you have a mentally ill loved one

Having a loved one that's mentally ill is a labor of love. For me, I did everything I could do to include having the man I loved picked up on a mental illness warrant. If you are living with or have close contact with someone who's mentally ill, seek out a support group, family therapy or counseling. It will help you keep things in perspective.

Mental illness and heredity

If your family has a history of mental illness be sure to take proper care of yourself by keeping stress to a minimum, exercising, eating properly, avoid alcoholic beverages and don't do drugs. Alcohol and drugs make mental illness worse. Drugs can take you from being a functioning person to dysfunctional and will intensify the mental illness. Never do drugs if mental illness runs in your family.

Therapy

There are various types of therapy available usually with a treatment program for the mentally ill person. The hospitals or clinics may have therapy sessions available for the family or mate. Take advantage of this opportunity for healing.

The longer you wait the worse it gets

Seek help as soon as you notice a problem. If someone that knows you tells you they've noticed you doing abnormal things and are concerned about you, listen. I know it may be difficult to hear but the last thing you want to do is allow the illness to become worse by refusing to acknowledge the symptoms. The worse it gets the harder it is to get a handle on.

Mental Illness Warrant

This is an extreme resort and nothing to play with. The mental illness warrant is a court ordered warrant which forces a person to go to a county hospital for observation and analysis. The hospital can hold the person for up to 72 hours and if they find the person does need help can request an extension for further examination.

To get a mental illness warrant, you have to contact the county courts or possibly the Justice of the Peace. They will have forms for you to fill in, you will have to speak with a judge or magistrate and swear that what you're stating is the truth. You also sign papers stating that you understand what you are doing is punishable by jail time and or fines. Essentially, you are required to list who the person is, why you are requesting an MIW, detailed facts. If the judge agrees the "white paper" warrant is necessary, he will order the warrant and the person is picked up as soon as possible.

Do not play with this. If you do, you will find yourself in a heap of trouble which may result in a warrant for your arrest.

Education, Income, Career

Notes

EDUCATION, INCOME, CAREER
INTRODUCTION

Intelllectual growth should come at birth and cease only at death. -Albert Einstein

Education, gained through college, university, continuing education programs, self-taught, or technical training, leads to a career and a certain income bracket. The more you learn and are able to prove your ability through credentials, the more favorable and better paying positions you can pursue.

Setting goals in life and working towards them will assure you progress. When choosing a career, consider the fastest growing occupations. There are certain skills that will get you a job regardless of your level of education. You can make more than minimum wage by learning the basic office skills such as typing, 10-key, using a word processor such as Microsoft Word and a spreadsheet program such as Microsoft Excel. You can either teach yourself many of these skills, take classes or learn them by working temp jobs, which can be obtained through a staffing agency.

If you think you're an entrepreneur at heart, learn business and the particulars of the industry you're interested in. If you desire to work independently, you must develop skills that are in demand so you can be in demand.

Regardless of whether you're an entrepreneur or an independent contractor, each requires a risk. Be sure you're ready to take that risk.

Before you start a business, read the chapter called "Ten Things You Should Do When Starting a Business." Don't stop there. Seek as much information as possible. Always make educated choices.

Educate yourself to maximize your career potential and, in turn, to maximize your income.

SETTING GOALS

Once we accept our limits we go beyond them.
-Albert Einstein

A goal is something you want to achieve. Goals can be set in every area of your life such as finances, career, family, and education. Setting and meeting goals will make your life much more productive and fulfilling.

Setting goals can be equally as difficult as reaching your goals if you don't have an idea about what you want to do.

To begin, you must decide what type of goals you're setting. Are they short-term or long-term? To what aspects of your life do these goals relate? Is there a particular something you need to accomplish? Do you want to learn a trade? Do you want to improve your eating habits?

Next, select a goal. Write down what you're currently dissatisfied with or desire to change or improve. Determine what tasks are required to accomplish this goal. Write those down.

Consider your current schedule and responsibilities and choose a realistic deadline for each goal. Avoid putting undue stress on yourself. Rushing or applying pressure to get something done can create problems and undue stress. You may forget important details that may affect the outcome of a particular situation and affect your health. Although you

293

may consider yourself to be superman or superwoman, some things are worth the time taken so it's done right!

Decide when you're going to start working on your first goal. Once you begin working, review your progress daily and cross off the tasks as you complete them. Repeat these steps for each goal and before you know it, you will see your life changing before your eyes.

Setting goals require you to take the time and love yourself enough to want to change your life. We get so accustomed to giving to others, our jobs, and everything else that it becomes easy to be outwardly focused.

If you're having a hard time developing your list, start with a "Top 10" list. Itemize the ten most important goals you need to achieve to get started. As you progress, add another goal to the list as you cross off goals you accomplish.

Use the same sheet of paper until you find it necessary to start on a clean page. As the paper becomes messy with marked-out words, you will recognize your progress and see your life changing in subtle to enormous ways.

This is an example of taking the goal "take classes" from the "Top 10" list and breaking it down into smaller goals to meet the large goal. You can use this process for each and every goal you have so you can see the progress you make as you complete each step to reach your goal.

TOP 10 LIST
1.Job
2.Car
3.Apartment
4.**Take classes**
5.New clothes
6.Read more books
7.Start savings
8. Set up mutual fund
9. New furniture
10.Establish credit

Educational Goals
Take classes
1. Locate local colleges
2. Select classes
3. Visit schools
4. Apply for school /enroll
5. Get manuscripts
6. Take tests if necessary
7. Enroll in school

EDUCATIONAL OPTIONS

> *The important thing is to not stop questioning.*
> *Curiousity has its own reason for existing.*
> -Albert Einstein

Since I had a difficult time in high school (due to depression sparked by my father's death), much of the preparation I heard my classmates speak of such as taking the SAT or ACT flew right by me. I had no clue taking the tests affected your acceptance into colleges or universities.

When I decided to go to college, I brought home some college applications and financial aid papers and presented them to my mother. When she told me I couldn't go, I didn't understand why. I later learned that due to her being uneducated in the process, she didn't know to make sure I took the necessary tests, nor did she understand the financial aid process. Tuition looked like another debt. A couple years later I decided to attend college and went through the process on my own.

Never allow ignorance to dissolve your dreams. If you don't understand something, ask questions and research to get the answers. But by all means, make an informed choice concerning education.

You must have some type of knowledge in life to survive, whether you acquire it through the educational system, self-study, or hands-on experience. Obtaining a specialized skill will allow you to advance quickly because your knowledge is certified. Being self-taught or having hands-on experience has its benefits, especially when you are able to prove yourself through demonstration. No matter which path you choose, you will have to learn and acquire information to succeed. Don't allow fear, money, opinion, a high school diploma, or the lack thereof, stop you from aggressively pursuing your educational interests. You always have options available: Choose one. Be aware that higher paying jobs often require at a minimum, a four-year college diploma.

Alternative schools

If you have not yet obtained your high school diploma and are not yet an adult, you can still earn a diploma or obtain an equivalent. Alternative schools evaluate what you know and give you the opportunity to complete your high school education through their program.

GED

If you are over 16 years old, you can attend a GED program. A GED, or General Education Diploma, is acquired through testing and is equivalent to a high school diploma. It does not replace a diploma but serves as proof that you are educated at a high school graduate level.

Once a GED is obtained, it allows you to continue your education at a higher institute of learning. It's never too late to obtain a GED. If you are concerned about your ability to pass the test, any of countless GED programs at local community colleges, outreach programs, on the Internet, or distance learning courses will help you prepare. For information on GED programs in your area, contact your local community colleges or your state's board of education.

Continuing education programs

Continuing education programs are credit and non-credit courses offered by colleges and universities that allow you to further your education in a particular field of study, refresh skills you haven't used in a while, or take classes for fun.

Continuing education programs offer certification programs for various fields of study such as computer applications and project management.

You can also obtain credits for a specialized field such as law, nursing, cosmetology, computer science, or business.

If you are looking for an inexpensive way to continue educating yourself, develop additional skills, or get your feet wet in a college environment, this is the way to go. For information on classes in your area, contact your local community college, university, or your state's board of education.

College

Will you be attending a college or university? What's the difference, you ask? A college is an institute of higher learning, which offers a four-year undergraduate program leading to a bachelor's degree. A university contains colleges offering undergraduate programs in various fields of specialization such as a college of law or business. At a university, you have the option of pursuing higher degrees of education such as masters or doctorate.

Whichever you choose congratulations on continuing your education! As you learn, apply your knowledge as often as possible so you have an experience as a point of reference. Degrees offer book knowledge; the real knowledge or wisdom comes when you actually begin to apply what you have learned.

College offers tremendous growth. Not only are you being educated but also you're growing as a person. It may be the first time you've ever been away from your parents for a significant length of time and been responsible for your own well-being. This is usually accompanied by the explosive revelation that you are free. With freedom comes responsibility. Don't forget any valuable lessons you've learned. There are a few steps that you must take before you actually get to college. If you're like most people, one of those includes obtaining financing.

Financial Aid

God Bless America! Everyone has the opportunity to attend college in the U.S.A. Thanks to the government; money has been set aside for student loans and grants to assist students in paying for college.

The following information is excerpted from the U.S. Department of Education, Funding Your Education Booklet. To receive the booklet in its full format, contact the Federal Student Aid Information Center 1-800-433-3243. For more information, visit www.fafsa.ed.gov or call 1-800-4-FED-AID.

The U.S. Department of Education offers a variety of financial aid programs for students. Federal student aid includes grants, work-study, and loans. Grants need not be paid back. Work-study allows you to earn money while loans are funds you can borrow for your education. You'll have to repay any money you borrow.

Scholarship search services

Many private scholarship search services provide lists of sources of financial assistance for which you may apply. If you decide to use one of these services, you may check its reputation by contacting the Better Business Bureau or your state's attorney general.

Plus Loans (Parent Loans)

To find information on federal student loans and to view related publications online, visit their web site at www.ed.gov/studentaid.

If you need to speak to a live person, call the Federal Student Aid Information Center at 1-200/4-FED-AID (1-800/433-3243).

If you're hearing-impaired and have access to TTY call: 1-800/730-8913.

U.S. Armed Forces

The U.S. Armed Forces also offer educational programs and ways to pay for school or reduce your school costs. Contact your local military recruiter for more information on these programs.

State higher education agencies

Your local State Commission on Higher Education or Department of Higher Education can also provide information on state education programs, grants, scholarships, continuing education programs, financial assistance programs, and career opportunities. For more information, please refer to your local telephone book or visit: www.ed.gov.

Scholarships and grants

Scholarships and grants are available to assist with costs of education through various private organizations. There are thousands of philanthropic organizations that award students various amounts of funding based on qualifications or statuses such as disability, minority, sexual preference, field of study, financial need, or religion.

COLLEGE CAMPUS AWARENESS

The choice you make today will impact the remainder of your life.

I never lived on a college campus but have had the opportunity to speak to some prior and current college students that have. There are a few factors that came up in each conversation that I'll address.

Peer Pressure

Peer pressure is when your friends or associates attempt to persuade you to change your beliefs, morals, speech, or behavior to fit into their group.

Peer pressure is predicated by you selection of friends. The type of people you hang around will determine what you're introduced to be it people or situations. By carefully choosing your friends, you better control your experiences.

With pressure/influence you can wind up in situations that you would not normally choose for yourself such as underage drinking, having sex with people you don't know or multiple partners, doing drugs including prescription drug abuse, etc., all because you're trying to fit in. The possible effects are your missing class, failing grades, bad reputations, possible addiction, etc.

You have a right to stand your ground regardless of what anyone thinks of you. Ultimately they will respect you even if you don't go along with what they want you to do. They'll learn you're not a pushover based on your ability to say NO! I understand everyone wants to be liked however, if the group you're hanging with doesn't respect your free will; your power to choose what's right for you - they're not the group for you.

Surround yourself with people like yourself or whom you aspire to be like. If you know ultimately you desire great grades, a great job, respect and accomplishments, surround yourself with those that are working towards the same. If this isn't your normal crowd but what you aspire to be, it's up to you to change and become what you dream of becoming.

Time management

Time management is managing your time to accomplish as much as you can. Between you and your parent's assistance you've managed your time. Now that you're in college it's all up to you. There are so many things to do and see and you don't have a curfew or set bedtime until you set it yourself.

My niece told me time management was her biggest challenge. I admire her because not only did she have a full load of classes, she worked as well. She chose to work because she had expenses and wanted things for herself. She struggled the first semester and was very disappointed with her grades. She pointed out that some classes may be more difficult and require more that others and all the classes are new unlike in high school where you do a refresher at the beginning of the class and the subject matter is a continuum of your previous one.

To deal with these issues:

- Plan your study time appropriately based on the level of difficulty or your grasp of the class.

- Buy a digital recorder and record your classes to help your review.

- If you're having difficulty with classes, seek tutoring or join a study group.

Credit

There will be credit card companies trying to get you to apply for cards. One or two cards are okay; preferably a major credit card such as Visa, MasterCard, or American Express. You can use these cards just about everywhere and the interest rates are less than department store credit cards. Avoid getting department store credit cards to avoid the high interest rate. Learn more about credit cards in the credit card section.

Smoking

You'll always see the kids or young adults that seem to always have a cigarette in their hand. It's amazing that so many young adults still associate smoking with being cool. Though there are many campaigns for smoking awareness, they refuse to acknowledge they're setting themselves up for addiction, cancer, ugly lips, bad breath and skin.

You are cool just being yourself. You don't need to endanger your life or others' lives via second hand smoke to prove to someone you're worthy of attention.

Prescription drugs

Never trust anyone enough to ingest drugs of any type no matter what the circumstance. Take only your own prescription medication.

Some think prescription drug abuse or "pill popping" is sophisticated because a lot of wealthy people are known to use prescriptions as a legal means of getting high. These people are also the ones that usually justify their addiction by convincing themselves it's okay because they're prescribed.

Sophistication is not risking your life to fit in. Sophistication is also not damaging your liver, the ability to function, and being vulnerable to the whims of others.

Sophistication is being wise about the ways of the world. Being wise is to know better than... knowing better than is having sense to not do something. Become sophisticated by having sense and using your knowledge to know that you don't have to put on a façade. Surround yourself with those secure enough to be themselves. Be secure enough to be you. If you're not secure and putting on an act is what you associate with being yourself, ask yourself why you think that you have to be that way in order to be liked. What are you ashamed of? Remember you are who you are for a reason, no matter where you came from, how you were raised, or whether or not you wear designer clothing. You are the perfect you.

Drinking

Many college campuses are surrounded by bars. Some bar owners don't card (ask for identification) or care about whether you get drunk and the effects of it. It is up to you to care about you.

To my understanding, a lot of high school students start drinking before they reach college and their habits continue in college. For some, drinking is a new experience. For all, I will warn you against drinking, drinking games, and alcohol abuse. Excessive consumption of alcohol is alcohol abuse. It can impair judgment, be addictive, and even deadly.

You may have watched movies and saw people doing shots, chugging, or just throwing drinks back. Yes, it looks fun but remember they are acting. Yes, this occurs in real life but you rarely see the repercussions of these acts in movies. Before you allow peer pressure get to you or make an attempt to be impressive, visit www.madd.org: Mothers Against Drunk Driving. You life is more important than proving you're cool.

Sex

Sex – wow, where do I begin? I had an intensive conversation with a man on his experiences while living on a college campus and was amazed at what he shared. Ladies pay extra attention to what I have to say since the examples come from true male experience.

It's safe to say most young men are horny, inexperienced and trying to get as much sex as possible. They will pass you around, set you up to be passed around, talk about how easy you are, and tell their friends to try to bed you. They'll even tell their friends how to get you; how to approach you, what to say and how to act.

If you fool with the wrong people, you may be subjected to guys trying to make you feel like you owe them or it's an honor to be with them, putting you in situations to allow a group of guys to "run a train" on you (several guys taking turns having sex with you). Some may use "Ghb" – Rohypnol, the date rape drug, so they can have their way with you. Some will even videotape having sex with you without you knowing.

- **Never be in a hurry to have sex with anyone. If a young man is really interested in you, he'll wait.**

- **You don't owe anyone anything – any access to any part of your body. You are the prize.**

- **You don't have to have sex with anyone to become popular or make friends. This is not the way to love. Love is felt first in the mind and heart. Sex isn't the only way to express how you feel for someone.**

- **Never put yourself in a position where you are the only female in a room full of men, especially if you don't know them, it isn't a study group, or something legit.**

- **Never go anywhere with a guy you've just met or are intending to meet. Meet in public until you get to know him better.**

- **If you've dated a guy and next thing you know you're being approached by his friends, cut him and his friends off. Also be leery of a sudden influx of guys trying to "holler" at you.**

- **Just because your friends are having sex doesn't mean you have to.**

- **Be leery of someone pushing drinks on you or trying to get you drunk. Make your own drink if possible and keep and eye on it to make sure no one drugs you.**

- **If you join a sorority, it is not your responsibility to sleep with the brother organization (fraternity).**

- **Oral sex is sex as well. You can get the same diseases as if you had intercourse in your mouth, throat, and chest.**

- **Always protect yourself and you may want to invest in a can of pepper spray (check if legal in your state before buying).**

Young men, yes I'm telling. Treat yourself with respect as well as the young ladies that you encounter. I know that sex, college, and freedom are possibly new experiences for you. You do not have to sneak anyone in your mother's house. You're free and a lot of you are trying or will try to "conquer" as many young ladies as possible. While you're doing this, remember this is a new age.

1. **Respect your and the young lady's body.**

2. **Men can catch, carry, and spread many STD's because you're either not aware you have one or are ashamed and won't go to the doctor to be treated. Wear protection at all times and go to the doctor if you catch something.**

3. **Before you disrespect a young lady by setting her up, sending you friends to her or schooling anyone on how to get this girl to have sex with them, ask yourself would you want this to happen to your sister, cousin, or friend?**

4. **You don't have to prove your masculinity or depth of cool to anyone.**

5. **If you ever encounter a group of guys violating a female, don't become a part of it. First, it's wrong. Second, you have no idea if any of these guys or this girl have diseases. Help her get away or call security.**

6. **It is illegal to drug anyone. Using Ghb or any other drug to sedate someone so you can freely have sex with them is rape.**

7. **Women don't owe you anything because you take them out.**

8. **Get to know a young lady before having sex with her.**

9. **Disease is spread through the mouth as well.**

10. **Manhood is not measured by the number of women you bed.**

Heterosexual or homosexual

I was told by a young gay man that he was surprised to learn how many gay males are "down low". He told me that even his roommate dated a female in the open and secretly dated other gay men. He used the female as a cover for his sexuality. If you are in a similar situation be it male or female, have a conscious. Don't put people in unsuspecting and possibly life-threatening situations. Be honest and allow them to make a choice. You may be surprised to find that there are males and females who will accept their mate's sexual preferences. Find those people. Don't hurt people you love because of your own insecurities. Maybe it's time to come out of the closet.

Social networking sites

The internet has broken down barriers and created a fresh experience in terms of socializing. You can email, blog, or have a dedicated web site to communicate your thoughts and ideals or post pictures and share your life.

Be leery of posting various aspects of your life. This information is accessible by the world and a potential employer. More and more, employers are using the internet to learn more about potential candidates and some people that are already employed have lost their jobs due to what they have posted on the internet. Keep in mind that if you'd be embarrassed to discuss what you've posted or a picture that may be considered distasteful, don't post it.

Each subject I've addressed is serious and can impact your life and stay on your campus. Take this information seriously. Make good choices. If you choose wrong, as soon as your realize it, choose again.

Sexting

Sexting is sending naked pictures via a text/picture message. Do not send naked pictures to anyone. These pictures will haunt and affect you for the rest of your life. Even if someone promises they won't send or show it to anyone doesn't guarantee that the photos will not been seen or sent in error. **Protect your future!**

I DON'T WANT TO GO TO COLLEGE, WHAT NOW?

Increase the possibility of earning a decent income by learning a skill or trade or by getting a degree.

What happened, have you figured school is a waste of time? Are you tired of being in class? You're ready to get a job and start making some *real* money? If you don't have a nest egg or wealthy parents who are going to spoil you forever, you'd better have a backup plan. Everyone doesn't like school but, the more the world changes, the jobs that are in demand and pay the most require specialized education that is obtained from an institute of higher learning. Many companies require you to have a four-year college degree.

Weigh you reasons for not wanting to attend college. Is it because you are not a "school" person; you don't like school? Do you feel you can't afford it or don't need to go? Whatever your reason, understand that people with college degrees are the people the employers retain and quickly promote.

If you're not comfortable committing to two to four years of college, you may want to consider taking a few continuing education courses to learn business skills, computer training, or other skill that will help you make more than minimum wage.

If you are not prepared to start at the bottom and work very hard to progress, think again. I have a tremendous amount of knowledge in various areas of business and have met all of the qualifications for consideration of employment in upper management employment but one, a college degree. Not having a degree caused my resume to be trashed many times. All the knowledge I had was overlooked for a candidate that more than likely didn't have the hands-on experience I had but did have a college degree. Before you totally give up on college, think very hard.

If you're sure you're not going to college, look into some continuing education certificate programs that will allow you to specialize in a field. If you want your own business, some business courses will help with marketing, accounting, and management.

College isn't for everyone but does provide knowledge, opportunities, and chances for a more substantial income. Before you totally decide to not pursue an education, think about where that leaves you. How much money can you make with limited skills or none at all? Is it your dream to live with your parents or live frugally, forever? You have to make a decision about how you want to live and what it takes to get there.

Speak to a counselor, your parents, or someone who is in college, and read about the occupations that interest you and what it takes to be hired. Make an informed decision. It will help you to not waste precious time and you can get on with your life.

There are many successful people who never obtained a college degree. Many have created wealth by starting a business, investing their money in the stock market or real estate. They applied themselves. With any success comes a form of education. **To succeed, you have to be knowledgeable in whatever endeavor you choose.**

TEMPORARY & STAFFING AGENCIES

Each skill obtained will prepare you for the next job.

If I were to state every skill that I have related to business, my resume would appear to be unbelievable. Much of my experience was gained through temporary employment. If ever you need to gain experience, definitely work through a temporary employment agency.

Temporary employment agencies provide temporary employees to their clients. In addition, they sometimes assist their clients with filling open positions by screening candidates and then referring them for interviews.

Staffing agencies are useful when you are seeking permanent employment. Their niche is filling their clients' available positions. Unlike temporary employment agencies, this is their specialty. Some companies will charge you a fee for helping you find employment. If you don't want anyone's hand in your pocket, stick to the agencies that charge the companies instead.

Temporary and staffing agencies usually specialize in a particular field of work. Be sure to find one that's suitable for you. Office personnel agencies can help you gain office experience. If you desire manual labor, choose an industrial agency.

The agencies make their money by charging their clients for your services, paying you a percentage, and then keeping the balance. The agency has a vested interest in you because many "temp" positions have the potential of becoming permanent. If you are offered a permanent position while working a temporary assignment, the agency will be paid a "finder's fee" which will equate to ten to thirty percent or more of your salary if you are hired.

If you are highly skilled, negotiate your pay rate. In some instances, they do have the power to increase your pay. Otherwise, the staffing representative and the agency will benefit but you won't. Be sure you're paid at least the average rate of pay for your position.

The benefits of working with a temp agency are:

- You gain hands-on experience
- Can be used as a stepping stone
- Free computer training
- Gets your foot in the door with companies
- The opportunity to increase your skills
- You work when you desire and you have the option to leave any job you are not comfortable with
- You have flexibility

To increase their revenue potential, temp/staffing agencies provide computer training in many software applications, including some specialized applications. They desire to make you more marketable so they have a diverse database of candidates, which ensures more clients for them.

As a temp, you should take advantage of every opportunity to increase your business knowledge and qualifications. You help the agency and yourself. The representative at the agency will take a particular interest in you as they see you develop. When they see an eager person, they are more apt to help.

At each job you accept, learn as much as you can. All the skills you learn will increase your marketability. Extend yourself and let your supervisor know you're interested in learning more. Learn each company's policies and procedures. No two companies are the same. You can learn a few new things at each assignment that will enhance your business skills.

When you register with an agency, the staffing representative will ask you what salary you're looking for. They will try to negotiate a rate that's best for the agency, so start with a higher dollar amount than you would accept and negotiate. Don't be unrealistic; know your skills and what you're capable of. If you know that the going rate for a receptionist is $10 per hour, don't request $20 and expect to get it. You may even mention you know the going rate, state it, and request that amount.

Agencies usually request close to or double the amount they're paying you from their clients. I'll give you an example. I was working in accounting (full charge bookkeeping) and making $15 per hour. I came across the bill for my services and noticed that the agency was receiving $26 per hour for my services.

Finish assignments

You do have the option to leave any assignment that you don't like. Don't make a habit of it. It should be a rarity. The representatives at the agency will keep notes on you. If the assignment isn't that bad, stick with it until it ends.

Accept only the assignments that are suitable for you. Do not feel bad or guilty if you can't do a particular assignment. The agency's representatives will call with offers that pay less than the pay you requested. Remember, the relationship is a give and take. They aren't just helping you; you're helping each other. The assignments you accept should be convenient for you. The hours or getting there on time shouldn't be a challenge.

Keep track of your responsibilities at each assignment. If they change drastically – if you were hired to answer phone calls and light typing and you find yourself doing spreadsheets and presentations on top of your other duties – you're being underpaid. Bring this to the attention of your representative and request higher pay. They will review the job work order and speak to the client. Do not allow yourself to be used.

You are representing yourself first and the agency second. Be sure you make a good impression by dressing appropriately, arriving on time, and completing your work in a timely manner. The impression you make reflects on you and the caliber of employees the agency hires. The impression you make will benefit you more than the agency. You have the opportunity to become a full-time employee. You will also have a contact at that company who knows your abilities and might be used as a reference in the future.

Never stop learning and use the agencies to your advantage. Never allow them to make you feel as if they're doing you a favor. They need you as much as you need them…probably more. If they don't want you, the next agency will. Register with a few agencies so you will always have options available. If a permanent job doesn't work out for you, you know where you can find work. Don't burn your bridges. If you burn a bridge, you can no longer use it to progress. You never know when you'll need that person or business' help. **Don't do anything detrimental to destroy your relationships.**

THE BASIC SKILLS THAT WILL GET YOU A JOB

It's the little things that mean a lot.

The basic skills you need to get a job depends, of course, on what type of job you desire. For now, we're going to address the basics for getting your foot in the door to a corporate environment.

Grooming

Dress professionally which includes slacks, dress shirts, dresses, blouses, suits, or skirts that are business attire, and always have excellent personal hygiene. Brush your teeth, comb your hair, iron your clothes, bathe and use deodorant.

Personality

Have a cheerful yet confident personality without being ditzy. Be approachable so that people won't be afraid to talk to you. Smiling is always good; sincerity is better.

Language

Eliminate all street language. For example, the "Yo' homeboy", or the "Naw mean", or other street terminology used to replace *regular* English language.

Telephone etiquette

Be cordial, professional, and polite. Did you know that you're being interviewed even before your interview? Potential employers pay very close attention to your voice, enunciation, personality, and etiquette on the initial phone call. These traits are all signs of the type of person you are.

Team player

Be a team player. Don't be afraid to lend a hand when necessary. The ability to work well with others as well as alone is a definite plus.

Computer skills

Learn a word processing program such as Microsoft Word or Word Perfect. If you know one and not the other, don't be intimidated. Word processors are basically the same. Nearly everything you need to know can be found in the "Help Menu." Learn a spreadsheet program such as Microsoft Excel and a presentation application such as Microsoft PowerPoint. These programs are now standard in most office jobs.

Math isn't everyone's strong point, nor is operating a calculator, but learn the basics of addition, subtraction, percentages, multiplication, and division.

Punctuality

Arrive for your interview fifteen minutes early. By arriving early, you have an opportunity to observe the employees.

Typing

Did you hate typing in school? Too bad; depending on your job it may have followed you to work. The difference is that typing skills can now help you to make money. Speed and accuracy command higher pay.

Filing

Know the order of alphabets and numbers. You may have to alphabetize or put files in numerical order. Practice this.

Research

If you have an opportunity, research the company at which you're interviewing. Learn as much as you can about the company. Your knowledge can possibly give you an edge on the next candidate. A candidate with knowledge about the company is impressive to an employer.

RESUMES

This is your opportunity to brag about your accomplishments.

There are several types of resumes but the main three are: chronological, functional, and professional.

The chronological resume is for those with more work experience. The resume highlights positions, responsibility and accomplishments beginning in order with the most recent position listed first and proceeding backwards. This resume is great for those that have stayed in their field. It gives them an opportunity to show promotions or increased responsibilities and accomplishments.

The functional resume is for those who may have none to a varied work experience. It highlights skills and not where the skills were obtained. A benefit of using this type of resume is that the listed skills could have been obtained from volunteering or hobbies.

The professional resume highlights professional achievements, such as increasing productivity, profits, or receiving awards.

Resumes should be kept short and sweet. They should be concise yet supply all pertinent information. You may have heard that a resume needs to be one page. If an additional page is necessary, try to keep the text to one-half of the second page.

The following information should be included in a resume:

- Name
- Address
- Phone number
- Email address
- Objective
- Work history
- Computer skills/ computer applications, ex. Word, Excel
- If you are bilingual, be sure to include this. Knowing more than one language can increase your pay.
- Extracurricular activities – only if relevant to the position your are seeking

The easiest way to write a resume is by using the Microsoft Word Resume Wizard or other word processing application. The resumes are preformatted and you just have to fill in the information.

Hiring managers or Human Resource departments search for key words in resumes that pertain to their particular field. They also look for other adjectives; descriptive words to help them sort through the resumes as well.

Tips

1. Research the job you are applying for to learn the requirements, key words, and salary range.

2. When creating your resume, use the key words that are applicable to your experience and tweak it to the company's needs.

3. Make sure you include an objective or a personal profile which will include your goals, the type of person you are and your abilities.

4. Don't lie about your experience or salary history.

5. Always do a spelling and grammar check. You may want to have someone else review it as well.

6. As a student with little or no work history, create a functional resume highlighting skills obtained but not how you obtained them.

7. Use the internet as a resource to locate additional information for your particular field and sample resumes.

What's in a name?

There is a whole generation of parents who made up or chose unconventional names for their children. These *unusual* names can cause the person reviewing the resumes apprehension about or judgment of a candidate, with the assumption that the person is *ghetto*, regardless of their skills. This often leads to the resume being trashed.

Now this isn't right in my eyes, but it is the truth. Some people are intimidated by having to attempt to pronounce the name correctly or are influenced by mainstream media.

For those of you that suffer from mispronunciation or judgment of your name, I suggest that you either choose a shortened version or a "more acceptable" name when conducting business.

A good example would be the Korean lady that does my nails. She changed her name to "Lisa" to avoid having to explain her name or get people to correctly pronounce her name.

If you notice, many of the Eastern people in America have an American name and the name they were born with. This is merely a suggestion that I can almost guarantee will make a difference in peoples' perception of who you are based on your name.

FINDING A JOB

> *Don't stress if you don't get a particular job. The job that's for your is already yours.*

Job search is different now than when I started out. Pounding the pavement (going door to door) is only one option now, because you have the Internet. The majority of your legwork can be completed without leaving the house.

Companies now have many options for advertising job openings, which offer many resources for finding a job. An example would be them posting jobs on their web sites and job posting boards to solicit applicants.

Internet

The Internet is full of job search engines, newspapers, company web sites, and job posting boards. The job search engines allow you to define your search parameters for jobs best suited for you in your preferred location(s). The Internet also lists many jobs that will not be advertised in newspapers.

Not only can you view job ads, you also have the option of posting your resume for potential employers to view. Potential employers or recruiters review resumes online to reduce paper-shuffling and fill positions more quickly by searching for keywords. Posting your resume allows companies the opportunity to solicit you for positions you may not have known were available.

If there is a particular company you're interested in, visit their web site. You can locate valuable information such as the company's history, benefits, job openings, and how to submit your resume.

Staffing Agencies

Staffing agencies work on your behalf as well as other clients (potential employers) to find a match for a particular job. When using a staffing agency, be sure to use one that won't charge you a fee for their services. The employer pays them quite well.

Job Fairs

A job fair is an event where several companies set up booths in a specified location to set interviews or screen candidates on the spot. If you decide to attend a job fair, dress to impress, take several copies of your crisp resume, and be prepared to interview.

Newspapers

The good old newspaper. If you're lucky, you'll have access to a paper with a well-organized job section. Newspapers are still a good source of job openings for job seekers. There is less competition for positions advertised in the newspaper than on the Internet. If you choose this route, purchasing a Sunday newspaper is best to have more options, but if not the Sunday paper, be sure to get the paper first thing in the morning, highlight the jobs that interest you, and call the company or submit your resume immediately to give yourself a better chance at the job.

Pounding the Pavement

Pounding the pavement (going door-to-door) is most beneficial for those seeking employment in retail. There is usually an open door policy for submitting applications. If you know that you're interested in working for a large or corporate company, call their human resources department or look on their web site to learn their application procedure.

The Local State Department of Employment Security

Many people are not aware of this resource. Your local state Department of Employment Security has a database of employers looking to hire. Many of the jobs are state government jobs. This department has job counselors available to assist you with your job search.

Family and Friends

When job hunting, you must plant as many seeds as possible. Utilize all your resources, including family, friends, and acquaintances. Mention to them you're looking for a job, and if they will take it, give them a copy of your resume to pass on.

THE INTERVIEW PROCESS

Manners, manners, manners.

You got the interview! Great! Now it's time to make your best impression. Below are some interviewing tips.

Punctuality

Be punctual by arriving at least fifteen minutes early. Do this by mapping your route and taking a test drive the day before, taking into consideration distance, time of day you'll be traveling, and traffic. Prepare your clothing the day before as well.

Appearance

It doesn't matter if you're applying for a job at a corporation or a warehouse, always look your best. This means wearing your best and proper grooming.

- *Men*

Buy clothes that fit. No sagging pants or oversized shirts. Wear a black, blue, or gray suit with a shirt and tie. Shine your shoes. Dress conservatively. If you don't own a suit, you can either go to a resale shop or make do with a shirt, tie, and a pair of slacks. Shave, brush your teeth, cut and comb your hair.

- *Ladies*

Wear a suit, black or blue, a dress, or slacks, blouse and jacket. Be sure to wear pantyhose or stockings, conservative shoes, and minimal jewelry and perfume. Do not wear low-cut blouses or miniskirts. Keep makeup to a minimum avoiding glitter, heavy eyeliner, mascara, and black lip liner. Bathe, do your hair, and brush your teeth.

Sitting

The way you sit says a lot about you. You are to appear as a professional today; no slouching, or sitting with your legs cocked or spread wide. Sit up straight and appear in a respectful manner. You never want to appear disinterested or disrespectful.

Research

Before you go to the interview, be sure to read as much information as possible about your perspective employer. Knowledge of the company is always a plus. In addition, research the position so that you know the required skill set and the average salary.

Resume

Always carry three copies of your resume in case the interviewer misplaces theirs or you need a copy for yourself. Your resume comes in handy as you fill in applications. Resumes provide your prior employers information.

Nervousness

It's natural to be nervous. You are put in a position where you have to explain yourself and your abilities. This is why arriving early is important. You have time to relax, freshen up, and take a deep breath. Treat the interview as a conversation and don't worry so much about being judged.

Personality

Personality is important. It's okay to smile. Smiling shows you're receptive and happy. Seriousness has its place, usually when discussing business – apply as necessary. Relax, yet have an upbeat spirit. Perkiness and enthusiasm is great if not phony or in excess. The interviewer is not only reviewing your experience but also assessing how your personality will fit in with the company. You know how you feel when you are happy and your day is going great – be this person.

Shaking hands

Remember, not too hard, not too soft, but just right.

Testing

Some companies require you to take skills and/or personality tests. The skills test may include math, spelling, filing, comprehension, typing, and computer applications such as Microsoft Word, Excel, or PowerPoint. The personality test will screen you to see if you're honest, ambitious, and consistent among other things. The questions are asked many different ways so be consistent and honest.

Potential interview questions

- What are your strengths? Make sure you state them.
- What are your weaknesses? Never state any weaknesses. You answer should resemble this statement, "I can't think of any that will stop me fulfilling the duties of this position."
- Give an example of when you resolved an issue.
- Give examples of good customer service.
- Where do you see yourself five years from now?
- What did you do that was notable in your previous jobs?
- How did you help the company you previously worked for?
- Why did you leave?
- Why do you want to work here?
- How can you benefit this company?
- When asked about employment gaps, state something positive such as, "I was seeking a better opportunity."

- How much do you want to make? Tell them you expect a salary suitable with the responsibilities of the position.

- What hours are you available to work? Do not commit to times you're not available.

- Do you have reliable transportation?

- Do you have special skills?

- What type of benefits do you desire?

Questions you should ask

Allow the interviewer to do most of the talking. Follow their lead and if they offer you something to drink, take it.

Always ask questions to understand anything that has been discussed so you know what you are getting into.

1. Why is the position available?

2. What is the average cost for health insurance?

3. Do they offer sick, personal and vacation days?

4. How often are employees eligible for raises? If applicable, ask about bonuses and commission.

5. How soon will they make their hiring decision?

Always say thank you for the interview and that you look forward to hearing from them and shake their hands.

The offer

If the interview goes well, you'll receive a call with an offer for employment. They will offer a salary. By this time you should know the salary for the position you've interviewed for. Based on this information, you should now if the offer is appropriate. If you disagree with the amount, make a counter offer for the amount of pay you need. If they ask you to take the pay they're offering and they will review your progress after 90 days of probation for an increase, and this is acceptable to you, get it in writing.

After you agree with their offer, depending on the position and company, you may receive an offer letter that you must sign. This letter may have a few documents attached to possibly include an arbitration, non-compete, or confidentiality agreement.

The **arbitration agreement** requires that if you have a grievance with the employer and you wish to be compensated, that instead of going to court, you agree to go to arbitration and be heard by a mediator.

The **confidentially agreement** basically states that you will not share any confidential or proprietary information obtained while in the employ of the company.

The **non-compete agreement** states that you can't work for the same type employer within a certain radius/miles for a certain number of years.

Drug test

Some companies have a no tolerance policy and in order to be hired you must pass a drug test. You will either provide urine or hair. If the hair on your head isn't long enough, you will have to provide pubic hair.

Credit report

Depending on your job, your credit history may come into play. It is important to have good credit when in financial industries such as banking or credit. The company wants to know your probability for theft.

If you pass all the screenings, you will be given a start date. Be on time. Ask questions and don't be afraid to ask for help if you're unsure about something.

Quitting your job

Don't burn bridges. If for some reason you need to quit your job, I hope you've found a better one or have another means of income. Besides that, give a two-week notice. For the next two weeks, provide the same quality service, be on time, and keep your commitments.

A lot of employers are at-will employers meaning they can fire you at anytime without explanation and you can quit at anytime. Professional courtesy is to provide a notice even if it's only one week. If you ever wish to return to that company, you employee record will reflect positively.

PROPER DRESS, PROPER PLACE

Your first impression is supposed to be your best impression, so always give it your best shot!

When I first moved to Dallas, I attended several job fairs in pursuit of employment. One particular job fair stands out in my memory because I couldn't believe the attire of the people who were supposed to be dressed professionally. I saw a man in an electric blue suit and another with his clubbing clothing on and a female who wore the same. Flash certainly has its place, but when you're trying to make a statement, make the correct statement in the proper situation.

Sorry guys and gals, jeans everyday all day is over. Well, at least from 8 to 5 Corporate America time. Changing your wardrobe is one of the adjustments you make as you become an adult. You have to dress appropriately for each circumstance.

In society, people first perceive who you are, rather than what caliber of person you might be, based on your appearance. They will scrutinize you from head-to-toe to gather information and form an opinion. Whether acquaintances or potential employers offer the once-over, you should expect it.

You know it happens because you do it yourself. Think about the last time you saw an attractive young lady or guy; you sized them up and determined whether or not they were approachable or your type based on their appearance. Therefore, what do you think happens to you on a daily basis?

"What difference does it make?", you may ask. "I don't care about what people think about me or the way I dress." You will need to start caring if you want to get ahead in this world. There is a proper way of dressing for every place you go.

Let's cover *grooming* before further discussing clothing. Be sure you are always well-groomed. Shave; bathe; wash, cut, or curl your hair; and apply deodorant. Cologne or perfume is cool, but don't overdo it.

When you go to a party, wear whatever cool clothes you desire. But when you're in society taking care of business, **the following will help get you in the door:**

- Wear clean clothing, underwear, and socks that match.
- Shine your shoes. Men are constantly judged by their shoes. Are they clean, shined, run over? Take care of your shoes. They tell a lot about you. If you can't quite afford new ones, try a resale shop.
- Wear a tie.
- Iron your clothes. Remove the wrinkles and add a little starch to your dress shirt.
- Ladies, wear pantyhose and a skirt that ends below or immediately above your knees.
- Don't wear low-cut blouses.
- Apply your makeup lightly and wear a conservative hairdo.

Let's assume you walked into a place of business for a job interview with a wrinkled shirt smudged with dirt stains, a mustard-spattered tie, mismatched socks, pants with lint balls on them, and greasy, dirty hair. What type of impression would you be making? The employer is going to think, "if this is his best, then what is his worst?"

I AM AN ENTREPRENEUR

Without a plan, you plan to fail.

Willingness to work hard is a known trait among entrepreneurs. Even when they are tired and can't see the light ahead for the fog, they persevere. When the hours are long and there are no friends or family around who still believe in their dreams, their hope and undying faith gets them through the night. Then one day, they see the light. All the darkness fades away, their dream becomes a reality, and everything they went through to get to that point was worth it. That is the life of an entrepreneur.

"The critical ingredient is getting off your butt and doing something. It's as simple as that. A lot of people have ideas, but there are few who decide to do something about them now. Not tomorrow. Not next week. But today. The true entrepreneur is a doer, not a dreamer."
- Nolan Bushnell, founder of Atari and Chuck E. Cheese's

Entrepreneurs usually know who they are at a young age. Some are born with the inclination. Others become entrepreneurs due to circumstance or the pursuit of happiness. You have a desire to run things. You are a leader. You believe in your dreams passionately and are willing to take the necessary risks to make them happen. You dislike working for others or work better alone and you are determined to succeed.

If this is you, I must warn you that this is not the easiest path in life. You usually spend a large portion of your time gathering information through experience to make your business a success. You will experience ups and downs. You may even take five steps back to make one giant step forward. Faith in yourself is what will get you through.

To be a successful entrepreneur, you must gather information, apply what you have learned in the past, make a plan (without it you plan to fail), and proceed with caution.

Your business relationships are important. Never take on more than you can handle. Keep your word; it's all you have in this lifetime. Don't abuse your resources and don't burn your bridges.

As much as you may dislike working for others, it may be necessary to pay rent, to learn something you need to know, or just to maintain.

Always take care of your responsibilities first. Don't sacrifice your family's life (style) for your dreams. You don't want to wind up homeless or without your loved ones to share in your joy.

Take advantage of the innumerable resources available to you. Submerse yourself in every bit of information you can find relating to your endeavor. Push on until you see the light.

To find out if entrepreneurship is right for you, visit the Small Business Administration (SBA) web site and take the free entrepreneur training course at: http://www.sba.gov/training/entrepreneurship.html.

The SBA provides various types of loans for startup to established businesses. Some of the most popular loans are the micro loan, which is a small business loan that is guaranteed by the SBA for up to $150,000. The SBA offers a variety of financing options as part of their primary goal of stimulating growth of small businesses.

In addition to loans, the SBA is a great resource for education and other types of assistance. For more information, visit www.sba.gov.

SCORE

The SCORE offices are usually in the same offices as the SBA. These retired business owners volunteer their time to assist entrepreneurs with developing their businesses. They offer extensive knowledge of planning and execution.

Minority Business Development Centers

These centers offer assistance and guidance to small business owners. These centers can be located through the Small Business Administration web site: www.sba.gov.

Chamber of Commerce

Look in your local telephone book, conduct an internet search, or contact City Hall to locate your area Chamber of Commerce. This organization provides networking opportunities, demographics, and other helpful information about the community.

Community Colleges

Many community colleges offer continuing education classes on writing business plans, starting a business, or even specialized fields of study or interest. Specialized classes can be an asset to a budding entrepreneur.

Internal Revenue Service (www.irs.gov)

The IRS offers a CD-ROM, the "Small Business Resource Guide CD," which provides information for startup businesses. The IRS also provides the necessary information concerning business taxes.

Many entrepreneurs have succeeded without attending college or university. Though a higher education may not be necessary to succeed, don't rule it out. More knowledge and understanding concerning any new venture is always a plus. Depending on what type of business you're interested in, it may even be necessary.

It is always important to obtain as much information as possible and always have something to fall back on such as a skill or savings.

SELF-EMPLOYMENT

> *Always have a skill to fall back on.*

If you want independence, flexibility, and the ability to choose where you work, being self-employed or an independent contractor may be for you. The catch is to have a skill that is needed and knowing your craft very well.

It can be something as simple as cutting grass or washing windows. If you know your craft, you can solicit business and become self-employed. You must be dedicated and willing to work hard because you're actually in business for yourself. No one is going to hand you business on a platter. You have to hustle and get your name and a great reputation out there.

The benefits are:

- You set your own hours
- You do the work you desire to do
- Flexibility
- Tax write-offs

The drawbacks are:

- You have to solicit business (which can be difficult if you're a shy person or don't like sales)

- Depending on the type of work you do, you can have a fluctuation in income depending on the length of your contracts.

- You are responsible for paying all your benefits and taxes including social security, federal and state taxes, health insurance, and liability insurance, to name a few.

- Generally, people who desire to own their own business like working alone or on their own schedules, enjoy flexibility, have difficulty being micromanaged, and offer a skill that is needed. You must treat being self-employed as a business at all times to maintain a continuous income.

Business cycles

Everything in this world has a cycle. The cycle for business includes times when business is slow. Be sure to save so you have money to get you through these times and create a retirement plan for your future. In fact you may consider creating an additional stream of income so you will always have income.

TAKING RISKS

> *You never know your true abilites if you never take a risk.*

Part of being an entrepreneur involves taking risks. Taking risks involves having faith and regardless of the outcome, you're okay. Anyone can take a risk, be it a gambler at the blackjack table or a broker purchasing stocks. As an entrepreneur, you must be an intelligent risk taker by gathering as much information as possible before placing your bet. This way you minimize risk and your losses.

Let's suppose, for example, that you're interested in opening a new hamburger joint. On the same block are McDonald's and Burger King. To reach your potential place of business, the traffic must first pass the other establishments. Would it be a wise risk to open your business on this street or elsewhere with less competition?

In another example, you acquire the patent to an invention that there is clearly a need for. You've researched the market through opinion polls, focus groups, and marketing firms. The only catch is that you would need to invest every penny you have to make this venture happen. Would this be a wise investment?

Clearly, I would find a better location for the burger joint to have a better chance of establishing a profitable business with less competition. For the second venture, I would take the risk because the research indicates a favorable outcome.

Your goal as an entrepreneur should be to maximize your profits. Utilize all resources available to you. Do as much research as possible. Spend frugally and within your means. You can also read the chapters, "I'm an Entrepreneur" and "10 Things You Should Do When Starting a Business."

There will be times where you will have to take a chance and follow your instincts when others don't believe in you. There will be times when you're not so sure of yourself but you have a hunch. **Whatever the reason** you decide to take a risk, learn about being in business and obtain all necessary information before signing that check or contract.

When starting a business, remember to gather as much information as possible. Don't rush or allow anyone to rush you into making a decision, and always maximize your profits.

10 THINGS YOU SHOULD DO WHEN STARTING A BUSINESS

Stick to your business plan!

Lots of people jump up and start businesses without an ounce of planning. These are the businesses that will more than likely fail. Below are some steps to get you on your way. As a future business owner, you can never gather too much information. Below is a list of ten things that I know are important when starting a business. (Do not limit yourself to this list).

1. *List your reasons for wanting to start a business.*

2. *Determine which business is best for you.*

Is there a need for your business? If so, why? What are you interested in? What are your hobbies? What would you like to improve? How much time are you willing to invest?

3. *Research your market.*

Visit the library and get on the Internet. Some libraries have books that will guide you through the complete setup of a particular business. How are other businesses doing? Who is your competition? What is going to set you apart from your competitors? Is there a demand for your business or can you create one?

4. *Strengthen your reasons listed.*

Once you have answered the three previous questions, continue by summarizing each answer and adding information such as:

- What service(s) or product(s) will you offer?
- What is the name of your business? Is it available?
- What skills do you have or need to learn to run the business?
- What equipment or supplies do you need?
- What are your resources and how will you fund the business?

5. *What will be the legal ownership status of the business?*

Will you operate as a sole proprietor, a corporation, or form a partnership? As a sole proprietor, you own the business. As a corporation, you must have a board of directors, and you can be the CEO and founder. Establishing a corporation relieves you from being personally liable for lawsuits or other legal matters concerning the corporation. The business is an entity responsible for itself. Before establishing a corporation, get a clear understanding of your responsibilities. A partnership consists of you and whomever you decide to partner with. You can have equal shares of ownership or less depending on each partner's investment.

6. *Develop a business plan.*

There are many guides available on how to do this at the library, bookstores, and on the Internet. The SBA provides a guide on their web site at www.sba.gov. Your business plan is critical as it will be your guide on how you will operate your business, obtain financing and meet your financial goals.

7. *Check your credit.*

To obtain financing, you must have a decent credit score. If you have delinquent or closed accounts, charge-offs, judgments, or any other bad debt, you will first need to clean it up. See "Credit Repair".

8. *Financing.*

With a complete business plan and good credit, you can now work on financing. The government offers several ways to obtain financing. See

"Entrepreneurship" and the reference section.

9. *Establish a banking relationship by opening a business banking account.*

Find a bank with minimal or no fees if yours is a small business. Keep you account in good shape by having minimal to no overdraft or non-sufficient funds occurrences. Use this account for business transactions only. Keep business and personal transactions separate.

Once you've developed a relationship with your suppliers, you may want to establish a business credit report through Dunn & Bradstreet. D&B is the business credit-reporting agency. You obtain a D&B number free but if you're interested in establishing a credit history, you must pay a fee and send them three good credit references. Having this credit profile will allow you to establish business credit in the same manner as personal credit.

10. Find your location, move in, set up telephone lines, review your business plan and get to work.

Finances

FINANCES INTRODUCTION

Let not the love of money but the love of mankind be your motivation to prosper.

As a young adult, learning and having financial discipline are two of your biggest lessons. With adulthood comes responsibility.

When I first made a substantial income for my age, I had no clue about the importance of saving, investment tools, the proper use of credit, or making my money work for me. I gave money away, spent it on others and myself, and really didn't have anything to show for it. I had moved out of my mom's home and got my own place and my own credit cards. I already had a car, so I was on my way.

I was good about paying my bills until I lost my job. Creditors called demanding money I didn't have. I really hadn't thought about the repercussions of not saving, spending money and maxing out my credit cards. I tried to make payment arrangements with the creditors and collection agencies, but how could I keep the arrangements when I didn't have any money? Therefore, I blew them off and had to deal with having bad credit for the next seven years.

I was inexperienced. I didn't have a clue about paying off debts, making agreements to remove negative files from my credit report, or the leverage

341

I had because the creditors wanted something from me – money.

It's common for young adults to spend money and enjoy a carefree life. It's also common for them to create debt, mismanage money, have nothing to fall back on in an emergency, and ruin their credit.

If you don't grasp anything else in this book, grasp the financial information. It will give you an invaluable head start. While your peers are complaining about how they don't have money to make it through the week, you can sail through. You can be ahead of the game by doing what is expected of an older adult. **Set yourself up so that you have something to fall back on, your money is working for you, and use credit responsibly.**

TIPS FOR FINANCIAL STABILITY

> *Stablilty is as stability does.*

Financial stability is obtained through research, work, discipline, and determination. Stability is having adequate finances to suit your living style as well as resources to accommodate unexpected occurrences. With stability, you gain freedom from financial stress and worry.

Use these rules to create financial stability and to assist you in keeping your money safe:

- *Pay yourself first.*

Deposit a predetermined amount of money in your savings account, mutual fund, CD or 401k. The standard is 10% of your earnings. If you are able to save more, save more! If you can't afford 10%, then do what you can. Just save consistently so that it becomes a habit.

- *Never allow anyone to access your accounts.*

If you do, you open yourself up to theft, fraud, and damaged credit.

- *Never spend above your means.*

Credit is a great tool when used properly. Instead of using credit to create debt, use it to build your ability to borrow. Don't create excessive debt for yourself. The funny thing about credit is that if it looks like you don't need it, they will give you more. Try not to use more than fifty percent of your credit line. When paying your bills, pay them off as soon as possible. Low minimum payments on credit cards allow finance companies to maximize their profits on a small investment.

- *Choose your bank, credit cards, and investment tools wisely.*

Read the fine print and ask questions if you don't understand. Pay attention to fees, interest rates, and penalties. In some aspects, no debt is good, but it's a Catch 22. Your credit rating is based on your management of debt and how you repay it.

- *Pay your bills on time.*

Credit bureaus are in the business of collecting and selling information about you. Whether you do or don't pay your bills on time is recorded on your credit report. This can help or hinder you in the future.

- *If you ever have a situation where you can't pay your bills, call the creditor and make arrangements.*

Communication will help keep your account in good standing. Creditors will help you because they have everything to gain—your money! They will sometimes reduce your interest rate, allow you to skip payments, or renegotiate your payment terms. Don't be afraid of them; you have the power.

- *Look into creating passive income; money you have coming in with a minimal amount of work required.*

One way of creating passive income is by investing in real estate.

Take financial management seriously. If you start early, you will be ahead of many people and on your way to a financially stable life.

BUDGETING

Following a budget reduces stress and worry.

Budgeting entails allocating money for expenses, savings, and investments. Often we spend money impulsively and when it's all gone or time to pay a bill, we're left trying to figure out where it all went or how the bills are going to get paid. Budgeting helps you to identify where you spend your money and how much you spend.

By budgeting, you can:

*   Stop overspending
*   Save money
*   Realize your investment potential and act on it
*   Appropriate funds more accurately

Planning your budget

Write down each mandatory expense such as rent, lights, gas, phone, food, and car note. Calculating this will tell you the bare minimum income you need.

Continue by listing other expenses such as laundry, credit cards, miscellaneous household, etc. These bills will fluctuate but should average the same amount each month. Total all the expenses and this will tell you what you need to make to maintain your current lifestyle.

Subtract the total of your bills from your total monthly income. Does your budget exceed your income? If so, adjust the amount you spend on unnecessary expenses. If there isn't any room for adjustment, you need to revamp your spending. You are living above your means and you will not get ahead this way.

If your expenses don't exceed your income, is the balance ten percent or more? If not, try to adjust your expenses that aren't mandatory so that you can have some money to save and/or invest. **When you do have ten percent or more left over, you have the following opportunities:**

- Save for a financial cushion
- Save with a specific goal in mind such as a vacation
- Investing
- Look into CD's, mutual funds, etc.
- Building your credit

Building your credit is a good option if you're trying to develop or repair your credit history. You can get a secured Visa or MasterCard, a line of credit, or a secured loan.

With either of these options, you will be depositing money into a savings account and borrowing money against it. You will have to make timely monthly payments, which will be reported to the credit bureaus, thus establishing a credit history.

Don't think you need a budget? At some point in everyone's life they experience financial problems. Budgeting helps you to prepare for those occurrences in the future. Save money to reduce stress in the future. Financial worries are stressful and affect your overall happiness.

Not sure about where your money goes? Track your spending habits for a week. Write down each and every purchase you make daily. After the week has passed, review how much money you actually spent. Were all the little purchases necessary? How much money could you have saved by taking your lunch for a few days? How much money could you have tucked away for emergencies?

Planning a budget is one thing but following it is another. By following your budget, you know how much money you need to make and how it will be spent. A good way to motivate yourself is to set a goal, reach it, and treat yourself.

For example, let's say your first goal is to save $1,000. When you reach your goal, you can treat yourself to a new dress or a pair of basketball shoes. It's a mental game, but you know what will motivate you. Eventually it will become a habit to budget and save. Financial stability is the real reward.

There are many personal accounting programs available such as MS Money or Quicken. These programs will help track your expenses, spending habits, plan for your future, assist with investing and allow you to download your banking and credit card information from the financial institutions web site.

WELFARE

> *Crutches are temporary and meant to be used only when necessary.*

Government assistance, welfare, public aid, public assistance, first of the month check, is all the same; food stamps and money the government gives as a temporary crutch until you are able to do better.

There have been times in my life that I needed public assistance to supplement my income. I wasn't making enough money to support my family so I received assistance.

This was always a blow to my pride but as a parent you have to do what you have to do to make sure you take care of your family. As soon as I was able, I'd let go of the assistance and go back to supporting my family the way I always had.

I remember as a teen visiting the Chicago housing projects with a friend. A lot of her friends lived in the projects. This was new to me. I heard young girls around my age talking about getting their own place (in the projects), getting a check and having babies. An aid check was a few hundred dollars a month but that's a lot when your rent is twenty eight dollars and you have food stamps. This was their reality, how life worked and their natural progression.

Their grandmother and mother lived in the projects so they would do the same. They were never told this ain't it. Welfare is meant to be temporary until you do better. It is not meant to be a way of life.

Because people don't understand this, they are afraid to give it up. I would challenge any one of you that are in this situation to dig a little deeper. Public assistance doesn't stop at food stamps and the meager amount of cash they provide. They also offer job training, skills training, school assistance, childcare assistance, etc., the opportunity for you to do better and let go of this limited way of life. What is $300 a month when you can have $3,000 a month? You can have a vehicle that isn't different colors and is actually dependable. You can have an apartment or home with clean well lit hallways and you don't have to be afraid of your neighbors or gang violence.

Remember I told you that you always have a choice in life? If your current reality doesn't make your heart sing, choose again.

I understand everyone has hardship. When that hardship is over, release everything associated with it, including the government assistance.

Remember, when you know better, you have the opportunity to do better.

CHECKING ACCOUNTS

Each time you write a check you are promising to pay. Don't make promises you can't keep.

I opened my first checking account after being solicited by a bank. A representative called and we set up the account over the phone. I knew that I could write checks to make payments; however, I also learned to play "beat the check" as well. I didn't win very often and, coupled with the fact that I let my boyfriend use my ATM card; my account didn't last very long. That was my experience. I had no knowledge about the do's and don'ts, so I did the don'ts.

How a checking account works

Having a checking account allows you to write checks, which serve as a "promise to pay." Once you write a check, the debtor presents it to your bank to cash it. The bank accesses your account for the funds (the amount you have written the check for) to cash the check. If the funds are available, the bank deducts the amount of the check from your account and pays your debt to the debtor. That is essentially how a checking account works.

Benefits of Having a Checking Account

* Build a relationship with your bank

- The ability to make purchases without carrying cash by having a Visa or MasterCard debit card or an ATM card

- A safe place to keep your money

- You can write checks for payments instead of purchasing money orders

- Depending on the type of account you have you can utilize privileges the bank offers

- Direct deposit of funds to your account

- Bill payment, Internet banking options and other benefits depending on your bank

Proper use of checking tools

Write checks when you have the funds available. Avoid playing "beat the check." If you must, however, keep in mind that checks usually clear a bank in two days.

Use the memo section of the check to note your reason for writing the check. This can come in handy when dealing with legal or tax issues or anytime you need to reference a payment.

ATM cards (Automatic Teller Machine) are used to access your account. You may use your ATM (Automatic Teller Machine) card to withdraw cash from an ATM.

Debit/credit cards are used to make purchases and to access your account. Using the debit option, money is deducted from your account immediately. Using credit allows you a day or two before the money is removed from your account. Purchases made with these cards are called POS or point-of-sale transactions. These options have been implemented to reduce business expenses and loss of profits due to bouncing checks.

Special Note: In 2004, banks implemented a new program for checking where as soon as you make a purchase by writing a check, the funds are immediately withdrawn from your account. This reduces fraud and NSF check collections for businesses.

The "beat the check" game doesn't work when making purchases at establishments that are making use of this program. So if you have a checking account, write a check and it is declined, this is probably the reason.

Safety rules to apply:

- Any account that is a monetary instrument should be safeguarded.

- Guard your checkbook like cash. Protect it so it is not stolen or misused.

- Do not allow anyone to use your ATM or debit card, not even your boyfriend or girlfriend.

- Do not leave your PIN (personal identification numbers) accessible or with the debit or credit cards that they are associated with.

- Protect your debit cards even more diligently because they are tied into your checking account. If the card is stolen, the thief will not be spending a credit card company's money; it will be yours.

- Do not write checks for which you know you don't have funds available. This will cause your account to become a NSF account (non-sufficient funds), which will not look good to your bank if this is a repeated occurrence. This can cause your account to be closed. At the minimum, your bank and the company to whom you wrote the check will charge you NSF fees.

- Always balance your checkbook by recording each transaction you make. This includes deposits, withdrawals, transfers, purchases, automatic debits and electronic payments.

Consequences of neglect or abuse

Bounced checks (checks that don't clear your account due to non-sufficient funds) and accounts closed by financial institutions can leave you with a negative banking history.

Banks subscribe to credit reporting agencies such as Chexsystems or Telecheck. These agencies operate in the same way as the "Big Three" agencies (Equifax, Experian, and TransUnion). The only difference is that their clients are financial institutions, banks or credit unions. Chexsystems,

Telecheck, and similar agencies will report any activity you have with a financial institution (such as bounced checks or closed accounts) and retain the information for up to seven years unless asked to remove the information by their client or the information is false.

Some retail businesses subscribe to their service as well to verify that you have a positive standing. Using a check verification machine, businesses verify that your check "is good." This protects them from having to deal with NSF checks and collections. If you've bounced checks before, your check may be rejected.

When you bounce a check, you and the person or business to which you wrote the check is charged a fee by your financial institution. In turn, businesses will charge you a fee for a returned check to offset the fee they were charged.

To avoid any negative situations with your account, avoid making purchases you don't have the money to cover.

Balancing your checkbook

- Record every transaction including checks written, deposits, debit and credit purchases, transfers, electronic payments, automatic debits, ATM withdrawals, deposits, and banking fees.

- If you're a forgetful person, purchase the checks that make a duplicate for your records. Keep receipts for easy reconciliation.

- Add deposits and subtract purchases or withdrawals.

Reconciling your checking account

- Reconciliation is checking your statement against your check register to verify each cleared and outstanding transactions.

- In your check register, mark all the transactions that have cleared your account with a checkmark.

- List the checks that do not appear on your statement on the register balance sheet on the back of your statement.

- Finally, subtract any deposits that haven't cleared your account and the ending balance should match your statement.

TRANS. TYPE/ CHECK NO.	DATE	DESCRIPTION OF TRANSACTION	PAYMENT/ DEBIT (-)		FEE (-) (IF ANY)	DEPOSIT/ CREDIT (+)		$ BALANCE	
Deposit	1/2	Deposit				600	00	600	00
411	1/10	Groceries	55	00				645	00
Debit	1/11	Office supplies	40	00				605	00
ATM	1/14	TM Gas	100	00				505	00
Deposit	1/18	Deposit				200	00	705	00
Transfer	1/22	Transfer to savings	100	00				605	00
412	1/22	Voided check						605	00
413	1/22	Light bill	60	00				545	00
414	2/01	Rent	400	00				145	00
Pos	2/05	Shoe store	40	00				105	00
Auto Debit	2/06	Internet	20	00				85	00

The fee column can be used to check off payments that have cleared.

A Second Chance

If you have a negative report with a reporting agency, don't give up! If you feel the information they have on file is inaccurate, ask the agency to verify it. If the information is correct, you can explain your side of the story. The agency will take a statement from you and include it in your report.

There are banks that offer second chance banking for people who have problems opening accounts at other financial institutions. These banks will allow you to open an account without checking your banking history. Their rates are usually higher, but it's an opportunity for you to establish a good banking relationship. Inquire with some of the local banks.

To obtain your report:

Chexsystems 800-513-7125 or 800-428-9623 www.chexhelp.com

Telecheck 1-800-Telecheck www.telecheck.com

Check Rite 800-766-2748

SCAN 800-262-7771

Equifax 888-832-0179

SAVINGS ACCOUNTS

Prepare yourself for that rainy day.

A paycheck away from being homeless is where millions of people are. If they lost their job tomorrow, they wouldn't have any money to fall back on. A lot of people do this because they just don't see where they have money to save; all they see are the bills they have to pay. It could be that they were never taught to save. In any case, savings accounts should be viewed as a bill as well.

Everyone has unexpected emergencies such as illness, layoff, car repairs, home damage, travel, or medical expenses. Saving provides financial cushioning. You have the comfort of knowing you have additional money available in case of an emergency, while your money is earning interest.

Choosing a savings tool

To begin saving, shop the banks or credit unions that you're able to join. When looking for a savings account, remember that the idea is to save money, so try to avoid paying extra fees for your account. Inquire about requirements, service fees, penalties, and interest rates. Some banks and credit unions require as little as one dollar to open a savings account.

Regular savings accounts are good if you don't mind the low return.

They are safe and usually insured by the government (FDIC) for up to $100,000. This is a good starting place to hold your money.

If you want your money to work for you and increase steadily, don't put your money under the mattress or leave it in a low interest-bearing account. Consult a financial planner and invest. You have several options such as mutual funds, CD's (certificate of deposit), and stock. Choose investments that are safe and will yield a higher return than the average savings account.

Open your account and pay yourself first! The norm is ten percent of your earnings. If you have a tight budget and can't do ten percent right now, set an amount you can stick with and when ten percent is not a problem, commit to it. If you can save more, save more.

You can also save with a specific goal in mind. In addition to your regular savings account, you can open additional accounts for vacations, school, retirement, down payment for a new house, etc. It's up to you.

Some credit unions and banks will offer special savings accounts for the holidays or family vacations. It is usually an opportunity to earn a decent interest rate on a short-term account. Always ask about these options.

Tips on saving

- If you're having trouble making a commitment, try this: Get a big container and at the end of each day, put your change in it. I know people who have saved hundreds and even thousands of dollars this way.

- Ride the bus or train to work. You can save on gas, time in traffic, and you gain some time for reading.

- Take your lunch to work a few days per week.

- Rent movies instead of going to the movie theatre.

- Try generic brands of foods vs. name brand. Some are equivalent or better.

The key to saving is to not touch it. Stick to it and you'll be prepared for that rainy day.

CREDIT UNION

Never limit yourself when deciding on a financial institution.

A credit union is a non-profit member-owned cooperative, which offers many of the services that a bank does.

To access the services of a credit union, you usually have to be affiliated with an organization, employer, or community that is a credit union sponsor. If someone in your immediate family is a member of a credit union, you can usually join as well.

Credit union accounts and banks function the same but have different names. A checking account is called a share draft account. A saving account is called a share account.

The benefits of establishing accounts with a credit union are:

- They usually have lower costs for banking services
- A higher yield on savings accounts and CD's
- More personalized service because they're usually smaller than commercial banks
- Transactions fees are lower, including specialty transactions such as wire transfers

- Fees and minimum balances are lower than local banks.

- To continue providing competitive service, many credit unions now offer ATM cards, credit cards, and debit cards.

- Credit unions provide a better opportunity to get a loan. They usually offer loans for cars, homes, education, holidays, and vacation.

- When choosing a credit union, be sure to choose one that is federally insured. Look for NCUA (National Credit Union Association), which will assure your deposits up to $100,000 per account.

To find a credit union in your area that you may be eligible to join, call the National Credit Union Association at 1-800-937-2644.

PARTS OF A CHECK

Educate yourself on all things that can affect your pocket.

1. The payor – person or company issuing the check

2. Check number

3. Date

4. The amount of the check in numbers

5. The Payee – the person or company the check is made payable to

6. The amount of the check in words- must match the dollar amount

7. Memo section – used to make a note as to why the check was issued

8. Payor signature or authorized signature

9. Check cashing deadline – states that you have that many days from the issue date to cash it. If that date passes, the check will be void.

10. Check number in MICR – MICR is Magnetic Ink Character Recognition. The magnetic ink and the special check characters

are used so checks validity can be verified and also read by various check reading machines.

11. Routing and checking account number in MICR

12. Endorsement area- is three lines on the backside of the check for you to endorse or sign the check when you are cashing or depositing. If you are depositing the check, put your account number on it. Never sign a check until you are ready to cash it. If you lose the check and have already endorsed it, anyone can cash it. Yes this will be against the law, but you have endorsed it which is signing the check over.

13. Watermark- is an identifying image or wording on the check that is viewable at an angle. This is used to protect the check issuer. Watermarks help verify authenticity.

Check stub

If you have a paycheck, you will have a check stub as well which will list the following:

- Gross Pay – your pay before any deductions

- Net pay – your pay after deductions are taken

- Hours worked

- Pay rate – your hourly or salary rate

- Deductions – can be your insurance or other deductions you've opted

- Taxes

- FED Withholding – taxes paid to the government to support the government's initiatives

- State Tax – state tax that support you state's initiatives

- Medicare – monies paid toward Medicare which is health insurance for the elderly

- OASDI – is the tax paid to social security for elderly retirees and disabled persons

ABC Company (1)
123 Main Street
Anywhere, TX 70555

(3) _____ Date

1211 (2)

Pay to the (5) John Doe _____ $ (4) 100.00
Order of

(6) One hundred dollars and no/100 _____

The Best Bank
1111 Main Street
Anywhere, TX 75000

Cash within 90 days (9)

Memo (7) _____   (10) (8) *Mary Smith*

⑆111222332⑆0013456799   1211

- YTD – year to date- will list your year to date totals for each detailed tax or deduction

For each check you receive, make sure this information is correct:

1. Your name is spelled correctly

2. Hours worked

3. Pay rate

4. Deductions

5. Taxes

If you find any discrepancies, either make a copy of your check, highlight the information, and note on the check or write them down and speak with your manager.

Cashing your check

You have a couple of options. The first option is to deposit the check into your checking or savings account. If you don't have one, now would be a good time to start one. You can avoid check cashing fees by depositing your check into your bank account. If you decide to open a bank account with your check, you may want to ask if they will put a hold on the check. A hold is when a bank does not make the funds available for a certain amount of days. Banks sometimes do this to verify your information and the validity of the check before they release funds. Once your account is established you will be able to cash your check at the bank without a hold or check cashing fees.

Check cashing business/Currency Exchange

Your second option is to use a check-casher or currency exchange. These companies are in the business of cashing checks for a fee. The fee is a percentage of the amount of your check. If the check is a manual or handwritten check they will call to verify the check before cashing. You can also pay certain bills and buy stamps or other products at these locations.

PREPAID VISA OR MASTERCARD

Prepaid means there is a fee. Educate yourself before "prepaying."

Having credit cards gives you the ability to rent cars, pay your bills online and more.

A prepaid credit card allows you to deposit money into an account and use the card to make credit transactions based on the amount of money you have deposited. There is often a fee associated for the use of the card and/or each transaction. You are paying a company for the ability to make credit card transactions or to have access to your money. Is this something you really want to do?

If you need a credit card, establish a bank account and request a Visa or MasterCard debit card. It works the same way as a prepaid card minus fees. If you have good credit, you may qualify for a credit card as well.

If your credit is bad, you can also apply for a secured credit card which will require your depositing money into a savings account that is controlled by the credit card company. This company is called a secured card because the money in the savings account secures the line of credit extended to you. If your security deposit is two hundred dollars, your line of credit will be the same. If you charge you credit card to the limit and for some reason the account becomes delinquent, the credit card company will apply the money from the savings account to your bill and close you credit card account.

A secured card will allow you to build your credit. You credit score increases as you pay your bills on time and remain below your limit. It's best to keep your balance lower than fifty percent of your credit limit. You will pay a finance fee if you don't pay your credit card in full before your billing cycle ends.

Read all agreements that you sign, so as to not be surprised by hidden fees. **Always try to keep as much of your money as possible.**

PAY DAY/TITLE LOANS

> *Be wise in your financial matters.*

Avoid payday and title loans like the plague. This is the absolute worst type of loan to have. Payday and title loans work the same way except the title loans give you a longer time to pay off the debt and the payments are in installments.

A payday loan is a loan that requires you to sign an extensive contract stating that by your accepting x amount of funds, you will, on your next payday, pay the loan, which is the money you borrowed, with interest, which can be as high as 800%. The loan is secured by your writing a check or checks to the loan company.

When you get paid, you are expected to return to the loan office and pay the amount you wrote the checks for. They will in turn stamp you contract paid and give it to you along with your checks. If you don't return, they will call and call asking when you're coming in to pay the debt. If you don't return, they will deposit your checks. If they clear the bank, you're all good. If not, here's where the issues begin.

Let's say you borrowed $100 and you don't have the money you borrowed and you return to the office to make a payment. The interest requires you to pay $20 per $100 that you borrow so you owe $120.00. You refinance or rollover the loan which requires you to pay interest on top of the interest you already have to pay.

Twenty dollars is not a lot of money with a simple example of $100. What if you borrow $400 with $80 interest for two weeks? You don't have all the money so you refinance a portion of it. They lender will only require you to pay the interest that will accumulate as if you are financing $480. So you still owe the $480. If you didn't have the $400 in the first place, and you couldn't pay the $480, what makes you think you can afford to continue refinancing the loan? This is how you will continue to dig yourself deeper and deeper into debt.

Here are some tips in case you are ever in a situation where you've exhausted your resources, such as asking family or friends for help, applying for a short-term loan at your bank, tapping into your savings, or using government assistance and a payday loan is your only out.

You are signing a contract. You have 72 hours to change your mind and not pay interest. Let's say you need $100 to pay a bill by Monday but you know you'll have the money on Wednesday. Avoid paying interest by borrowing the money on Monday and paying it back on Wednesday before the exact time you took out the loan on Monday.

When you go to payoff the loan, I don't care how many times they ask if you'd like to refinance the loan or do you want another loan, **pay it off and do not get another one.**

Look for a special where they aren't charging interest on your first loan. Take advantage of it, pay the loan and don't go back.

Never ever get a loan for someone else and expect them to pay it back. There was a guy I heard about that had multiple girlfriends that he coaxed into getting loans for him that he never paid. If you don't pay the loans, this will affect your credit, not theirs.

If you know you're going to pay the loan but don't have it on the due date, call the lender and tell them when you will have it. If you don't have the money in your checking account, the lender will hold your check, you don't have to refinance, and you've extended the amount of time you have to pay the loan. This will only work for a few days. Do not go in and refinance the loan.

Another thing to be aware of; if you don't go back to pay the loan, the company will deposit your check. If it is rejected due to non-sufficient funds, you'll incur bank charges. The company is smart. They know they can only deposit a check up to three times. If the check is returned for non-sufficient funds, you and the lender will incur bank fees. The lender will transfer their fees to you. After one to three attempts to cash your check, the lender will then turn the check into an electronic debit. The lender is no limited to the amount of times they can hit your account.

A title loan is a loan that requires you to use your vehicle as collateral. The interest rates for these loans are as high as 300%. The loan is usually for half the resale value of the vehicle. The lender may or may not take possession of your vehicle during the course of the loan. An alternative for them not possessing the vehicle is to install a GPS device so they are able to locate the vehicle if you default on the loan.

If you default on the loan and still have a car note, you will owe your original finance company and the lender for the title loan. In some instances, the title loan company will auction your vehicle or sell it for the amount owed and you will still have to pay your original finance company.

Every financial tool has its place, time and season. Be extremely careful, especially when dealing in pay day or title loans.

AVOID THE CREDIT CARD TRAP

Remember, what you choose today will affect you for the rest of your life.

Credit is a loan extended to you that has to be repaid. It is not free money. Always be aware of your limit, due date, grace period (the length of time your purchases are free from interest charges) and APR.

The credit card trap is most often related to college students and credit, but is actually relevant to everyone. The trapping begins when you receive one card, establish a good history and suddenly you're bombarded with pre-approved credit cards and offers from numerous companies. The trap occurs when you accept the credit offers and run up your balances. You wind up with debt that you can't possibly maintain and the juggling starts. You rob from Peter to pay Paul, meaning you pay one credit card bill only to use the now available funds to pay another bill and so on.

The stress isn't worth it. Avoid the trap by acquiring only a few cards; designate their use. Try to limit charging to ten percent or less of your monthly income and pay that off when you get the bill. Don't spend unreasonably to keep up with the Jones'. You have choices.

CREDIT REPORTING AGENCIES

When it comes to credit, someone is always watching.

Credit reporting agencies are companies that make money by collecting and supplying information about you such as:

1. Your name, social security number, address, marital status

2. What credit cards you own, loans you have

3. Length of employment

4. Your payment history (how you pay your bills)

5. Inquiries from companies who have considered granting you credit

6. Information from public records such as court cases, liens, judgments, or bankruptcy

7. This information is sold to various companies from whom you wish to borrow or with whom you want to establish credit.

There are three (3) major credit-reporting agencies. The smaller bureaus usually purchase their information from one of the three larger bureaus. The major credit reporting agencies are TransUnion, Equifax, and Experian.

Equifax www.equifax.com
P.O. Box 740241, Atlanta, GA 30374-0241
1-800-685-1111

Experian (formerly TRW) www.experian.com
P.O. Box 949, Allen, TX 75013-0949
1-888-EXPERIAN (397-3742)

TransUnion www.tuc.com
P.O. Box 390, Springfield, PA 19064-0390
1-800-916-8800

Credit reporting agencies and wrong information

Credit reporting agencies are not exempt from making mistakes and reporting wrong information. In the case of similar identities, such as same name and birth date, information often winds up on the wrong report.

Based on this information, it is wise to review your credit report at least twice a year to check for inaccuracies. If you apply for credit and are denied, you are able to receive a free report. Request the report from the agency that supplied your credit information within 30 days after being denied. If you find information in error, dispute it. See the Credit Repair section for more information.

Take advantage of the free annual credit report by visiting the site:

www.annualcreditreport.com.

CREDIT REPORTS

Always take the opportunity to review the information gathered concerning your credit worthiness.

Your credit report is established the first time you apply for credit. The information you supply on the credit application is used to do a query. The credit reporting agency's computer does a search to match identifying information such as your name, address, and date of birth to their existing database. When the information doesn't match any of the existing records, a credit report is created based on the information you have supplied. This begins your credit history.

Receive a free credit report

You are able to receive a free report from each of the three major bureaus by visiting www.annualcreditreport.com

You can also receive a free report if you:

1. Have applied for credit or employment and have been denied based on the information supplied in a report generated within the last 30 days

2. Are unemployed

3. Are currently receiving government assistance

4. Live in doesn't allow the credit agency to charge for the report

If none of the above circumstances apply to you, purchase a report by contacting the agency and mailing the fee or by visiting their web site. The fee usually ranges from seven to nine dollars.

What in the world is a credit rating and who gives a hoot?

CREDIT SCORE/ RATING

Try to stay below 50% of your credit limit.

It was never explained to me what a credit rating was and I really didn't care because I didn't know it existed. I just thought I was "all that" because I had credit cards. Then one day I lost my job and couldn't pay my bills. I began receiving collection letters saying that nonpayment would adversely affect my credit rating. Still, I thought, "No big deal," not knowing the "adverse" information would remain on my credit report for seven years. I figured that I wasn't going to stress myself over something that at the moment I could not fix. When I finally got on my feet again, I applied for credit again and was denied. I was told that I would get a letter in the mail from the credit bureau that supplied the information concerning my credit history. This is how I learned about credit ratings.

A credit rating is a score given to you based on your credit history, which is derived from information that you and creditors supply about you. The scores may be called FICO or Beacon or Vantage score.

In an effort to more consistently *grade* a person's credit score across the board, the three major credit reporting bureaus recently developed something called a Vantage score. The bureaus use the same scoring system but do not guarantee the same score due to differences in the amount of information that each bureau may have on a person. The system grades credit with a range from A-F.

Your credit history includes and you are graded on:

- Bill payment history

- Your creditors

- Credit inquiries (what companies have looked at your report because you've applied for credit)

- Any bills that have gone to collection agencies

- Your high and low credit limits

- Residency

- Employment history

- Public record information such as bankruptcies, liens, or judgments

Your score is also based on:

- Debt management – the types of debts you have—revolving, installment, retail. Credit cards like Visa, MasterCard, Discover, or American Express are better debt to have than retail store cards.

- Stability of career and residency – have you moved and changed jobs a lot.

- The number of credit inquiries you have. Credit inquiries stay on your report for two years from the date they appear. They can work against you if you have too many in a short period.

A credit grantor will decide whether you are a credit risk or not based upon this information. If you are deemed a credit risk, you are considered someone who may not pay back the credit a company has extended. Therefore, for the company to issue credit to you, they would be taking a risk. Each company has its own scoring criteria. One company may be more concerned with how you pay your retail debt and how long you've had the accounts while another company may be concerned with whether or not you've had a bankruptcy.

To view your credit report and learn about your credit rating, you can order a credit report from all or just one of the three major credit-reporting agencies. Included with your credit report will be an explanation of how to read the report and how to correct any inaccurate information. For more information about correcting inaccurate information or credit repair, please see the Credit Repair section.

CREDIT REPAIR

Be cautious when paying for something you can do yourself.

If you ever need to repair your credit, I recommend your working on it before paying someone. Credit repair is not as difficult as it may seem. It takes time and patience, which is something you should be willing to have when receiving a second chance.

If you want to repair your credit, first you need to order copies of your credit report from the three major credit-reporting agencies. Their contact information is listed under "Credit Reporting Agencies."

Review each credit report one at a time for any negative entries, delinquencies, charge-offs, liens, and any inaccurate information such as amounts owed, wrong account, or not your account at all. Check your personal information for inaccuracies in your birth date, the spelling of your name, and addresses. Lastly, check for inquiries by companies that you did not authorize.

Make a list. Under the heading, "Personal Information Inaccuracies," include all inaccuracies with your name, address, social security number, birth date, spouse's name or employer.

Under the heading, "Possible Credit History Inaccuracies," include every negative entry on your report. Dispute the true inaccuracies first. If you disagree with the amount or validity of any entry, dispute that as well. On this particular list, which you are using strictly for ease of reference at this time, create one column that lists your last payment date and another column that lists what year the debt is to be erased from your account. Highlight the oldest debts. You will dispute these first. If you have ten negative entries, you may want to dispute three to five this time and the balance next time. Be reasonable, if the debt is five months old you certainly don't want to dispute that one just yet. Save it for last.

Under the heading, "Inquiry Inaccuracies," list all the companies who have requested your report that you didn't authorize. You can either dispute inaccuracies on the Internet at the agency's web site or by writing a letter. If disputing online, you can check progress and it eliminates the curiosity that comes with waiting. Be mindful that your choices for dispute reasons and the space in which you can type information are limited.

Do not use the form the company sent you. Write a letter including a reference to the report or file number referenced on your credit report, list your social security number, current address, and birth date so the company is able to identify you. I've learned that letters that don't include identifying information are pushed aside.

Credit reporting agencies have thirty days in which to investigate disputed information. If within those thirty days the agency can't verify the disputed information, it must be removed. The agency will send you an updated report as well as the lenders who have requested your report within the past six months.

Your initial letter should be similar to this:

January 1, 2009

Jane Doe
1111 Mulberry Lane
Detroit, Michigan 12345

Experian
P.O. Box 949
Allen, TX 75013-0949

In reference to Jane Done, credit file/ report # 3334405412
Social Security Number: 111-11-1111
Birth date: 01-02-56
Current Address: see above
Previous address: list your previous address here if you have moved recently, also include a copy of a utility bill and your social security card as identifying information.

To whom it may concern:
After reviewing my credit report, I have located several inaccuracies. Please investigate and correct them within the 30 days allotted to you by the Fair Credit Reporting Act and send me an updated report with the inaccuracies removed to my current address.

"Personal Information Inaccuracies"
Social Security Number: 112-11-1111 (please list my correct number and remove this inaccuracy)

"Credit History Inaccuracies"
ABC Department Store
John's Telephone Service
Gulf Credit Collections

"Inquiry Inaccuracies" (I did not authorize these inquiries)
Ski Gold Credit
Best Bank

Thank you,
Jane Doe

ALWAYS KEEP A COPY OF THE LETTERS YOU MAIL.

This is the first letter you will send by certified mail. After receiving your letter, the company will usually send an acknowledgment letter. If you haven't heard from the credit reporting agency within fifteen days, prepare your next letter. The only difference will be that you state: "This is my second request. On January 1, 2009, I mailed the following information. I do expect a response from the original letter dated January 1, 2009 by February 1, 2009."

Mail this letter including the information from the original letter. If you have not heard from the credit reporting agency within 30 days, write your final letter stating: "This is my third and final request. I have mailed two letters, dated January 1, 2009 and January 15, 2009, and have not received a response from your company. Under the Fair Credit Reporting Act, you are allotted 30 days in which to respond to my request. The 30 days have now been exceeded and I am requesting that you correct the following inaccuracies and send me an updated report immediately." Be sure to include copies of your first and second letters. You may even mail this letter certified to confirm that the agency actually receives your request.

Repeat this process for entries you wish to have removed from each credit report by the three agencies. If they do not respond to your requests, you now have the opportunity to report them to The Federal Trade Commission, www.ftc.gov or 877-FTC-HELP.

When you receive your updated reports, they should list all of the investigated and deleted inaccuracies. If they were able to verify the information with the creditor, the report will list the information as verified.

If this doesn't work and you're in a hurry to correct your credit, it's time for negotiation. You have the power! The creditor wants something from you—your money. Many companies will work with you to settle a debt. They are happy to obtain a portion if not all of the outstanding debt.

Verify the debt with the creditor and their mailing address. You have a couple of options. You can write a letter stating what you are willing to pay a settlement or arrange to pay off the full debt. I would try the first option first.

The letter should be similar to this:

To Whom It May Concern:

I am writing in reference to account number _____. I am currently in a distressed financial situation. In an effort to clear the debt with your company, I am willing to pay $_____ as a final payment.

(or you can type) In an effort to clear the debt with your company, I am willing to make monthly payments of $___ for # months.

Upon receiving the full payment, it is agreed that you will remove the negative entry from my credit report and/or do not respond should I dispute the information.

Agreed:_____   Date:_____
Authorized Financial Representative for (insert company name)

Agreed:_____   Date:_____
Jane Doe

Mail two copies of this letter with your signature, requesting that one copy be sent back to you, signed by a person authorized to make such agreement.

Do not send any money until you have this agreement in your hands. Make a couple of copies and put it away for safekeeping. Whatever agreement you have made, you must keep it or the agreement becomes null and void.

Taking these steps should enable you to clear your credit and begin to rebuild a positive report.

To further build your credit, obtain a secured credit card (Visa or MasterCard). After paying this card on time, apply for a store department card or a gasoline card. Make small purchases and pay them on time. You will have then established good credit for two or three accounts. See the Secured Cards section.

Additionally, you can improve your credit further by opening a savings account at a bank with a $300 deposit, then return to the bank in a couple of weeks and apply for a line of credit. Request to use your savings as collateral, which will secure the loan for payment. The bank will more than likely allow you to do this because at this point they won't lose a thing.

If you have a negative report with a reporting agency, don't give up! If you feel the information they have on file is inaccurate, ask the agency to verify it. If the information is correct, you can explain your side of the story. The agency will take a statement from you and include it in your report.

Credit is a huge responsibility. You can handle it by not living beyond your means or overspending and by paying your bills on time.

Notes

UNSECURED AND SECURED CREDIT CARDS

Be selective when deciding on credit cards to build your credit.

Companies are making a killing right now by charging astronomical fees when offering secured or unsecured credit cards to people who need to rebuild or establish a credit rating. If used wisely, secured cards can benefit you greatly.

The unsecured credit cards offered to rebuild your credit are those with which I would be most cautious. Many companies on the Internet advertise unsecured credit cards. When you qualify on the web site for the card, they stress that you read the terms of agreement. I strongly recommend that you read it very closely. In the terms you will often find a fee ranging from $49.99 to $500 assessed solely for their extension of credit to you. This may or may not be the processing fee. They often assess astronomical finance fees for the annual percentage rate (APR), over-the-limit fees, monthly fees, and yearly membership fees, to name a few. If the intent is to repair or establish credit, an unsecured card is not worth it. You should not have to pay a company to receive credit.

Some companies split their membership fee into monthly installments and won't allow you to pay in one lump sum. This is so their potential to make additional money from late or over-the-limit fees are increased.

Avoid these companies if you can.

Some credit card companies assisting with credit repair require you to pay a minor fee for yearly membership or a small processing fee that is reasonable. Other credit card companies will extend credit to persons rebuilding or establishing credit with minimal charges.

Some secured credit card companies have established good reputations. Even though they are in business to make money, they seem to be more concerned with giving you a chance to do better. If you're working on your credit now, consider these companies before you resort to desperate measures such as paying $500 for the privilege of having a having a credit card.

Secured Cards

Secured cards are secured by the funds that you deposit into a savings account, which is opened by the issuing bank. These funds are not accessible by you but can be returned to you should you pay off your debt and close the account or the company chooses to give you a regular unsecured card based on your good payment history.

Secured accounts are great for reestablishing your credit. The card will usually have a spending limit equal to the amount of your savings account deposit. In three to twelve months, your account may be reviewed for a credit increase based upon your credit history and your deposit may even be refunded to you depending on which company you are dealing with.

Secured cards don't have (as many) hidden fees and can be obtained from banks with a reputable history. When you apply for these cards, always read the fine print, ask questions if necessary to make the most of the situation.

Check with your local bank to see if they offer a secured card. In addition you may want to visit Orchard Bank at www.orchardbank. com.

IDENTITY THEFT

Secure important documents as if you were securing your money.

Identity theft is a billion dollar industry. If your identity is stolen it can cause nightmarish problems.

Identity protection tips:

- Do not carry your social security card unless absolutely necessary.

- Do not leave your purse/wallet or important documents in your vehicle. It's not wise to use your glove compartment as your filing cabinet.

- Invest in a paper shredder for your home. Shred all documents that have account numbers or vital data such as your birth date or social security number.

- Watch for changes in your credit report such as an influx of new credit card offers or denial of credit.

- Do not write your PIN numbers or passwords on your credit cards. Do not store your PIN numbers or passwords in your wallet with your credit cards.

- Do not share your personal information with telemarketers.

There are scams where people will call requesting your account information or for you to verify your social security number.

- Always make a copy of the front and back of your credit cards, social security card, and driver's license. This way if any of this information is stolen, you will have a backup copy. You can call your creditors and cancel your cards.
- Do not share your personal information with anyone.
- Do not allow anyone to open accounts in your name.
- Only take the credit card you will use with you.

Web sites

- Scams – do not reply to any emails requesting your bank or credit card information. Your bank and credit card company already has your information so why would they request it from you?
- Do not reply to emails requesting your account passwords.
- Create a difficult password for all accounts.

If your identity is stolen:

1. File a report with the police and give as much information as possible.
2. Contact your creditors.
3. Add a statement to your credit report and place a fraud alert.
4. You may want to sign up for a credit monitoring program.
5. You may want to call 888-5-OPT-OUT to remove your name from unsolicited mailing lists.

Apartment Leasing

Choose a home that you can afford.

There are two types of rental agreements: lease and month-to-month. With a lease, you rent a property for a set period. The landlord can't raise your rent and you don't have to move unless you elect to do so when the lease expires.

Month-to-month usually involves a period of thirty days at a time. Each time you pay your rent it renews your month-to-month agreement until you decide to move or the landlord requests that you move.

Consider the following when apartment hunting:

- A **credit check fee** – the property management will check your credit rating and report to see if you've been evicted or own any other property owners.

- A **security deposit** that may amount to a month of rent – is used as security in case the apartment is damaged.

- A **cleaning fee** or deposit – is used to get the apartment back in renting condition. You are usually required to clean the apartment before leaving.

- Read your lease carefully to learn the rules of the property, and any special terms that you will be required to follow (such as a non-smoking clause or lease renewal information).

When you move in, the landlord will usually provide you with a walk-through form that you should use to write down any problems or repairs needed within the apartment. This can be very important because it instructs your landlord to fix various problems and protects you when you move out from being accused of damages that were previously there.

Be aware that the owner can enter your apartment in case of emergency, if you request repair service and no one is home to allow the repair service entry, or if you intend to move out. Your landlord can show the apartment.

If for some reason someone doesn't pay their rent, they may be subject to an eviction suit. After you receive either a three-day or 30-day notice, the owner will send you a "complaint." This states that you are being sued. You have five days, including weekends, to reply to the complaint. You will also receive a "summons", which tells you when and where to respond. If the owner sues in municipal court, you must reply to the complaint in writing. If you do not, the case will likely be decided in the owner's favor.

You may believe that the owner of an apartment or house won't rent to you or is evicting you because of your race, religion, national origin, ancestry, age, sexual preference, sex or disability. Perhaps the owner will not rent to you and a person of the opposite sex because you are not married. If so, write or call the nearest office of either the **Department of Fair Employment and Housing or the U.S. Department of Housing and Urban Development (HUD)**. You should be aware, however, that owners of housing for senior citizens do not have to accept families with children.

SHOULD I MOVE OUT

{ *Don't make this decision based on emotions.* }

Moving out of your parent's home is a big step. I'm sure you're thinking about your own private space, no one telling you to clean up or to be at home at a certain time, but are you really ready?

When I moved out of my parent's home, I just wanted to move. I didn't think about anything but the fact that I was ready to be on my own. I wanted my independence. I was making decent money for my age and I knew I could pay my rent. Things turned out just fine. I managed to pay my bills and have an excess of cash.

A benefit to having a new start is that you don't have any bills except the ones you create. When pondering your readiness to move out, consider the fact that your responsibilities will include more than rent. Depending on where you live, it may include any or all of the following expenses; rent, electricity (lights), gas, water, parking, phone, and cable. You have to pay for your own toiletries: toothpaste, soap, toilet paper, deodorant, etc. If you don't have a washer and dryer, you may opt to buy or rent or if available, use the onsite laundry facility in your apartment community. You must buy cleaning items, such as dishwashing liquid, detergent, bleach, cleanser, etc. Don't forget that you have to eat, so let's include food. What about entertainment and more importantly, furniture. You have to furnish your apartment unless you get lucky with one that comes furnished or someone leaves the furniture. Don't get the term furnished confused with furniture when you're looking for an apartment. Sometimes it simply means the apartment has a stove and refrigerator so be sure to ask questions. Try to find a place where the stove and refrigerator are supplied so you won't have to purchase your own.

So as you can see, there's a lot more to think about when contemplating moving.

First things first. How much money do you make? How long have you been on the job? What can you afford? Not sure? Then, it's time to figure it out.

Rent should be no more than thirty percent of your monthly income. For example, if your income is $2000, 30% is $600. When you find an apartment you like, be sure to ask what utilities you will have to pay and what the average bill is.

On the next page is a mock budget that gives you a rough idea of how quickly money can be spent. This probably doesn't cover all your necessities but gives you an idea. It is very important to write a realistic budget that you will stick to. You may have to tweak it a few times to get it where it needs to be. There may be several adjustments you can make but always remember to save – pay you first, and pay your rent, utilities, and insurance on time.

If you make a budget and find you can't afford to move out yet, then you may consider having a roommate to share expenses. This should cut the major expenses in half. Try doing a budget as if you had a roommate. If you find it's doable, then start looking for a roommate.

If your expenses are still too high after decreasing your budget by associating a roommate, you may want to wait. Consider finding a better paying job or asking your parents to convert the apartment over the garage to your own special place. Whatever you do, don't move and put yourself in a bind causing you to stress on the "hows." How am I going to pay my rent? How am I going to pay my light bill? How am I going to get back and forth from work and school? How am I going to eat? It's not worth it. Remember, everything happens exactly when it's supposed to.

This is a sample budget based on an income of $2,000.00 per month.

Expense	Amount
Rent	$600
Electricity	$100
Gas	$30
Water	$30
Phone	$50
Laundry	$50
Car fuel	$200
Car note/bus fare	$200
Auto insurance	$70
Renter's insurance	$20
Cable	$50
Parking	$15
Cleaning supplies	$50
Food	$200
Savings 10%	$200
Entertainment	$85
Credit card bills	$50
Total	$2,000

FYI...BEFORE YOU MOVE IN

A little work on the front end will save you a lot of frustration.

- *Change of address*

When you move from any residence to a new one, you need to do a change of address at your local post office. Go to the post office and request a change of address form or visit www.usps.gov online and click on "Change of address." Follow the instructions. It usually takes a week or two before you start to receive mail at your new address.

It is important to call your creditors or other important contact and update your address.

- *Walk through*

When you sign the lease for you apartment, the leasing agent will walk the apartment with you. Point out any concerns with the carpet, paint, windows, any imperfections in the walls, and anything else you notice. Check the faucets, shower, tub, and toilet making sure the water runs properly. If the carpet is dirty, request it be replaced or cleaned. If anything is broken request repairs.

- *Utilities*

When you sign the lease for your apartment, the property management office will usually supply you with a list of utility providers for energy, phone, cable, etc. If not, you can always locate this information at the front of your local telephone book.

Before you decide on any one particular service, call around to get the best deal. Remember you budget and don't allow yourself to be upsold or convinced to buy features or products you don't need.

- *Home Security*

It is very important to examination the security of your new home. Check your front and rear doors. Do you have a deadbolt lock on your doors? If not, request one. This will deter easy entry.

- *Patio/sliding doors*

Sliding doors are equipped with additional security besides the lock that you move to lock the door. At the bottom of the door, there is usually a hole for a metal pin to be placed. If that is not available, there should be a metal bar that can be placed at the bottom of the track against the sliding door to prevent it from being opened.

- *Windows*

All of your windows should open, close, and lock. Make sure they are not painted shut. If they are, request they be fixed immediately. Always lock your windows before leaving your home. If you live on the first floor, don't leave your doors or windows open while sleeping or when your leave your home.

- *Smoke alarms*

Smoke alarms are mandatory. Check the batteries and test the alarm to see if it's working.

- *Alarm*

Some apartments are equipped with an alarm monitoring service. The provider monitors your apartment for the alarm. If the alarm is activated and you don't turn it off, they provider calls you to verify it's you in the apartment. If when called, you or someone else is either unable to provide the correct code or you don't answer the phone, the police is called and sent to your residence.

Having this service may require you to pay a fee. If the property management feels it necessary to offer this service, I suggest you subscribe for additional protection.

- ***Renters Insurance***

Renters insurance protects your property if damaged or stolen and damage that you may cause to the apartment. It is usually one of the least expensive insurances. The coverage also extends to most of your personal items if they're stolen or damaged while in your car. Most auto insurance policies don't cover items not permanently installed in your vehicle.

- ***Keys***

Don't leave a spare key under the flower pot or share it with your neighbors or friends. If necessary, leave a spare key with your parents or someone trustworthy. Realize you are allowing someone access to your property and personal information.

ROOMMATES

{ *Every relationship requires communication.* }

Being roomies has its pluses and minuses. The main benefit is financial because your expenses are cut in half. You also benefit from companionship and feeling secure knowing you're not alone.

Before discussing the potential roommate, let me ask you a few questions to get your mental wheels turning. Why do you want a roommate? How is your credit? How would you describe yourself? Are you willing to share? Are you clean? Are you responsible? Do you pay your bills on time? Are you a party animal? See, many of these are the questions you will be asking your potential roomies but are also questions they may ask you. You know your personality. Though you may think you are the coolest, most awesome person in the world, how are you to live with? What was your parent's or siblings' biggest complaint about you while you were living at home? What has changed and do you feel anyone will be willing to deal with this/these issues?

Now, back to the roomie. In addition to the questions above, here are a few more questions you may want to ask. Are they employed? How will they pay rent? How long have they been working? You want to scrutinize here. If they bounce from job to job, there may be a time when they don't have a job or money for rent. How much can they afford to pay for rent? How is their credit? What hours do they keep? Are they up all night? How do they feel about partying and having company? Do they do drugs, drink, or smoke? If the do drugs, this is a definite no go. You are taking a serious chance of coming home one day and finding all your possessions gone. Are they neat and clean? What are their least favorite chores? Is it important for them to pay bills on time? Do they usually share their keys with people? The list can go on and on. You want to find someone with similar morals and ideals so you know what you're getting into. In addition, it's great if the person complements you, for example, they like to wash dishes but you hate to wash dishes, you like to vacuum but they hate to vacuum.

Could you imagine always being on time but having to wait for your roomies' rent payment? What about cleaning your home only to have it trashed by your roomies' company or having to study and the apartment is full of people that you don't know playing loud music while smoking, dancing, and drinking? What if you have a roommate that never buys food? While looking for a roommate, consider asking a relative or someone you know and trust to room with you. They may even be able to refer someone to you.

Advantages of a having a "Roomie"

- You only have to pay half the rent and utilities
- Additional security because you won't be living alone
- They may provide companionship
- They can possibly be a study partner

Disadvantages of a having a "Roomie"

- You are dependent on someone keeping their agreement to pay their half of bills on time.
- You share space.
- You may have different ideals about upkeep and care of the apartment.
- You have to trust this person and their friends to not steal or

damage your property.

If you do get a roommate, you may want to set ground rules before moving in together. ***Discuss:***

- Food: Will it be purchased separately or together?
- Bills: Will you split bills or each pay a particular bill?
- Furniture: Who's bringing what?
- Cleaning: Who's responsible for what?
- Respect: Discuss your space, quiet time, study time, bed time.
- Company: How often and how much is too much?
- Keys: Don't share or make copies for people that don't live with you.
- Personal space: How do you feel about someone entering your bedroom, wearing your clothes, or using your personal items?
- Pets: Yes or no?
- Boyfriends or girlfriends: Sometimes people slowly move in and before you know it you have two roommates instead of one.

Every relationship requires communication. Be sure to discuss any concerns before you make the commitment. This way you both know if one another's terms are agreeable.

TIPPING

An expression of gratitude is always welcome.

Tipping is an expression of gratitude for having received good service. People working as wait staff, valet attendants, host, etc., are dependent on the tips they receive. Many make minimum wage or less per hour and their tips increase their pay to above minimum wage.

Should you tip? Absolutely! I tip to show my appreciation as well as critique the service I've received. For example, a friend and I visited a restaurant for lunch. Our server was experiencedbut new to this restaurant as a waitress. She was attentive, promptly greeted us, and we never had to ask for a refill on our drinks. She was "Jane on the spot." Because we'd received such outstanding service, we spoke to her manager and acknowledged her. We learned this was her first day on the job. She served us like the professional she was. Our individual bills were about twelve dollars each. 15% of $12 is $1.80. I left her a $5 tip to show my appreciation.

Okay, same restaurant different day and I was accompanied by a coworker. It took the waiter 15 minutes to greet us. It took him another 10 minutes to come back and take our orders. From there it took 10 more minutes to get a glass of water. At that point we spoke with the manager and advised her of the poor service we were receiving. The manager spoke to the waiter and he instantly appeared. By this time I knew I was going to tip a lot less than my norm. The bill was about $12.23. I gave the waiter a twenty and he returned with dollars and no change and quickly left the table. I politely stood up and told my coworker, "The change he kept is his tip", and we left. He had a lot of nerve assuming I didn't want my change. You can clearly see the difference in the service.

Tipping is based on a percentage of the bill. The minimum is 10 percent but the new standard is 15 percent. Anything above 15 percent is great. Remember, people that wait on you depend on your tips to take care of themselves and their families. Always be conscious of the golden rule, "Do unto others as you wish them to do unto you."

Some nationalities have been labeled as non-tippers and often receive less than the best service they could based on the wait staff's experience. Break the assumption by always showing your appreciation for good service.

CAR BUYING TIPS

Be an informed buyer.

I guess since my first car was used, my mindset was to purchase another used car when I was needed another vehicle. Not understanding credit and running into deceptive salesmen didn't help. So, I encountered several lemons, a salesman that I paid to reduce my interest rate, and paying more than what one of my cars was actually worth.

My first good car buying experience and my first new vehicle purchase occurred when I was in my thirties and tired of settling for pieces of trash as a mode of transportation. I finally told myself that I was worth more and I deserved better.

I spoke to friends of mine and several told me that they had owned several new vehicles. I don't know what the devil happened to me and my mindset thinking that I could only purchase used cars. Before you subject yourself to possibly buying used cars that will eventually cost you as much or more than a new one, read on. The tips I am providing can be used as a guide to purchasing new and used vehicles. After all, there are plenty of used vehicles that are suitable and in good condition.

1. Research. Visit Edmunds.com and kbb.com to learn about

vehicles, their value, and what you should expect to pay.

2. Use dealer and manufacturer web sites for incentives and rebates that dealerships can allow if you purchase a vehicle.

3. Know that the sticker price is negotiable. You can purchase vehicles for well under the sticker price.

4. Do price comparisons on the Internet and newspapers and locate the best deals. Once you locate the best deals, contact/email the dealerships to start a bidding war. Each time you get a lower bid, advise the other dealerships to see if they will bid lower. Some will try to play hard and refuse to bid. If so, tell them if they don't bid, you won't do business with them.

5. If you choose to speak with a salesperson in person or on the telephone, let them know that you are researching vehicles on the Internet. They tend to change their tune when they learn you're an informed consumer.

6. Never mention a trade until you find out the lowest price you can get for the vehicle you want. You need your selling price.

7. It is to your benefit to know your credit standing. Get your credit score to learn what interest rate you qualify for. Do not allow the dealership to mess over you with the interest rate.

8. Be budget conscious. Don't try to purchase more car than you can afford. Avoid unnecessary accessories or those that you can live without.

9. Pay attention to your paperwork. Do not allow them to add in extra items like extended warranties. Many times your vehicle is already covered for what they may try to sell you. Inquire about the difference between the extended warranty and the warranty your car already has.

10. If buying a used vehicle, request a Carfax report so you can get the history of the vehicle. Be leery of vehicles that have been in accidents.

11. Check the tires and if they are balding or have low tread, request

the dealer to either replace the tires with new ones or reduce the selling price of the vehicle so you can purchase new tires.

12. If you car is used, make a vehicle inspection a part of your test drive, and request reimbursement from the cost of the vehicle. There is a law called the "Lemon Law" that prohibits car dealers from selling defective vehicles. If you get a vehicle that is a headache from the start, try to return it. If the dealer won't accept it, get on the Internet and find out who you need to contact locally concerning being sold a lemon.

13. The 3-day contract cancellation period is not available in many states when it comes to vehicle purchases. Once you drive off the lot, the car is yours, unless it's a lemon.

14. If you can't afford a new vehicle, you may have to deal with some cosmetic defects as long as the car runs well.

15. It may take you some time to make your purchase, but when you do, you'll know exactly what you are getting.

16. Females, a male's presence will save you a lot of strife. Dealers often look at women as easy prey. For whatever reason, they tend to respect you and your purchasing power when a man is present.

17. Inquire about gap insurance. If your vehicle is stolen and unrecovered or is totaled (it costs more to repair than what it is worth), gap insurance will pay the balance you owe to your finance company less what the insurance company pays.

There is also new insurance options that will pay your car note for x amount of months if you become unemployed and some auto dealers/manufacturers will allow you to return your vehicle without a negative report to your credit history.

Be sure to inquire about all of your options and take someone with you that will keep you alert and has your back!

Happy car buying!

GENERAL VEHICLE MAINTENANCE

There's something about a maintained car.

Every car comes with an owner's manual which states a scheduled maintenance program. Follow this schedule to keep your vehicle well maintained.

Basic maintenance includes:

- *Tire rotation*

The tires are moved around the vehicle to even the wear. This should be done each time you have an oil change.

- *Oil change*

The mileage at which an oil change should be performed varies dependent upon the vehicle. The standard is every 3,000 miles. With the oil change the oil filter and oil are changed. Depending on where you have the vehicle serviced, they may offer to change your air filter, windshield wipers, clean your vehicle and top off your fluids. Perform these additional services as needed:

- *Windshield wipers*

If you notice your wipers tearing or not working properly, replace them.

- *Car wash*

It's important to wash your vehicle especially in areas that have snow. The salt that is put on the ground will rust your vehicle. It's good to wash this off your vehicle often.

- *Wheel alignment*

If you ever feel your vehicle pulling to one side; if you take your hands off the steering column as you're driving and it veers to the left or right, you wheels are not aligned. This can cause your tires to wear unevenly and also affect the ride of the vehicle.

- *Fluid maintenance*

Read you manual to find out how often you should have your fluids changed. This may include a transmission flush or a brake flush. Power steering fluid and antifreeze needs to be maintained as well.

- *Filter changes*

The oil filter is changed when you have an oil change. The air filter needs to be changed because it will affect your gas mileage.

- *Tune-ups*

Every so often you will need a tune-up which is the replacement of your spark plugs and other maintenance. Spark plugs help to start the engine and if they need replacement, your vehicle may not start up properly.

INVESTING

Invest properly and wisely.

(DISCLAIMER: THE INFORMATION IN THIS SECTION IS NOT INTENDED TO BE USED AS FINANCIAL ADVICE AND IS NOT TO BE USED AS A GUIDE FOR INVESTING. IT IS PROVIDED STRICTLY FOR USE AS REFERENCE INFORMATION.)

To invest properly and wisely requires research. You must first determine your goals and the risks you are willing to take. Some investment tools provide a higher risk with a higher chance of gain, but you take a chance on losing as well.

Are you less of a risk taker? If so, mutual funds and CD's are a good way to start investing. They certainly offer more opportunity for growth than a regular savings account.

You can begin your research by viewing various investment web sites such as MSNMoney.com, Bankrate.com, InvestorGuide.com, or The U.S. Securities and Exchange Commission: www.sec.gov. There is a wealth of information available on the Internet. Other learning tools include: investment magazines, financial planners, and the local library. You may even contact your local community college's continuing education department and inquire about classes they may offer. Gather as much knowledge as you can so that you're able to make wise decisions when you're ready to invest and you're an active participant in your money's future.

I have included brief information on various investment tools. Investing is a way to increase your worth and financial security. **Research first. Invest second.**

CD OR CERTIFICATE OF DEPOSIT

This type of CD can make you dance too.

A certificate of deposit requires your depositing money into an account, leaving it there for as little as a few weeks to a few years and allowing it to earn interest. The financial institution uses your money for investments and they pay you interest on the money in your CD account. A CD account pays higher interest than a checking or savings account.

Some points to remember are:

1. Shop around for interest rates.

2. Don't limit yourself to local banks or credit unions. You may find a better interest rate in another state. It doesn't matter where you have the account; you'll continue to earn interest.

3. Be sure to use money that you know you're not going to need.

4. Be sure to find out if the institution offers early withdrawal. (If they do, find out if there is a penalty and what it is).

If you're looking to invest safely, CD's are a good choice. They are federally insured up to $100,000.

MUTUAL FUNDS

Mutual funds provide an opportunity to invest without putting all of your eggs in one basket.

A mutual fund is a company that invests money for a group of people (shareholders). Each person who owns shares in the mutual fund is a shareholder. Mutual fund companies invest in stocks, bonds, and other securities. Mutual funds do carry a risk but are less risky than other types of investments.

The benefits of using a mutual fund as an investment tool are:

• You become part owner of several companies because your investment dollars are spread over several opportunities or companies.

• A professional manages the mutual fund.

• Investing in mutual funds lowers your cost of purchasing stocks, bonds, or other securities because the fund usually buys and sells in large amounts.

Mutual fund companies, banks, brokers, financial planners, and insurance agencies sell mutual funds. Mutual funds earn money for you through the income it earns by sale of shares or by making a gain. The latter occurs when an investment increases in value and the fund doesn't sell it.

There are three types of funds: the **money market fund** (not to be confused with the money market account that banks offer), **bond funds**, and **stock funds**. Each of the funds has unique risks and benefits. The bond fund is riskier than the money market fund because it is not restricted to the type of investment in which it participates, whereas the money market fund. Stock funds are the riskiest of all but have a tendency to do better over a long term of investment.

When shopping for a mutual fund, gather information from the fund itself and a financial planner, bank or insurance company. Compare various funds by reviewing each fund's prospectus. The **prospectus** includes a description of the fund, the cost to you in expenses and fees, and the past performance of the fund. The prospectus also includes ongoing fees, which include management expenses and other expenses of the mutual fund. Past performance does not guarantee future performance but may act as an indicator of the fund's future.

Check to see if the fund is **loaded** or **not loaded**. A loaded fund charges sales loads and transaction fees, but offers the assistance of broker services. You are charged each time you buy, sell, or exchange your shares. The fees often go toward commissions to brokers and advertising costs.

A no-load fund doesn't charge sales loads and you don't have the assistance of broker services.

A loaded fund does not guarantee that the fund is necessarily better than a no-load fund. Because of the overhead, loaded funds usually have to out-perform a no-load fund to equate the same profit or greater.

RETIREMENT PLANS, BENEFITS & SAVINGS

Never depend on anyone to take care of you. Whatever the government provides should be a bonus.

Depending on the size of the company, an employer may offer various retirement plans to its employees. If you work at a company that offers 401(k), employee stock ownership plans, profit-sharing plans, or others, take advantage of them.

The two types of plans are **defined benefit plans** or **defined contribution plans**. A defined benefit plan promises a specified monthly benefit at retirement. The plan may state this promised benefit as an exact dollar amount, such as $100 per month at retirement.

A **defined contribution plan**, on the other hand, does not promise a specific amount of benefits at retirement. In these plans, the employee or the employer (or both) contribute to the employee's individual account under the plan, sometimes at a set rate, such as five percent of earnings annually.

A **Profit Sharing Plan** or **Stock Bonus Plan** is a defined contribution plan under which the plan may provide, or the employer may determine annually, how much will be contributed to the plan (out of profits or otherwise). The plan contains a formula for allocating to each participant a portion of each annual contribution. A profit-sharing plan or stock bonus plan includes a 401(k) plan.

A **401(k) Plan** is a defined contribution plan that is a cash or deferred arrangement. Employees can elect to defer receiving a portion of their salary, which is instead contributed on their behalf, before taxes, to the 401(k) plan. Sometimes the employer may match these contributions. Employees who participate in 401(k) plans assume responsibility for their retirement income by contributing part of their salary and, in many instances, by directing their own investments.

An **Employee Stock Ownership Plan (ESOP)** is a form of defined contribution plan in which the investments are primarily in employer stock.

A **Money Purchase Pension Plan** is a plan that requires fixed annual contributions from the employer to the employee's individual account.

A **Simplified Employee Pension Plan (SEP)** is a relatively uncomplicated retirement savings vehicle. A SEP allows employees to contribute on a tax-favored basis to individual retirement accounts (IRAs) owned by the employees.

This information has been supplied by the U.S. Department of Labor, Retirement Plans, Benefits, and Savings Publication:

Social Security Retirement Benefits

Many people wonder where their Social Security tax dollars go. Generally, out of every dollar you pay in Social Security taxes:

Eighty-five cents goes to a trust fund that pays monthly benefits to retirees and their families and to widows, widowers and children of workers who have died; and 15 cents goes to a trust fund that pays benefits to people with disabilities and their families.

Your Social Security taxes also pay for administering Social Security. The administrative costs are paid from the trust funds described above and are less than one cent of every Social Security tax dollar collected.

The entire amount of taxes you pay for Medicare (1.45 percent of your earnings) goes to a trust fund that pays for some of the costs of hospital and related care of Medicare beneficiaries.

Money not used to pay benefits and administrative expenses is invested in U.S. government bonds, generally considered the safest of all investments.

- ***How Do You Qualify For Retirement Benefits?***

When you work and pay Social Security taxes (called FICA on some pay stubs), you earn Social Security credits. Most people earn the maximum of four credits per year.

The number of credits you need to get retirement benefits depends on your date of birth. If you were born in 1929 or later, you need 40 credits (10 years of work).

- ***How Much Will Your Retirement Benefit Be?***

Your benefit amount is based on your earnings averaged over most of your working career. Higher lifetime earnings result in higher benefits. If you have some years of no earnings or low earnings, your benefit amount may be lower than if you had worked steadily.

- ***Full Retirement Age***

The usual retirement age for people retiring now is age 65.

Because of longer life expectancies, the Social Security Law was changed in 1983 to increase the full retirement age in gradual steps until it reaches age 67. This change began in the year 2003, and it affects people born in 1938 and later.

You can start your Social Security benefits as early as age 62, but the benefit amount you receive will be less than your full retirement benefit.

This information is available in its entirety through the Social Security Administration, SSA Publication 05-10035. It can be viewed on the Internet by accessing www.ssa.gov. Their toll-free number is 800-772-1213 or TTY number: 800-325-0778

INSURANCE

Insurance provides protection and security.

There are several types of insurance that you will need in your lifetime if you drive a vehicle, own a house, or value the welfare of your loved ones. Insurance requires you to pay a premium, which is the amount you pay for the insurance policy. You may also have a deductible, which is a payment you must make, as your participation in the loss (claim). A claim is a demand for payment made to the insurer.

Insurance provides protection and security. It can protect you from having to pay for things such as accidents, property loss due to theft, damages, and expenses relating to death. It provides security because the insurer will pay for the loss or damage.

When shopping for insurance, be sure to get a full understanding of the policy you're purchasing. You may even want to do your own research to be a more informed shopper.

Automobile insurance is mandatory in the United States. There are two main types of insurance that you can purchase: *general liability* and **full coverage/property damage**. General liability will not cover the cost of damages to your vehicle, but it will cover the cost of damages and bodily harm to other vehicles and persons involved in the accident. Full coverage will cover all costs related to any damage or loss to your car and another vehicle if you are in an accident and at fault. **Uninsured/ underinsured motorist coverage,** besides the obvious, offers coverage if your vehicle is involved in a hit and run. It also reduces your deductible, and includes rental coverage.

Renters insurance or **homeowners insurance** provides coverage against loss or damages to your belongings and the property that you own or are renting.

There are several types of **life insurance**, which are all payable upon the death of the insured. Life insurance is a way to provide for your family or loved ones after your death. Life insurance can also be used to pay your debts or costs for your burial. When purchasing life insurance, be sure that you understand exactly what you are getting. Ask many questions and compare the different policies. Be sure to purchase the policy that will best benefit you and your loved ones.

- **Whole life insurance** provides insurance over the person's lifetime. It also has cash value that can be borrowed against.

- **Variable life insurance** value is determined by the value of the underlying investments.

- **Universal life insurance** can be used as an investment tool. It provides term life insurance and a tax-deferred savings account. This account may also be borrowed against.

- **Term insurance** provides coverage for a specific period of time.

- **Cash value life insurance** accumulates a value that can be paid out before and upon death.

If you are unsure of the best insurance for you, research online or contact a financial advisor or insurance sales agent.

HOME BUYING TIPS

Take your time and find the house that's right for you.

Buying a home versus renting has many perks. For many years the majority of your payment goes to interest for the home loan, which is deductible from your federal and sometimes state tax as well. A home is an investment and hopefully your property value will increase.

For people with bad credit, the first step for buying a house is increasing your credit score. There are homebuyer programs that will assist you with this or you may begin on your own by using the "Credit Repair" section in this book.

Homebuyer programs

Many cities offer a new homebuyer's grant, which may be $5,000 or more. These programs assist you with developing your credit, qualifying through lenders, and sometimes referring you to home builders or real estate brokers.

Brokers

Real estate brokers will guide you through the home buying process. They can help you locate properties, find a lender, possibly save money, and educate you about different types of mortgages. There is no fee for their services to you; the home seller pays them.

Cost of purchasing a home

There are three costs that you should concern yourself with:

Earnest money: A deposit you invest towards the purchase to show the owner you are serious (which will be applied to the down payment or closing costs). Inquire if the money is refundable if the deal doesn't go through.

Closing Costs: Fees associated with paperwork processing. These fees can be negotiated to be paid by the seller.

Loans: Use a mortgage calculator, to calculate the mortgage payments you can afford. Mortgage calculators can be found online at web sites such as: Bankrate.com or money.msn.com.

Lenders

There are many options to financing: banks, credit unions, private mortgage companies and even state government lenders. Lenders have different fees and rates. Take your time and shop around to get the best deal.

Mortgages

There are many types of mortgages. The most common are fixed rate (the interest doesn't fluctuate) and ARM (Adjustable Rate Mortgage); your interest rate goes up and down during the year. The adjustment is tied to a financial index such as the U.S. Treasury Securities Index. The FHA (Federal Housing Administration) is not a mortgage company, but a department that insures loans given by lenders to encourage loans to people who ordinarily wouldn't qualify.

When you find a home, discuss with your realtor:

- The asking price
- Condition of the home
- Home inspection

- How long the house has been on the market
- Negotiating the price
- Is the location suitable for you, your children, commuting to work, closest to conveniences such as food stores.

Negotiation

Always negotiate the price of a home. Don't cheat yourself of possibly saving money. If the asking price is a good deal, go for it.

Closing

Closing the deal usually takes up to three hours. Read all the information and ask questions about what you don't understand! Before you go to the closing, read the information provided by your lender concerning closing costs.

HOUSEKEEPING TIPS

It's a dirty job but somebody's gotta do it!

1. Establish a place for everything and after use, return that item to its place

2. **Dirty clothes:** Purchase a hamper, set a day to wash, or wash as soon as you have a load of like colors.

3. **Dishes:** Keep the sink empty. You can designate one cup, plate, and individual silverware items for yourself and use them repetitively, cleaning after each use and placing them in a dish rack. This will eliminate the sink filling up with dirty dishes. If you do decide to use several dishware items and you have a dishwasher, rinse and load the dishwasher after use. Decreasing your electricity bill by hand washing the dishes.

4. Immediately make your bed upon rising.

5. Before you go to bed straighten your home, leaving nothing out of place.

6. **Trash:** Avoid having trash throughout the apartment by having a large trash can in the kitchen. If you are good about emptying the trash, place cans throughout the house and empty as they fill.

7. **Bathroom:** Clean the counter, toilet, and tub after use or as needed. You can use disposable wipes for the counter and toilet for quick tidying and foam wash for the tub.

8. Dusting is very important. Do this as often as possible to keep down allergens.

9. **Recycling:** You can do your part to help Mother Earth. You can recycle glass, plastic, paper, and metal by placing each item in separate recycling bags (often blue bags) before garbage pickup. There are many stores that sale pre-labeled containers or you can purchase slim garbage containers and line them with the recycle bags.

10. Daily maintenance reduces the amount of work necessary on your general housecleaning day on which you do an extensive cleaning of your home.

Happy house cleaning!

REAL LIFE,

Real Choices

A Young Adult Life Reference Book

FROM THE AUTHOR

Thank you for the opportunity to communicate information that will hopefully prove to be useful in your life or that of a loved one.

Remember to use what you need and feels right to you. With wisdom comes the responsibility to enlighten others. Be a light to those in need by passing on information that very well may change their lives.

Please keep in contact by visiting the Real Life, Real Choices website at www.realiferealchoices.com and www.copiouspublishing.com to place orders, Discounts are available for non-profit, government, or other business organizations.

Remember, when you know better you have the opportunity to do better. Take care and I wish you more success and happiness than you could ever dream of!

Love,

Kijana

BIBLIOGRAPHY

Consumer Information

Federal Trade Commission, "Free Annual Credit Reports", Federal Trade Commission, 2009, www.ftc.gov/freereports, Catalog of Federal Domestic

Federal Trade Commission, "Fighting Back Against Identity Theft", Federal Trade Commission, 2009, www.ftc.gov

Health

Jack Ritchason N.D., *The Little Herb Encyclopedia*, Pleasant Grove, Utah:Woodland Health Books, 2004

Michael Castaleman & Sheldon Saul Hendler, *The Healing Herbs*, Rodale Press, 1991

Jethro Kloss, *Back to Eden*, Loma Linda, CA.:Back to Eden Books Publishing Co., 1994

Varro E. Tyler, PhD, *The Honest Herbal: A Sensible Guide to the Use of Herbs and Related Remedies*, New York: Haworth Press, Inc., 1982

James Grun, Herbalist, *The Male Herbal*, Freedom, CA:The Crossing Press,1997

John Heinerman, *Heinerman's Encyclopedia of Healing Herbs, & Spices*, West Nyack, NY: Parker Publishing Company, Inc., 1995

U.S. Department of Health & Human Services, "Populations", 2009, www.aids.gov

Centers for Disease Control and Prevention, "Health & Safety Tips", 2009, www.cdc.gov

National Institute On Drug Abuse, "Drugs of Abuse Information", 2009,www.nida.nih.gov

Natalie Staats Reiss & Mark Danbeck, "The Nature of Suicide", 1995-

2009, CenterSite,LLC., www.mentalhelp.net

Cancer Care.org, "Cancer Care: Get Help", 2009.Cancer Care Inc., www.cancercare.org

Healthy Women.org, National Womens Health Resource Center, 2009, www.healthywomen.org

Westside Pregnancy Clinic, "Fetal Development", 2001-2009, www.wpclinic.org

Sister Zeus, "Living With Our Fertility", 1998-2008, www.sisterzeus. com

Men Can Stop Rape.org, "Men Can Stop Rape", 2007-2009, www.mencanstoprape.org

Finances

Grace W. Weinstein, *The Lifetime Book of Money Management*, Visible Ink,1993

Lawrence J Gitman & Michael D. Joehnk, *Personal Financial Planning*, Fort Worth:The Dryden Press, 1993

Eric Gelb, *Eric Gelb's Checkbook Management*, Austin, TX: Career Advancement Center, Inc., 1994

Lisa Berger, *Feathering Your Nest: The Retirement Planner*, New York: Workman Publishing Company, Inc., 1993

Jordan E. Goodman, *Everyone's Money Book*, Wisconsin: Dearborn Financial Publishing, Inc., 1998

Johnathan D. Pond, *The New Century Family Money Book*, New York: Dell Publishing, 1993

Mary L. Sprouse, *Financial First Aid: Smart Remedies for Hundreds of Curable Money Ailments*, New York:John Wiley & Sons, Inc., 1998

Bankrate.com, "Debt Management", 2009, Bankrate, Inc., www.bankrate.com

Chex Systems, "Chex Systems Consumer Assistance", 2009, Chex Systems Inc., www.chexsystems.com

Investor Words.com, "Investor Glossary",2009,www.investorwords.com

REFERENCE SECTION

Abortions
Planned Parenthood: www.plannedparenthood.org
Medline Plus: www.nlm.nih.gov/medlineplus/abortion.html

Adoption
Planned Parenthood: www.plannedparenthood.org
Child Welfare Information Gateway: www.childwelfare.gov

Alcohol Abuse
National Institute on Alcohol Abuse & Alcoholism: www.niaa.nih.gov
Alcoholics Anonymous: www.aa.org

Birth Control
Planned Parenthood: www.plannedparenthood.org
Medline Plus: www.nlm.nih.gov/medlineplus/birthcontrol.htm

Breast Exam
Susan G. Komen Breast Cancer Foundation: www.komen.org
American Cancer Society: www.cancer.org

Career/Jobs
Monster.com: www.monster.com
Careerbuilder.com: www.careerbuilder.com
U.S. Department of Labor: www.dol.gov
Bureau of Labor Statistics: www.bls.gov

Death

National Mental Health Association, Coping with Loss- Bereavement and Guilt: www.nmha.org/reassurance/coping.cfm
Dental Care
American Dental Association: www.ada.gov

Drug Abuse
National Institute on Drug Abuse: www.nida.nih.gov
Narcotics Anonymous: www.na.org
Sober.com: www.sober.com

Education
U.S. Department of Education: www.ed.gov
Students.gov: www.students.gov

Employment
www.monster.com
www.careerbuilder.com
www.indeed.com

Entrepreneurship
Ewing Marion Kauffman Foundation: www.kauffman.org
Blackenterprise.com
United States Small Business Administration: www.sba.gov

Exercise
American Council on Exercise: www.acefitness.org

Finances
Federal Reserve: www.federalreserveeducation.org
Bankrate.com: www.bankrate.com
MSNMoney: www.moneycentral.com

Foot care

National Diabetes Education Program: www.ndep.nih.gov/campaigns/feet/feet_overview.htm

Herbs

Mothernature.com: www.mothernature.com
Herb Research Foundation: www.herbs.org

Health (General)

National Health Information Center: www.healthfinder.gov
U.S. Department of Health and Human Services: www.hhs.gov
WEBMD: www.webmd.com

Homosexuality

Queer Resource Directory: www.qrd.org

Human Anatomy

Innerbody.com: www.innerbody.com

Investing

Investorguide.com: www.investorguide.com
Stockmaster.com: www.stockmaster.com
CNN Financial News: www.cnnfn.com

Mental Health

National Institute of Mental Health: www.nimh.nih.gov
Substance Abuse and Mental Health Services Administration:
www.samhsa.gov

Parenting

Americanbaby.com: www.americanbaby.com

Focus on your child.com: www.focusonyourbaby.com

Rape

Rape Abuse & Incest National Network: www.rainn.org ; operates national sexual abuse hotline. 1-800-656-HOPE 24/7. Provides counseling services, statistical information, etc.

Men Can Stop Rape: www.mencanstoprape.org 202-265-6530

Sexually Transmitted Diseases (STD's)

Medline Plus:

www.nlm.nih.gov/medlineplus/sexuallytransmitteddiseases.htm

Planned Parenthood: www.plannedparenthood.org

Smoking

Center for Disease Control and Prevention: www.cdc.gov/tobacco

Step Parenting

Bonus Families: www.bonusfamilies.com

Suicide

Center for Suicide Prevention: www.suicideinfo.ca

SuicideHotline.com: www.suicidehotline.com

Suicide Awareness Voices of Education: www.save.org 1-800-SUICIDE

Index

www.ingramcontent.com/pod-product-compliance
Lightning Source LLC
Chambersburg PA
CBHW052027090426
42739CB00010B/1815